A LEGION PARA IN ALGERIA

Tony Hunter-Choat's War, 1957–62

Peter Hoskins

Helion & Company

Helion & Company Limited
Unit 8 Amherst Business Centre
Budbrooke Road
Warwick
CV34 5WE
England
Tel. 01926 499 619
Email: info@helion.co.uk
Website: www.helion.co.uk
Twitter: @helionbooks
Visit our blog at blog.helion.co.uk

Published by Helion & Company 2022
Designed and typeset by Mary Woolley (www.battlefield-design.co.uk)
Cover designed by Paul Hewitt, Battlefield Design (www.battlefield-design.co.uk)
Cover Artwork by Mark Stacey © Helion & Company 2022

Text © Peter Hoskins 2022
Images © as individually credited
Maps by George Anderson © Helion & Company 2022

Every reasonable effort has been made to trace copyright holders and to obtain their permission for the use of copyright material. The editors and publisher apologise for any errors or omissions in this work and would be grateful if notified of any corrections that should be incorporated in future reprints or editions of this book.

ISBN 978-1-915113-72-6

British Library Cataloguing-in-Publication Data.
A catalogue record for this book is available from the British Library.

All rights reserved. No part of this publication may be reproduced, stored in a retrieval system, or transmitted, in any form, or by any means, electronic, mechanical, photocopying, recording or otherwise, without the express written consent of Helion & Company Limited.

For details of other military history titles published by Helion & Company Limited contact the above address, or visit our website: http://www.helion.co.uk.

We always welcome receipt of book proposals from prospective authors.

Sergeant Hunter-Choat in a studio portrait taken following his promotion in November 1959, having passed out top of his course. NCO status (from caporal-chef upwards) is indicated by the Legion's seven-flamed grenade badge in gold (rather than green) on the collar patches and shoulder boards of the service and walking-out uniform, which is worn with a khaki shirt and dark green necktie. (Linda Hunter-Choat).

Contents

List of Photographs		vi
List of Maps		vii
Foreword		viii
Preface		xi
Acknowledgements		xii
1	The Beginnings of an Adventure	13
2	France in Algeria: 1830–1954	20
3	The Legion Paras: 1948–54	29
4	From First Blows to the End of 1956	36
5	Basic Training: May–October 1957	50
6	Parachute Training	64
7	Operations November 1957–May 1958: The Sahara and Guelma	70
8	May 1958: Turmoil and Change	112
9	Caporal-chef	123
10	Sergeant	138
11	The Beginning of the End	143
12	The Last Months of 1st REP: January–April 1961	167
13	Final Months	178
Epilogue		186
Bibliography		189
Author's Note		190

List of Photographs

Frontispiece – Sergeant Hunter-Choat.	iii
November 1957: parachute training at Blida, with Nord Noratlas.	67
The gorge of El Kantara in the Saharan Atlas, Biskra province.	75
Tony (left) and Ray Palin (right) with a captured ALN flag.	78
December 1957: family encampment in the desert near Mrhaïer.	79
Guelma, January 1958: Tony with his FM24/29 before his first operation.	81
January 1958: paras of 1st REP on the way to Guelma near the Tunisian border.	83
H-21 'flying banana' helicopter delivering supplies in the field near Guelma.	84
Captured photo of ALN *fellaghas* posing with an MP40 and a flag.	87
Paras of 1st REP taking a break during operations.	95
Mascara, February 1958: 'the love of my life – my Emma.'	98
Captured ALN weapons at Guelma, April 1958.	102
9 May 1958: General Vanuxem presents Tony with his first Cross of Military Valour.	106
Tony's much-admired regimental commanding officer, Lieutenant Colonel Jeanpierre.	109
On operations, 1958–59: 'How's that for marching country?'	128
Tony armed with a MAS49 semi-automatic rifle with telescopic sight.	129
Zeralda, Camerone Day 1959: Tony after his promotion to caporal-chef.	135
Sergeant Choat in Kabylia.	148
Unloading arms captured during an operation in Kabylia.	156
A captured Algerian boy adopted by the regiment.	157
Tony while serving with 1st RE near Sidi Bel Abbès, late 1961.	180

List of Maps

General Map of Algeria with principal towns, ALN wilayas, and Legion bases.   21

North-East Algeria: Places mentioned in Chapters 7, 9, and 11 relating to operations involving 1st REP. I have been unable to precisely locate the topographical features Kalaat Renadjil and Koudiat Megroun El Ougami. However, the former is close to Beni Mezline and the latter Guelma.   71

North-West Algeria: Places mentioned in Chapters 9, 10, and 11 relating to operations involving 1st REP and 7th Intervention Company, 1st RE.   124

Foreword

Peter Hoskins has already made his mark as a military scholar, researcher, and writer with his books on the Hundred Years' War. So when I became aware from Tony Hunter-Choat's widow, Linda, that Tony had left an account of his time as a *légionnaire* and she gave it to me to read, I realised that it would make a fascinating, indeed an essential, book and that Peter was probably the man for the job. Linda agreed. I knew from my close friendship with Tony that, by any standards, his life had been extraordinary and not just his time in the Legion. There is much that will have to remain secret, at least for the time being. But the story of his time in the Legion deserves to be told, and Linda was keen that it be told properly.

Tony wrote a foreword for his friend Tony Geraghty's book about the Legion, *March or Die*.[1] A part bears repetition here, as it illustrates Tony's attitude towards his Legion service: 'Without any doubt, every *légionnaire* owes a great and unpayable debt to the France who provided him with the escape and refuge he sought so desperately; every *légionnaire* owes a great debt to France for the comfort and succour she gave him when he needed it most.' There is no doubt that his experience as one of the very few Britons in the then 26,000-strong Legion shaped Tony as a man and as a soldier, and provided the foundation for a military career probably unmatched in recent times for its variety and impact. He later became President of the Foreign Legion Association of former *légionnaires* in the United Kingdom.

I first met Tony at the end of my first tour with 22nd Special Air Service (SAS) Regiment. I had just returned from a task in the Far East to attend a junior officers' staff course at Warminster. I was a captain, and Tony was my syndicate directing staff, a major in the Royal Artillery. Rumours abounded amongst the students about this unusual and somewhat eccentric officer, about his previous service as a sergeant in the Legion and as a Gurkha officer with service in the Indonesian

---

1   Tony Geraghty, *March or Die, France and the Foreign Legion* (London: Grafton Books, 1986), p.7.

confrontation. Tony and I hit it off immediately, but what I did not know at the time was that the then Director of the SAS, Brigadier Johnny Watts, already had his eye on Tony to become the commanding officer of 23rd SAS, one of the two Territorial Army volunteer SAS regiments. This in itself was unusual: to reach such a position, you would generally have passed the SAS selection course, including the demanding officers' week, and served as a captain troop commander and a major squadron commander in 22nd SAS. There was no such suitable candidate available at the time, and Tony's reputation on active operations impressed Johnny Watts. Thereafter, Tony popped up in my life frequently: during my next two tours with the SAS and, subsequently, when we were both staff officers at SHAPE (Supreme Headquarters Allied Powers Europe) in Belgium. From this point, the rest of his service was spent mainly with special forces units of one type or another and, once he retired from the Army, in the specialist security world. We remained close friends for the rest of Tony's life.

When Tony died from lung cancer in 2012, Linda asked me to give the eulogy at his memorial service in Hereford Cathedral. The cathedral is big, but extra seats were required and hurriedly obtained to accommodate the crowd of family, friends, and military colleagues and comrades from around the world who arrived to make up the huge congregation. A senior delegation from France – five generals – could not make it as their helicopter was weathered off. At the service, the French Military Attaché spoke for the Legion and for France. He had only recently visited Linda at home, where he had presented her with the insignia of a Commander of the *Légion d'Honneur* for Tony – a remarkably rare honour for a non-French citizen. Sadly, Tony had been too ill to travel to London for formal presentation of the insignia before he died.

I have been lucky enough to work with some renowned and highly competent warriors. I have learned that every man has his flaws, and, in this respect, Tony was no different. He was an unusual and complex man and sometimes difficult to work with, especially if you were one of his subordinate officers. There is a British military aphorism that there are no bad regiments, just bad officers. Tony had served as a soldier in combat under some officers for whom he had the greatest respect and some who did not measure up. I believe he was therefore deliberately demanding of his officers, and, for some, that may have proved an uncomfortable experience. However, what was undeniable was Tony's exceptional courage, his military competence and professionalism, and in particular, that essential quality for special operations – a different way of thinking. These qualities, along with his character, in particular his modesty, usually engendered loyalty and affection.

Tony spoke five languages and was a gifted artist. His sometimes-idiosyncratic behaviour made him an interesting companion, too interesting for some.

Personally, my life would be diminished had I missed my friendship with this singular man and indeed his remarkable family.

I am delighted that Linda has agreed that Tony's personal record of his time as a *légionnaire* should be published and that it has been brought to life by Peter Hoskins.

John Griffin
Brigadier (retired).

Preface

This book does not set out to provide a comprehensive history of the Algerian War. It is first and foremost the story of an exceptional and much-decorated soldier fighting in the French Foreign Legion between 1957 and 1962. His record and reputation were such that a eulogy was written by a Legion general for ex-*légionnaire* Tony Hunter-Choat's memorial service. As the general wrote:

> After basic and advanced training during which he became first in his intake, he joined 1st Foreign Legion Parachute Regiment (1st REP), one of the most selective and exclusive regiments of the French Army. There he took part in the most ferocious episodes of what is now known as the Algerian War. Tony did very well, and for his gallantry received three citations [for] the Cross of Military Valour ... Being selected for the non-commissioned officer (NCO) course, he again came first in his class, and became the youngest NCO of the entire French Foreign Legion and one of the most promising. Then he went on and on fighting, got wounded, and was awarded the Military Medal, which in France is awarded only to NCOs and field marshals ... [The Legion was] where through hardship and comradeship he learnt the hard way to be a man you can rely on: loyal, faithful, terrible to his enemies, generous to his friends.

After completion of his initial five-year engagement, Tony was offered a commission in the Legion, which would have brought with it French nationality. As we shall see, he elected not to take up the offer and joined the British Army. Subsequently, in 2011, Tony was appointed as *Commandeur de la Légion d'Honneur*.

The account in this book of this outstanding soldier's career in the Legion is largely drawn from his own modest and self-effacing account. However, although the subject is Tony Hunter-Choat, to fully understand his story it is necessary to set it within the context of political and military events before and during the war – a war that sucked in up to 500,000 French soldiers and cost the French Army 25,600 dead, 2,000 of whom were *légionnaires*.

Acknowledgements

I am first of all grateful to Tony Hunter-Choat's widow Linda for having had the confidence to let me read and draw on the memoirs of Tony's life with the French Foreign Legion. In these days when one can be expected to apologise for the acts of one's ancestors, perhaps I can be excused for thanking Tony posthumously for the privilege of reading his modest, unassuming, and, at times, highly amusing account of his extraordinary, action-packed life as a *légionnaire*. My thanks are also due to Brigadier John Griffin, a very good friend since we served together at SHAPE in the mid-1980s. Not only did he facilitate my contacts with Linda and write the foreword to this book, but it was also through him that I was fortunate enough to meet Tony, who was also serving at SHAPE at the time. Thanks to that introduction, I was able to spend some good moments in Tony's amusing, stimulating, enjoyable, and never-boring company. My thanks are due to both John and Linda for reviewing the text of this book and providing valuable and helpful suggestions to correct errors and remove ambiguities. Finally, I am particularly grateful to Martin Windrow for devoting a great deal of time to reviewing a draft of my typescript. He has written extensively on the French Foreign Legion, and he provided invaluable advice on matters of style, historical fact, and terminology – indeed he has saved me considerable embarrassment.

1

The Beginnings of an Adventure

Enlistment

On Sunday, 17 March 1957, 21-year-old Tony Hunter-Choat arrived at Fort Neuf – adjacent to the medieval Chateau de Vincennes, a five-mile walk from the centre of Paris. As the red words '*LÉGION ÉTRANGÈRE*' on a green background made clear, this was a French Foreign Legion barracks. He knocked on the large studded wooden door of the fort, and a Judas hole opened. The reception was hardly encouraging: 'What do you want?', 'I want to join the Foreign Legion,' 'No you don't, fuck off.', 'But I do!', 'Why?' The young Hunter-Choat was at a loss for an answer and simply replied that he really did want to join the Foreign Legion. The Judas hole closed: 'Stay there!'

The door swung open, and Tony stepped into the courtyard of the nineteenth-century fortress. Five years of adventure were about to begin. By 1957, three years after the end of the French war in Indochina, hundreds of thousands of French troops were deployed in Algeria. There could have been little doubt in his mind that if he joined the Legion, he would be sent to Algeria, to participate in one of the most savage wars in the post-Second World War withdrawal from empire by the European powers.

Tony's background would not, perhaps, lead one to think that he would take the dramatic step of joining the Legion. The popular stereotype of a Legion recruit is of a young man seeking to escape either a murky past or a broken love affair. This was not the case with Tony. He came from a conventional middle-class family: his father was in insurance and his mother was a schoolteacher. He had been educated at Dulwich College, and he went on to study architecture at Kingston College of Art. In March 1957, his final examinations were approaching. Although he did not consider that he had what was required to become a first-rate architect, the road to a successful, but perhaps unexciting, career would be open to him. However, he preferred adventure to the humdrum. As he wrote:

> For no particular reason that I can remember, I woke early on Thursday 14 March 1957, and lay there in the darkness, waking up and thinking. I came quickly to a decision; I would go away that day from four-and-a-half years of architectural studies at Kingston College of Art and Architecture, away from all my friends, away from my wonderful Head of Architecture, Eric Brown, and away from my family. Now. The other two students whose names I cannot now even remember in our small ramshackle cottage were still asleep. I gathered up my passport and everything that I could sell to fund my travels, which amounted to only an electric portable gramophone and a watch, and crept quietly out. Since I had wrecked my lovely BSA 350 motorbike, I had to walk into Kingston.

Tony had taken a decision that would take him down an entirely different career path from that envisaged. He had no fear of roughing it. He had already developed a taste for foreign languages, adventure, and travel by hitchhiking around Europe in his holidays and had once hitchhiked from Oslo back to England without any money. Once the pawnbroker in Kingston was open, he raised money against his possessions then set out by rail for Dover and the ferry to Calais. The watch had been a fifteenth-birthday present from his parents. No doubt parting with it was a wrench, but five years later he was reunited with it thanks to a friend retrieving it from the pawnbroker.

On arriving in France, Tony hitched his way to the centre of Paris. There he met an attractive young woman who took pity on the plight of the young, almost broke Englishman. She insisted that Tony stay with her, which he did briefly before setting out on the Sunday to enlist despite some reluctance on his part and much pleading for him to stay on hers. (Uncannily, the writer Douglas Boyd, without any knowledge of Tony's experience, many years later started a novel, *The Eagle and The Snake*, with his hero selling his watch to fund his journey and staying with a girl he met in Paris before joining the Legion.)

Fort Neuf had been constructed between 1841 and 1844 as one of 17 forts built around Paris to defend the capital. Tony entered a paved courtyard surrounded by offices and dormitories. There were other potential recruits lounging about who had been brought in from outlying recruiting depots in Lille, Belgium, and on the German frontier. Once enough recruits had been gathered to fill a railway carriage, they would move south to Marseille. In the meantime, there were formalities to complete. Tony was interviewed in a sparsely furnished office by an 'extremely friendly and helpful non-commissioned officer', who recorded his personal details and removed his passport, with the promise that he would get it back on his discharge five years later.

Next was a haircut, a procedure that all who have served in the armed forces will recall. No matter how short your hair on recruitment, it is never short enough. In Tony's case, this was taken to the extreme: the traditional Legion haircut known as *boule à zero* (the ball to zero), with repeated passages of clippers reducing the hair to a fuzz one millimetre in length.

After a medical examination, Tony handed in his civilian clothes consisting of a leather jacket, two pairs of trousers, four shirts, four pairs of socks, and a pair of shoes. With the pawning of his watch and gramophone, he had now parted with all that he possessed in the world. In return, he received a motley selection of uniform items: First World War boots without laces, a Second World War-style battledress and overcoat, and a red and green Legion forage cap. The night was spent in dormitories, not dissimilar to those that Tony had experienced in French youth hostels: bunk beds with straw mattresses with bed bugs for company. His first experience of Legion food was that it was simple and filling; it would remain so throughout Tony's five years of service:

> Legion food was always good; it was never fancy but was exactly what hungry légionnaires needed after a hard day's work. It followed a fixed pattern: Hungarian goulash on Mondays, omelette on Tuesdays, pork on Wednesdays, spaghetti on Thursdays, fish on Fridays and so on, so at least you always knew which day of the week it was. The cooks were good and nearly all had been chefs before joining the Legion.

The next day Tony, under the name of Anthony Choat, signed his engagement papers: 'Engagé volontaire provisoire pour 5 ans au titre de la Légion Étrangère à l'Intendance Militaire de PARIS, le 18 MARS 1957'. (Probationary volunteer for five years in the Foreign Legion). The probationary element meant that, in theory, the recruit could change his mind during the first three months of his service, and the Legion could also dispense with his services during this period. As Tony pointed out, the reality was somewhat different. The recruit could change his mind as often as he wished, but the Legion could drag things out beyond three months and then say, 'Sorry, too late.' Similarly, a *légionnaire* could be discharged whenever it suited the Legion. At some point, Tony's mother got wind of his departure to join the Legion. She pursued him to Paris to try to prevent him making what she considered would be a huge mistake in abandoning his architectural career. In the event, she was too late: the contract had been signed, and she was refused access to her son. As Tony was to say later, he owed everything to the Legion; far from making a mistake, he had made one of the best decisions of his life.

Early on Tuesday, 19 March, the recruits were woken early. Dressed in their cast-off uniforms they resembled, in Tony's mind, a group of German POWs returning after five years in a Soviet prison camp. There were about 40 recruits in the batch: two other Englishmen, some Hungarians – one of whom, Laszlo Horvath, quickly became a close friend although neither spoke the other's language – several Germans, a Norwegian, a Dane, and a couple of 'uncouth' Belgians. Recruitment to the Legion is inevitably effected by world events: Spaniards arriving after the Spanish Civil War, Germans after the Second World War, and former Yugoslavs in the 1990s. The year that Tony joined was no exception: some Germans disillusioned with post-war Germany, some continuing to seek sanctuary from Allied authorities, and Hungarians escaping the aftermath of the 1956 anti-Soviet Hungarian uprising. Tony described their mood:

> After the strangeness of the last two days we were all unsettled and seeking strength through numbers; we stuck together as we knew already that we could never beat the system but needed either to work with it or to not let it find us out. This knowledge was to stand us in good stead for years to come; those that thought they were smarter than the Legion soon disappeared from the scene, and continued to leave as the Legion whittled us down to exactly what she wanted.

The day was spent cleaning everything, peeling potatoes, setting out the dining room, eating, smoking, and talking until late evening, when the recruits climbed into trucks to take them on the first leg of their journey to become *légionnaires*. They rumbled and bumped their way to the Paris Gare de Lyon station for the long, slow journey by train to Marseille. They were locked in their own carriage accompanied by a handful of NCOs, kept well away from the civilian population 'who would probably have run screaming at the sight of us'. They slept through the journey.

Tony found Marseille a delight: bright sunshine after the grey and damp of Paris in March. They were marched down the steps of the station to waiting trucks and driven to join 1st Transit Company at the Petit Bas Fort St Nicolas. This was the lower part of the citadel built by order of Louis XIV between 1660 and 1664 – not to protect Marseille from invasion, as might be supposed, but to control a sometimes rebellious and volatile population. The fort, facing the harbour on three sides and with the main gate on the other, was the principal transit point for Legion recruits, those who had re-enlisted and those returning from leave *en route* for Algeria. It fulfilled this function for many years, but today this part of the citadel, which has been renamed Fort Ganteaume, serves as an officers' club and mess for the French armed forces in Marseille.

Tony observed how agents of secret services and police forces from around the world lurked outside the fort to pick up wanted men rejected by the Legion or who had completed their service. Many who were to be discharged on completion of their initial engagement took one look at who was awaiting them and promptly decided that a further five years in the Legion was preferable to running the gauntlet of leaving the fort.

Tony and his new Hungarian friend found adjacent bunks in a large, airy dormitory. Together with the other recruits in their batch, they whiled away their time for almost three weeks awaiting the next ship to Oran. Smoking the free packets of Troupe cigarettes, distributed every two days (described by Tony as similar to the famous Gauloise but more loosely packed), featured, along with talking and drinking beer and wine. Their days started with breakfast at 0645 hours: coffee or hot chocolate, coarse bread, and cheese or pieces of chocolate or an apple or jam. Although much of their time passed in chatter and getting to know one another, life also started to take on a military dimension. They were paraded or, as Tony wrote, '… at least pushed and shoved into some semblance of order'. Such parades were repeated until, in due course, they started to get the hang of things. They were also vaccinated and interviewed. Such interviews included a long interrogation by French military intelligence, the *Deuxième Bureau*. He was intrigued, and perhaps somewhat disconcerted, to find that his interviewers were already well informed of his previous visits to France and other countries. Tony pointed out that the commonly held view that the Legion would accept anyone despite their past was a myth. The weeding out was severe and thorough, with a number of their batch, including one of the two other Britons who had joined with Tony, rejected and released into the clutches of those waiting outside the fort.

It is part of the legend of the Legion that NCOs indulged in gratuitous cruelty, particularly towards new recruits, but this was not Tony's experience. He found that the NCOs at Vincennes, Marseille, and later in Algeria were neither cruel nor unkind. They were certainly not soft or overly friendly, but they did all that they could to help the new and lost recruit to settle in. He believed that the stories of cruelty were put about by those who were simply unable to adapt to the Legion lifestyle. For Tony's part, although admitting to being often confused and bemused, he felt perfectly at home in the Legion from the start. He never felt that he was in an alien environment.

One aspect of his new life in the Legion was less savoury: the introduction to bed bugs, with which Tony developed 'a long and lasting relationship'. They were to be found everywhere: in the straw mattresses, the wooden bunks, and indeed the fabric of the buildings. Their bites resulted in almost unbearable itching, although with time he became immune to them. As his career progressed the bed bugs were joined by fleas, mites, and head lice.

At long last, early on Saturday, 6 April 1957, those of Tony's batch who had survived the weeding-out were trucked down to the port and embarked on the SS *Sidi Bel Abbès* bound for the Algerian port of Oran. The *Sidi Bel Abbès* was a very handsome ferry with smart cabins for paying customers. The story for the 100 or so Legion recruits, including those from other batches who had been waiting in Marseille, was very different and their conditions were far from luxurious. They were crammed into the lowest deck in the bow of the ship. The men slept in deck chairs and were fed from huge soup kettles, much like witches' cauldrons, swinging on tripods. As the crossing became rougher the contents slopped onto the deck to mix with the vomit of those suffering from seasickness. To add to the squalor, the 10 toilets were soon blocked and overflowing and added their contents to the mix of soup and vomit. This unpleasant voyage was to last until Sunday night when the ship arrived off Oran. The first impression was the smell of Africa, the distinctive odour of Algeria.

Joining *Les Événements*

Tony's arrival in Algeria came at a time when events were taking on a new dimension. The National Army for the Liberation of Algeria (ALN) had gained in strength and confidence, and the French Army was engaged in the urban Battle of Algiers. At home in Metropolitan France, there was growing disquiet about the conduct of the war, with a parliamentary commission established in early April 1957 to investigate reports of brutality and torture by the French Army.

The war was rarely referred to as such, with the euphemism *les événements* (the events) generally used. How could there be a war? Algeria had been occupied by the French since 1830; it was not considered a colony but an integral part of France, with a substantial proportion of the population of European origin, organised and administered in the same manner as mainland France. There could only be a war against a sovereign nation, not against rebels in 'France Overseas'.

To set Tony's experiences throughout the remainder of the war in context, it is time to look at the country in which he was to spend the next five years: a brief history since the arrival of the French more than 120 years before and the progress of the war to date. We shall also look briefly at the history of the Legion parachute units, which had started life in 1948 in the midst of the Indochina War, since the experiences of those who had fought there, and were to do so later in Algeria, had a significant impact on the conduct of that war. We shall return to Tony's story in due course in Chapter 5.

2
France in Algeria: 1830–1954

Invasion, Conquest, and Pacification

In the early years of the nineteenth century, the Ottoman Empire was in decline, and the Sultan was preoccupied with events closer to home rather than the more distant territories of his empire. Algeria was not a state but rather a land with many tribal groups, Berber and Arab, some of which were nomadic and others sedentary. It was largely rural with only small cities and towns. Its frontiers were ill defined, even fluid. This loosely bound part of the Ottoman Empire was ruled by the Dey of Algiers.[1] Barbary pirates operating from North African ports, including Algiers, had for centuries been an irritant for the European powers and continued to be so into the nineteenth century. Between 1801 and 1804, the US Navy had fought the corsairs of Tripoli, and, in 1816 and 1824, the Royal Navy had bombarded Algiers but had been unable to occupy the town due to its strong defences.

During the French Revolutionary Wars, when famine threatened in France, the Dey had supplied grain to the French government on favourable terms – indeed, he also loaned them the money for the purchase. Small repayments towards the loan had been made under the reign of Napoleon I, but a large part of the principal remained outstanding with significant interest having accrued. This debt was a long-running sore in relations between France and the Dey. Under King Charles X, a commission had been appointed in France to try to resolve the issue. However, the Dey could see nothing coming from this initiative, and, in April 1827, matters came to a head. The Dey wrote to the responsible French government minister who,

---

1   The Dey, possibly a corruption of the common Ottoman honorific title, Bey (lord), was the title given to the rulers of the Regencies of Algiers, Tripoli, and Tunis under the Ottoman Empire from 1671 onwards.

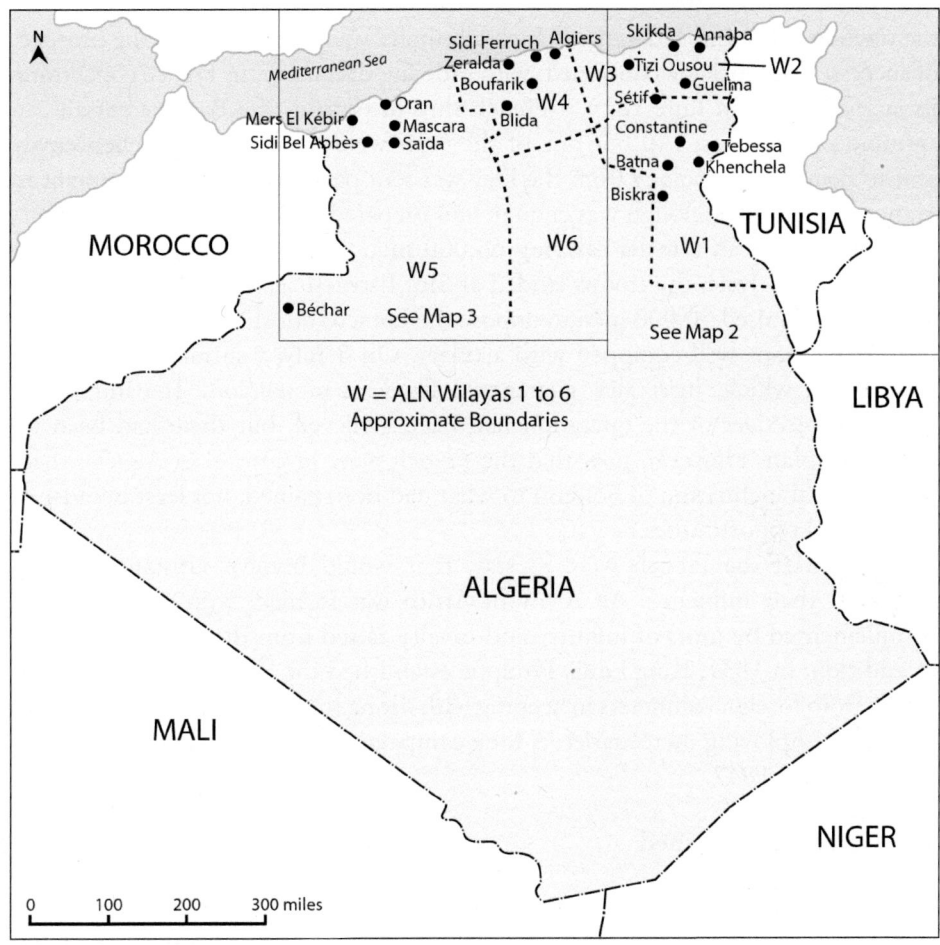

General Map of Algeria with principal towns, ALN wilayas, and Legion bases. (Author's illustration). (Map drawn by George Anderson)

instead of replying, sent the French consul to meet the Dey. In a bad-tempered meeting, the Dey expressed his outrage that the minister had not replied in person. He was also angered by what he saw as the lack of the respect shown by the consul and struck him with a fly whisk at the end of the meeting.

In August 1827, the French established a blockade of Algiers in retaliation for this affront to their consul, but it proved ineffective. The French squadron had few ships, and the shallow draft Barbary galleys were easily able to avoid the French ships standing off from the coast. A landing was proposed to take Algiers, but, in view of the strength of the landward defences and the failures of the Royal Navy to take the town in 1816 and 1824, the French admiralty was sceptical about the prospect of success. The blockade continued, with growing discontent in France concerning its lack of effect. In June 1829, a French ship in pursuit of a Barbary corsair ran aground on the coast. All but one of the crew were massacred. A French envoy sent to demand an apology from the Dey was sent packing. A new government in France decided that enough was enough and prepared plans for an invasion.

In May 1830, an armada carrying 65,000 men and 3,000 cannon set sail for Algiers. On 14 June, the troops landed at Sidi Ferruch, 12 miles west of Algiers. The Dey had raised 50,000 men to oppose the French, but they were no match for European troops well equipped with artillery. On 5 July, a surrender agreement was signed, which, inter alia, guaranteed freedom of religion. The immediate punitive objectives of the operation had been achieved, but there had been no long-term plan. However, now that the French were in control of Algiers, there was a natural inclination to hold on to what had been gained, not least because of commercial opportunities.

However, if the French were to stay, that would involve substantial forces to extend their influence. An Army of Africa was formed, with French troops complemented by units of infantry and cavalry raised from the local population. In addition, in 1831, King Louis-Philippe established the French Foreign Legion, drawn from foreign volunteers in keeping with a long tradition in pre-revolutionary France of employing mercenaries. A long campaign of expansion and pacification followed until 1847.

The Colony Established

Encouraged by the French, European settlers soon started to arrive, initially in their hundreds and then in their thousands. The first official statistics reveal 117,360 Europeans in the country in 1849. Contrary to what one might expect, they came not just from France. Some 46 percent were French in origin and 30 percent from Spain; the remainder came from Italy, Germany, Switzerland, British Malta, and Great Britain. The figures for the indigenous population are perhaps less reliable than for the Europeans but were estimated at 2,598,517. There were patterns of colonisation: the French generally opted for the region of Algiers, the Spanish for Oran in the west, and Italians and Maltese for the Constantine region towards the Tunisian frontier in the east.

Until pacification was approaching completion in the late 1840s, the colony was administered by the French Army, but, in 1848, it attained a status unique among French overseas possessions: it was declared to be actual French territory. The roughly 200-mile-deep settled coastal region was divided into three *départements* centred on (from west to east) Oran, Algiers, and Constantine. To the south, the sparsely inhabited pre-Saharan and Saharan wilderness was divided into six territories still largely administered by the Army through a network of intelligence (native affairs) officers. This structure was to remain essentially unchanged until the 1950s.

Although based on the farming of the fertile coastal region, by 1870 European settlement had become 70 percent urban. In addition to the businessmen and administrators in the three main cities, many failed homesteaders had sold out to larger landowners and drifted into small, scattered towns and villages. Replicating most aspects of those in southern Europe, these acted as hubs of settler life and administration.

Meanwhile, the wealthier *colons* (settlers) continuing hunger for territory produced chronic tensions with the semi-nomadic Arabs, whose concept of land ownership was entirely different: while they farmed family plots, pastoralism was more important and traditionally based on communal access to grazing lands. While demanding the rights of French citizens, the settlers resented any attempt by Paris (or the Army) to limit their voracity. In the 1860s, they were enraged by reforms attempted by the liberal-minded Napoleon III (whom they cursed as an 'Arab Emperor'). After Napoleon lost his throne following defeat by Prussia in September 1870, the *colons* rose in revolt against the republican government that replaced him.

The new government became more acceptable to them in February 1871, when a widespread Muslim rebellion by the plains Arabs and Berber highlanders, who eventually put as many as 100,000 tribesmen into the field, was suppressed. The rebels' bloody attacks on farms and villages were poorly coordinated; Army reinforcements defeated the main rebel groups by September and hunted down the last diehards in January 1872. Following this shock, the settlers abandoned any pretence of even-handed relations with the Muslims. In this, they would be shielded by an increasingly influential colonial lobby in Paris, with the governor-generalship becoming a civilian political appointment after the departure of the last military governor in 1879. More or less forced land purchases accompanied outright confiscations, and many Arabs were reduced to sharecroppers and hired labourers.

Another fundamental problem in French Algeria came from the promise to respect the freedom of religion for the indigenous peoples. This policy, laudable as it was, resulted in a contradiction. Native Algerians who wished to see greater integration with the European population in terms of rights were subject to Islamic civil law and not the French civil code. Despite the official respect for Islam, the religion of the Europeans was Roman Catholicism, and the Church wished to spread Christian beliefs. In 1867, a new archbishop of Algiers had become more proactive, creating orphanages where Muslim children were baptised and schools both to educate Muslim children and to convert them to Christianity. The French administration was hostile to the archbishop's evangelism, but resentment between the two populations was aggravated. In 1912, a senior member of the Church summarised matters: 'The Arabs will only be French if they are Christian.'[2]

A further differentiation between Europeans and the indigenous populations emerged as the French extended military conscription to French citizens in Algeria from 1864. With the granting of French citizenship to the Algerian Jewish population in 1870, conscription was extended to Jews, but Muslims were still excluded. By 1912, however, obligatory military service was extended to the Muslim population but without extending to them the rights of citizenship. There were disturbances among the Muslim population, with some families going into exile rather than see their sons recruited into the French Army against their will. Another grievance had been created.

Meanwhile, French influence was extending in Africa, most notably for the story of Algeria with the creation of French protectorates in Tunisia in 1871 and Morocco in 1912. However, in neither case were they considered as part of France nor was there widespread colonisation in the way there had been in Algeria. Thus, when pressure came for independence from France, the French would let go of Tunisia and Morocco relatively easily in 1956, while they fought ferociously to hold on to Algeria.

The First World War

With the coming of the First World War in 1914, both European and Muslim Algerians were conscripted into the French Army. Of the Europeans, 22,000 lost their lives, while 25,000 of 175,000 recruited from the Muslim population were killed fighting in Europe. The need for labour during the war also resulted in a wave of immigration by Muslims to France, and this expatriate population would later be a source of financial support for the Front for National Liberation of Algeria (FLN). However, the loyalty to France was not universal. In 1916, the population in the east of the country refused conscription; two French administrators were assassinated, and those refusing conscription withdrew into the hills to establish armed resistance. It was necessary to withdraw troops from France to restore order. The return of peace brought expectations among the Muslim population for recognition of their contribution to victory. Prime Minister Clemenceau issued decrees in 1919 to allow all Muslims who wished to do so to acquire French

---

2   Pierre Montagnon, *La Guerre d'Algérie, Genèse et engrenage d'une tragédie (1954–1962)* (Paris: Pygmalion, 1984), p.60. (Author's translation).

citizenship. However, to do so, they would be required to renounce Islamic civil law and accept the French code of civilian law. This created a dilemma for the indigenous population, but nevertheless some took the opportunity.

Between the Wars

The centenary of the French arrival in Algeria was celebrated with due pomp in 1930. Algeria was the jewel in the crown of the French Empire. Notions of social or political reform, let alone independence, were not on the agenda. The French saw themselves not only as colonists but also as liberators who had driven out anarchy and poverty and brought justice, education, peace, and well-being. In the intervening century, the European population had grown to 880,000, and the indigenous Berbers and Arabs now amounted to around 5,500,000. The Europeans remained largely urban, with 80 percent living in the towns and cities. Although there were inequalities between the Europeans and the indigenous people, there was no institutionalised racism: all took their turn in queues, mingled in public places, and shared public transport. If Arabs and Berbers were hesitant to sit on the terrace of a European bar, or a Frenchman to take coffee in a local Muslim café, that had more to do with cultural and religious differences than racism.

In contrast to the Europeans, 90 percent of the Arabs and Berbers lived in the countryside. All the large land holdings were held by Europeans, and the majority of the rural Arabs and Berbers eked out a poor living with small holdings. In the towns, and the countryside where there were substantial numbers of Europeans, there were 298 communes – towns and villages organised in the same way as in metropolitan France with an elected mayor and council. Around 25 percent of the indigenous population lived in these communes. Since 1919, Muslim councillors had been permitted, but they could not exceed one-third of the councillors. Thus, the power for decision making and allocation of resources, through the mayor and the enforced majority of councillors, rested with the Europeans. There were also 70 *communes mixtes*, but the term is misleading: these were not towns or villages with mixed populations but were vast areas of land as large, or often larger than, a good-sized English county. Around 75 percent of the indigenous peoples lived in these *communes mixtes*. They were administered by Europeans with the assistance of local *caïds*, who were Muslim notables in whom the French had confidence. They were appointed in return for service rendered or perceived loyalty and paid a salary by the central government. The *commune mixte* also had, from 1919, the right to an elected assembly, but its powers were negligible. The imbalance of European and indigenous settlement between town and country would be significant problem for the French Army in the face of rebellion from 1954.

As the century of French rule was celebrated, few French people and European Algerians saw much need for reform in Algeria, but among the Muslim population the demand for change was growing. For some, the search was for equality within French Algeria. Others wished to go further, calling for independence. Despite a general resistance to change among the European population, there were some who could see the way things were moving, with one governor-general on his departure from Algiers warning the European population: 'Take care. The indigenous people of Algeria, through your fault, do not yet have their motherland, they are looking for one. They ask you for the French motherland. Give it to them quickly, without that they will make their own.'[3]

The Second World War

The Second World War brought many Muslims loyally to the French colours, putting aside for the time being their thoughts of nationalism, though others saw a German victory as in their interests. Initially, after the French defeat in 1940, Algeria was in the Vichy camp but passed across to the Free French after the Anglo-American landings in 1942. In 1944, General Charles de Gaulle introduced reforms: equality between Europeans and Muslims, universal suffrage for Muslims, an increase in the number of Muslims on councils and assemblies, and the right for Muslims to retain their use of the Islamic civil code without prejudice to their French citizenship. A few years earlier, these reforms would have been well received, but now they were judged inadequate by the Muslim elites.

With the regeneration of the French Army from 1943, some 160,000 European Algerians and 50,000 Muslims enlisted for the liberation of Europe and the final defeat of Germany. With the focus on the war in Europe, few troops remained in Algeria. Garrisons were at skeleton strength, and many of the men who remained were either recruits waiting for enlistment or convalescents. The police were also below strength. With underlying nationalist resentment, a series of poor harvests, and little help with supplies from mainland France or the Allies, conditions were ripe for insurrection. There had been reluctance among some nationalists to take advantage of France during the war, but, as it drew to a close, there was a chance to exploit the circumstances.

On the day that the war in Europe came to an end, 8 May 1945, violence erupted when police fired upon demonstrators in Setif, near Constantine. Armed Muslim groups then fell upon Europeans there, and, in nearby Guelma, some of them

---

3   Montagnon, *La Guerre d'Algérie*, p.88. (Author's translation).

proclaimed jihad – holy war. The police, local European militias, the Army, and even the Air Force responded more-or-less indiscriminately. When the violence ended days later, 113 Europeans had lost their lives, but the number of Muslim deaths in this Setif massacre (including loyalists slain by the rioters) was vastly higher. It was certainly underestimated by the French at 2,000, though claims by nationalists of up to 45,000 killed were probably highly exaggerated. Whatever the true figures, this bloody episode was a turning point in the movement for Algerian independence.

General Duval, who had restored order, was under no illusions. In his prophetic report, he wrote, 'I have given you 10 years of peace. But we must not deceive ourselves. Everything must change in Algeria.'[4] Although food had been in short supply, the insurrectionists did not raid food stocks. First and foremost, this was a revolt against perceived injustice and those who represented injustice: France and the European Algerians.

The result was not, however, a recognition of the need for reform amongst the European *pieds noirs*.[5] On the contrary, fearing further uprisings, they refused all compromise: authority and firmness became the watchwords. Many Europeans also started to desert the countryside and villages to move to the perceived safety of towns and cities. The gap between the European and the Muslim populations widened. Elements of the Muslim population remained supporters of France and engaged in democratic processes. However, much of the population provided fertile ground for the more radical nationalists who believed that an armed revolt was the only answer. They bided their time in the uneasy peace that followed the events of 1945.

1945–1954

The Second World War had changed much. Aspirations for assimilation with France had taken a back seat to full independence. The government in Paris was not entirely blind to the need for change, but, in the immediate post-war years, Algeria was just one of many problems – not least of which were the political, social, and economic reconstruction in France and the war in Indochina.

In 1947, the French parliament approved a number of reforms that, inter alia, granted a degree of autonomy to the Algerian *départements*, including for financial

---

4   Montagnon, *La Guerre d'Algérie*, p.99. (Author's translation).
5   The term '*pied noir*' describes the population of French Algeria of European origin. The origin of the term is obscure.

affairs. A new Algerian Assembly was created with 120 members. Sixty members were to be elected by each of two electoral colleges. The first college comprised predominantly French citizens and a small minority of Muslims; the second college comprised the remaining Muslims. On the face of it, this should have given considerable power to the Muslim population, but all decisions required a two-thirds majority and were, in any case, subject to approval by the French administration. The Algerian Muslim leaders denounced these measures as insufficient.

Nevertheless, in these post-war years, Muslim political parties participated in the democratic process. From early 1947, one party served as cover for the paramilitary OS (Special Organisation). The OS carried out a number of low-scale attacks on Muslims identified as being too close to the French administration and, most notably, raided the post office in Oran to raise funds. However, the OS was predominantly concerned with preparation for an armed rising rather than carrying out terrorist acts at this stage: the purchase of small-arms, recovery of weapons abandoned during the war, and creation of hidden stockpiles of arms.

The OS was the nursery for what would become the FLN and the ALN, the political and military arms of the independence movement. The leaders were clear that independence would need to be torn from France. This mission of the OS was to prepare for revolutionary war: an insurrection of all the people, in which the mass of the rural population would play the determinant role. There were two strands to the independence movement: those who saw the future as Arab-Islamist and those who supported a broader Algerian solution that took into account the non-Arab-speaking Berbers, who accounted for 30 percent of the indigenous population. With many Berbers active in the movement, this latter view prevailed. In 1950, much of the OS network was dismantled by the police, but the movement remained active, if low key. Playing in their favour was the growing demographic imbalance – with, by 1954, a Muslim population of 8,000,000 in comparison with 1,000,000 Europeans. However, with 80 percent of Muslim children having little or no education, the Arabs and Berbers suffered disproportionally from unemployment. The result was the migration of 300,000 Muslim workers to mainland France. Of the Muslims who remained in Algeria, many lived in extreme poverty in the countryside or in shanty towns on the fringe of the cities, where the divide between Europeans and the indigenous peoples was more evident than ever. In these conditions, those seeking independence did not need to emphasise the nationalist card: the struggle against inequality, injustice, and poverty sufficed to fan the embers of rebellion.

3
The Legion Paras: 1948–54

The parachute units of the Legion had a remarkable history, from their formation in 1948 and throughout the wars in Indochina and Algeria. As Pierre Montagnon wrote in the preface to *Les parachutistes de la Légion, 1948–1962*, this period was:

> ... in every way exceptional ... [marked by] intense operational activity [and] heavy sacrifices. Very often the same personalities were present. A good number of combatants of the rice paddies and limestone hills of Indochina found themselves in the djebels of Algeria ... gaining a reputation as 'the best of the best'. The great names of 1948–1962 became legendary ... to have served [with the Legion para units] in these moments of glory and blood remained a matter of pride for life.[1]

The war in French Indochina (modern-day Vietnam, Laos, and Cambodia) began soon after the end of the Second World War, as the communist Viet Minh insurgency resisted France's attempts to re-establish its hold on the colony following the departure of the defeated Japanese. Much of the war was fought by the badly underequipped CEFEO (French Far East Expeditionary Corps) in the difficult terrain of Tonkin (North Vietnam) – rice paddies in the lowlands and nearly impenetrable jungle in the almost roadless highlands. While initially limited to guerrilla warfare, by 1950 General Giap's VPA (Vietnamese People's Army) was sufficiently organised and equipped to attempt more conventional operations.

It became apparent to the French that mobility and rapid deployment would be essential to counter the Viet Minh. Movement by road was slow and hazardous, with convoys exposed to the risk of ambush. There were a number of parachute

---

1 Pierre Montagnon, *Les parachutistes de la Légion, 1948–1962* (Paris: Pygmalion, 2005), p.11. (Author's translation).

units in the country, but the Foreign Legion did not initially include any paras. If the capabilities of the Legion were to be exploited to the full, an airborne element would be required. In early 1948, an independent para company of 150 officers, NCOs, and men was formed from 3rd REI (Foreign Infantry Regiment). Later in the year, two Legion para battalions were formed in Algeria, 1st BEP (Foreign Parachute Battalion) and 2nd BEP. The two units each had a complement of around 500 officers, NCOs, and men; 1st BEP deployed to Indochina in October 1948 with 2nd BEP arriving in theatre in early 1949. In June 1949, the company from 3rd REI was absorbed into 1st BEP.

From the outset, 1st BEP was heavily engaged in operations in Tonkin, operating at an often-frenetic pace in demanding conditions. French airlift capacity was limited to a couple of squadrons of French-built Junkers Ju-52 three-engined transport aircraft. Helicopters were then virtually unknown even for casualty evacuation, and, with the paucity of fixed-wing transport aircraft, the unit often had to be deployed by road. Even when they were airdropped, or flown into a forward airstrip, they were often operating without support, carrying rations with them and walking out of the jungle at the end of the operation. Initially, 2nd BEP was dispersed with several companies in Cambodia and one retained in Saigon to support 1st BEP when required; subsequently, the two BEPs were both heavily engaged.

The pace of operations for the two BEPs was unremitting, and casualties were part of everyday life. However, an operation in September and October 1950 proved to be catastrophic for 1st BEP and a disaster for the French overall. The operation was centred on the road south-east from Cao Bang (RC4, Route Coloniale 4), some 15 miles from the Chinese border, to the Gulf of Tonkin. There were several French outposts close to the border, and, with the victory of Mao Tse Tung over the Chinese Nationalists in late 1949, there was growing concern over their vulnerability in the case of Chinese intervention in the war. Not only were these outposts dangerously exposed, but RC4 was also notoriously hazardous, with convoys frequently subject to attack. In early September 1950, it was decided to evacuate posts along the northern half of the road, from Cao Bang down to Lang Son, where the HQ of the Frontier Zone was located.

This operation was planned to begin on 1 October 1950, but it was forestalled on 16 September when Giap launched an assault on the post at Dong Khe to cut RC4 south of Cao Bang. There were no mobile units within reach to relieve the two-company-strong Legion infantry garrison, and air support – limited to about a dozen Bell P-63 Kingcobra fighter-bombers – was always badly hampered by the morning fog. After desperate resistance, the *légionnaires* were virtually wiped out early on 18 September.

A brigade under Lieutenant Colonel Le Page, mostly Moroccan light infantry but including 1st BEP, was sent up RC4 from the south to That Khe but with only hesitant and muddled orders. On 2 October, Le Page, already embattled at Dong Khe, was finally ordered to meet up with and extract Lieutenant Colonel Charton's Cao Bang garrison. This force – mainly a battalion of 3rd REI and one of Moroccan troops – retreated from that post the following day. Apart from the difficult terrain and inadequate maps, both columns would suffer from poor communications and from delayed and unrealistic orders from the badly informed Frontier Zone HQ. General Giap orchestrated a concentration of his units to cut off and destroy both columns; about 15 VPA battalions finally achieved this on 7 October, less than 24 hours after Le Page's and Charton's exhausted remnants had finally linked up.

Forced to abandon their wounded, the survivors attempted to escape and evade through the jungle hills in small parties. Led by Tony's future commanding officer, the then Captain Jeanpierre, fewer than 30 paras of 1st BEP, from an initial field strength of some 500, managed to reach the post at That Khe before it was abandoned on 10/11 October. The Frontier Zone command then virtually collapsed; all the remaining small post garrisons fell back on Lang Son, and that major town – with its substantial arsenals and supply depots – was itself abandoned by 20 October. General Giap was left in possession of almost all territory north of the Red River Delta and enough captured materiel to equip a 9,000-man division. French casualties included 5,987 killed and missing from a total of 7,409 in the two columns and the post garrisons.

The disaster of RC4 had many simultaneous causes: inadequate levels of equipment and transport and limited intelligence information – but also poor coordination and a fatal complacency at senior command levels. Accustomed to relatively small numbers of French troops successfully resisting significantly larger VPA forces, the staff underestimated both General Giap's ambition and, crucially, the transformative aid that he had received from the Chinese People's Army following the communist victory in China in mid-1949. As Pierre Montagnon wrote, in the view of the commanders, 'In a set-piece battle a Viet Minh brigade could not hold out against a small battalion of paras.'[2] But by the autumn of 1950, greatly expanded programmes of conscription and of Chinese logistic and training assistance had brought Giap's main force in Tonkin up to some thirty 700-man battalions, each with organic machine-guns, mortars, and bazookas. He also had

---

2   Montagnon, *Les parachutistes de la Légion*, p.42. (Author's translation).

dedicated units of heavy anti-aircraft machine guns, and he could support assaults with up to a couple of dozen 75mm mountain guns.

This defeat, and the annihilation of eight-plus French battalions, badly shook morale both throughout the CEFEO and in France. One of many heads to roll was that of the C-in-C, General Carpentier. His replacement was the respected Second World War commander General Jean de Lattre de Tassigny, who accepted the post only on condition of being given unified authority as civil high commissioner and military commander-in-chief. His military deputy in Tonkin was the experienced General Raoul Salan, who had years of local experience and who we shall come across later in Algeria. This new regime set about a whirlwind programme of reforms, and, in early 1951, the overconfident General Giap played into de Lattre's hands by launching three premature offensives against the French heartland of the Red River Delta, which failed with huge losses. De Lattre would also benefit indirectly from the simultaneous involvement of China in the Korean War from November 1950, which finally brought the CEFEO ever-increasing levels of US equipment and funding.

One month after its near annihilation, 1st BEP was officially disbanded, but a nucleus was immediately reformed from survivors and men drawn from its base depot. This nucleus formed a 150-strong company, which was attached to 2nd BEP, while additional replacements were recruited and trained in Algeria to reform 1st BEP. The battalion was reformed on 1 March 1951, and, when the replacements arrived at Haiphong on 13 March, the unit was back to strength with around 500 men. In addition, both 1st and 2nd BEP were reinforced, each with a locally recruited company of around 290 Vietnamese, in accordance with General de Lattre's process of creating an effective ANV (Vietnamese National Army) by on-the-job training.

For two-and-a-half years from the reformation of 1st BEP in March 1951, until they were committed in November 1953 to the operation that would lead to the fateful battle of Dien Bien Phu, the Legion para battalions fought without pause in operations in Laos and throughout Vietnam, although the focus of most activity was in Tonkin. After Giap had recovered from his losses in 1951, the war would move inexorably in favour of the Viet Minh, with much of Tonkin nominally still French but, in reality, being to all intents and purposes under enemy control. General de Lattre, and in 1952 his successor General Salan, fought an offensive war, exploiting to the maximum the mobility and fighting qualities of the para units. The result was that the pace of operations for the paras was intense, often with only brief periods of respite from combat. Conditions were harsh, in remote and difficult terrain, and, despite the provision of increasing numbers of C-47 Dakota transports by the US, the paras frequently had to walk out after being dropped into hostile territory. They were involved in a range of operations: rapid deployment to defend threatened positions, offensive operations to interdict Viet Minh lines of communication and infiltration, and intervention behind enemy lines, sometimes in coordination with units moving by road, to destroy logistic infrastructure.

In January 1952, General de Lattre died from cancer and Salan became commander-in-chief. However, by May 1953, the inevitability of eventual peace talks had been accepted by the French government, and a new commander-in-chief, General Navarre, was appointed with a remit not to achieve a military victory but to punish the VPA sufficiently to gain France a favourable edge in such negotiations. Navarre remained predominantly on the defensive in Tonkin while concentrating on a major operation on the coast of Annam (Central Vietnam). However, he aimed to divert Giap's attention and reserves away from this, and from the Delta, by establishing an air–ground base at Dien Bien Phu in the Thai Highlands near the Laotian border, 185 miles west of the French airbases around Hanoi. A similar operation in the same region, at Na San, had proved successful the previous winter (though on more favourable ground and against relatively weak opposition).

Dien Bien Phu had an airstrip in a flat river valley, about 11 miles north-to-south by three miles wide, surrounded by hills. Navarre's objectives were threefold: to block any repeat of Giap's previous advance south into Laos; to create a hub for offensive sorties by paras and French-led partisans; and, if it came to it, to win a defensive battle against the VPA main force by means of artillery and tactical airpower. *Opération Castor* – the largest airborne operation of the war, committing two para brigades with six battalions and supporting units – was launched on 20 November 1953. The second wave included 1st BEP, along with colonial and metropolitan units and one Vietnamese unit (in all, about one-third of Dien Bien Phu's defenders would be Vietnamese). The repaired airstrip received its first C-47 on 25 November.

Over the next four months, increasing numbers of troops and amounts of equipment and supplies were flown in, including nine batteries of artillery, 10 tanks, and a squadron of F-8F Bearcat fighter-bombers. The garrison grew to about 10,000 men; the initial para units were progressively replaced by Legion, Algerian, Moroccan, and local infantry, but 8th BPC (Colonial Parachute Battalion) and 1st BEP remained in the valley. The response of the Viet Minh and VPA was equally unprecedented: by means of national mobilisation, Giap was able to concentrate and supply a siege army of nearly 60,000, with new field and anti-aircraft artillery. On 13 March 1954, a massive artillery bombardment opened his first assault phase, and, two weeks later, his guns finally closed the airstrip: French casualties could no longer be evacuated nor men and supplies flown in.

This is not the place to discuss the battle of Dien Bien Phu in depth.[3] Suffice it to say that the French high command had gravely underestimated the strength, resourcefulness, and endurance of the VPA and had not anticipated having to supply and reinforce the garrison solely by parachute. The VPA's artillery was masterfully dug in and camouflaged on the surrounding hills, and French counter-battery fire completely failed to silence it. French airpower also proved largely ineffective, allowing the VPA siege divisions to dig trenches ever closer around the French perimeter strongpoints and to overwhelm them one by one with support from heavy mortars. The assault units paid a bloody price for these successes but had received up to 20,000 replacements and reinforcements by early May. French para battalions were dropped into the steadily shrinking perimeter piecemeal – the 6th BPC and 5th BPVN (Vietnamese National Army Battalion) in March, the 2nd Battalion 1st RCP (*Régiment de Chasseurs Parachutistes* - light infantry paras.) and 2nd BEP during April, and finally part of 1st BPC at the beginning of May. These, and volunteer untrained parachutists, brought the garrison up to 15,000 men, but attrition never allowed the assembly of a sufficient reserve to check the VPA's progress for more than a day or two at a time.

By 7 May, dwindling stocks of ammunition, mounting casualties, the successive loss of strongpoints, and the end of all hope of relief left the garrison commander, General de Castries, no option but to order a ceasefire. All estimates of casualties at Dien Bien Phu must be treated with caution, but the French Ministry of Defence put French losses at 1,700 killed, 1,600 missing in action, 4,400 wounded, and 10,300 (including the wounded) captured. About 800 of the most seriously wounded were repatriated, but the majority were force-marched hundreds of miles to prison camps along with the other prisoners. The Indochina War came to a negotiated end in July 1954, but only some 4,300 at most of the Dien Bien Phu prisoners survived the march and the camps to be repatriated.

As for the Legion paras, both battalions had been effectively wiped out. Pierre Montagnon quotes 1st BEP and 2nd BEP losses as 316 and 99 total killed and missing in action, respectively. He is cautious over figures for the wounded since, as he says, some men were wounded more than once, but cites 609 for 1st BEP

---

3   The reader interested in knowing more of the Indochina War, and the Battle of Dien Bien Phu in particular, can do no better than read Martin Windrow's *The Last Valley, Dien Bien Phu and the French Defeat in Vietnam* (London: Wiedenfeld and Nicholson, 2004) and (London: Cassell, 2005).

and 334 for 2nd BEP.[4] Only a third of the Legion paras made prisoner returned from captivity. Once again, 1st BEP had to be reformed from men at the depot, recovering wounded, and reinforcements sent from Algeria. 2nd BEP went through the same process, and, by the autumn, both units were back to strength – just in time for the outbreak of the Algerian conflict.

The experiences of the Legion paras left deep scars. They had paid the price of poor planning and execution of operations by higher command. The lack of support for the CEFEO from Metropolitan France – both from the constantly changing governments and the general public (which had been indifferent at best and often strongly opposed to the war) – left a bitter taste. Many of the officers and NCOs with whom Tony served had fought with the parachute units in the bitter Indochina War. Their experiences had left them battle hardened but inward looking and distrustful of higher command. For them, Algeria could not be allowed to become a repeat of Indochina. Their attitude had a significant influence on the conduct of the war in Algeria and Tony's life with the Legion.

4   Montagnon, *Les parachutistes de la Légion*, p.147.

4
From First Blows to the End of 1956

On the surface, the early months of 1954 in Algeria gave no cause for concern to the French authorities. The French government's attention was focused on the disastrous end of the war in Indochina, and there were no overt terrorist acts. However, below the surface, rebel plans were taking shape, and in June a number of key decisions were taken by the leaders of the incipient rebellion. They defined three stages for achieving independence: put the means for rebellion in place, create a feeling of insecurity among the French administration and the European population while encouraging popular Muslim support, and create liberated zones. It was appreciated that it would be impossible to exercise a unified command, and much would have to depend on local initiatives. Thus, the country was divided into six zones, which later would be known as wilayas. As military preparations progressed, the political side of the movement was riven by dissent over objectives and means. Those involved in launching the armed rebellion got on with their jobs but suffered from unfulfilled promises from exiles to deliver arms and munitions, so they had to rely on existing stockpiles. Some in the French administration were alert to something brewing, but with the war in Indochina still under way and French troops having been sent to deal with growing problems in Tunisia, most eyes were elsewhere. There was also a certain complacency. Nevertheless, General Cherrières, commanding the Algiers Army Corps, was sufficiently concerned to put an airborne division stationed at Pau in southern France on alert.

The First Blows – 1 November 1954

In the early hours of 1 November 1954, All Saints Day, a series of rebel attacks was planned across Algeria. The date was chosen deliberately as a day of particular importance for the Europeans of the Roman Catholic faith. However, misfortune, ill-discipline, and lack of resources all contributed to the start of the rebellion being close to a fiasco.

In the mountainous Aurès (Wilaya 1), in the east of the country towards the Tunisian border, the local commander planned a series of operations: against the town of Batna, seat of a subprefecture, two communes (Biskra and Khenchela), and in the countryside. Operations were planned to begin at 0300 hours. Unfortunately, the commander of the group allocated to attack Biskra opened fire 45 minutes early. Attacks on the police station and the power station resulted in some Europeans wounded, but there had been rumours of something afoot in recent days, and the local forces reacted quickly. The rebels were forced to withdraw.

At Batna, the targets were the gendarmerie, the offices of the subprefecture, and army barracks. At 0200 hours, the chief of the rebels had the subprefect in his sights, but respecting H Hour, he held his fire. Suddenly, a few minutes before 0300 hours, lights came on throughout the town. The premature attack at Biskra had been reported, and the alarm had been raised. The rebels opened fire: two unarmed guards at the barracks were killed, but having lost the element of surprise, the commander withdrew his men.

At Khenchela, a town of 10,000 inhabitants 60 miles to the east of Batna, there was a small garrison of platoon strength to supplement the police. The rebels penetrated the police station and disarmed the police officers, leaving with their weapons. The platoon commander was shot and killed as he rallied the meagre defence; a sentry suffered the same fate, but the reaction was sufficient for the rebels to withdraw. In the countryside, there was a fruitless attack on a gendarmerie and, just after first light, the ambush of a bus carrying two French school teachers and a local *caïd*. One of the teachers and the *caïd*, who attempted to defend the two French passengers with his revolver, were killed and the other teacher wounded. There were scattered incidents further north in Wilaya 2 towards Constantine, with shots fired without effect against a gendarmerie and an army fuel depot. Some arms were seized from Muslim guards.

Ambitiously planned operations in Algiers (Wilaya 4) envisaged attacks on the radio station, the telephone exchange, a fuel depot, a gas production plant, and a cork warehouse. The result was a fiasco. The local commander had had problems with his men, and, as the fateful day approached, they refused to rise against the French. Reinforcements had to be brought in from elsewhere, but, inevitably, they lacked local knowledge. The commander charged with the attack on the cork warehouse got cold feet and decided at the last moment that he was too ill to take part. Elsewhere, rebels designated to plant incendiary devices got rid of them as quickly as possible. The devices were in any case rudimentary, and this, coupled with the timidity of the rebels, meant that they had little effect. Operations were ill coordinated, with some devices being detonated prematurely. The result was that the alarm was raised before other attacks could be launched. A small number of arms was seized but at the cost of several killed. The rebels withdrew.

In Kabylia (Wilaya 3), the results were derisory: a few bullet impacts on the walls of gendarmeries and some tobacco and cork warehouses burnt. To the west, in Wilaya 5, action was limited to raids on European farms and a failed attack on a gendarmerie. A few days later, local Muslims tracked down some of the perpetrators and handed them over to the French authorities.

The cost in human lives for the French had been light: six Europeans and two Muslims in French service. However, the concern for the French was not the scale of operations but that there was an organisation capable of coordinating simultaneous attacks, even if badly executed, across the breadth of the country.

This first day of widespread armed rebellion was the start of a war that was to last for seven-and-a-half years. The first wave of terrorist operations was accompanied by a proclamation from the FLN setting out the case for independence and expressing a desire for a peaceful settlement through negotiations.

Only five months earlier, the French had suffered their crushing defeat at Dien Bien Phu in Vietnam, and agreement for a ceasefire and French withdrawal from North Vietnam had rapidly followed. The loss of the Indochina War was to be regretted; the loss of Algeria, as an integral part of France, either through negotiations or military defeat, was unthinkable. There were also moves for independence in the French protectorates of Tunisia and Morocco, but the situation there was different from Algeria. They had never been colonised to the same extent or integrated into the French administration in the same way. The French Prime Minister, Pierre Mendès France, made the attitude of the government clear in parliament:

> Between her [Algeria] and the metropole [France], secession is inconceivable. This must be clear once and for all for everyone, in Algeria and in the metropole and overseas. France will never, no government – no French parliament, no matter what their political beliefs – concede this fundamental point. Ladies, gentlemen, several members have compared the situation in Algeria with that in Tunisia. I state that no comparison is more false, more dangerous. Here [Algeria], it is France![1]

---

1   Montagnon, *La Guerre d'Algérie*, p.128. (Author's translation).

The Minister of the Interior, the future President François Mitterand, was equally forthright: 'I accept no negotiations with the enemies of the motherland', and later, 'The only negotiation is war. Algeria is France.'[2] The governor-general in Algeria reinforced the point in mid-November: 'Here we are in France, and we are going to show it.'[3]

The Opposing Forces

Two years later, the FLN stated that the forces available to the ALN at the start of the war amounted to some 900 men. They were poorly armed with a mixture of rifles from many nations dating from the Second World War or earlier. There were few automatic weapons, some rare British Sten guns and Italian Berettas. Munitions were in short supply and needed to be used parsimoniously. There were also numerous shotguns, used with solid shot normally employed for hunting large game.

To counter this small, poorly armed force, there were around 50,000 French troops in the country, but only a small proportion were considered operational. The majority of the professional army was still in Indochina, deployed in Germany, or employed in training roles in France. Most of the troops in Algeria were in training bases or base depots and were poorly equipped for the war that was to face them. Their small arms were not well suited to guerrilla warfare, and some dated back 30 years. There was no artillery. Road transport relied heavily on old American vehicles, which proved ill-suited to the poor roads away from the main cities. Troop deployments depended heavily on movement by rail. Radios were poor: the standard infantry radio weighed 45 pounds and had a maximum line-of-sight range of two-and-a-half miles. There was no aviation support of any consequence. Mapping was limited to a scale of 1:200,000 – of little use for pinpointing a group of a dozen men. On the plus side, munitions were plentiful, but, at this stage of the war, every round expended had to be accounted for. It would be another year before hunter and hunted began to become appropriately organised and equipped.

In the meantime, the airborne division, which had been placed on alert in France in anticipation of trouble, was deployed to Algeria in early November. However, this was neither a division nor airborne other than in name. It consisted of only two parachute regiments, a few thousand men in total, but came without the means to use them in the airborne role. The men were largely conscripts who

---

2 Montagnon, *La Guerre d'Algérie*, p.128. (Author's translation).
3 Montagnon, *La Guerre d'Algérie*, p.128. (Author's translation).

had volunteered for parachute duties. After 1 November, the most significant activity was in the Aurès (Wilaya 1), and it was here that the reinforcements were deployed.

The French command was yet to appreciate the nature of this war, which would depend on the physical endurance of soldiers, individual courage, and speed of reaction. Troops were deployed in convoy or columns. The terrain was ideal for ambushes, but the rebels watched and waited: if a column passing on the road looked too strong, it would be allowed to pass. Also, the rebels were used to the terrain and lightly equipped – they could move more rapidly than the French troops – and simply evaporated into thin air when the slow-moving French infantry approached. The commander of one of the parachute regiments was an experienced soldier from Indochina. He appreciated the need for flexibility and speed, but without artillery, air support, or helicopters he could only do so much in his vast area of responsibility. Engagements were limited, and, as the year drew to a close, many could be excused for thinking that the events of 1 November were no more than a repeat of the short-lived insurrection in 1945.

1955

During 1955, the war developed in the countryside, where the European population was sparse. The primary targets were Muslims identified with the French administration, such as the *caïds*, or those suspected as having French sympathies. The objective, through terrorism, was to convince the indigenous population to come over to the FLN.

In January 1955, a new governor-general took office. Jacques Soustelle was a loyal Gaullist, a young and talented administrator. He was faced with the tension between the need for reform, within the framework of Algeria as part of France, and the trenchant hard-line position of the European Algerians, who believed that firmness was the only answer. His attempts at reform were seen as too little too late by the leaders of the independence movement and as an encouragement to the rebels by the hard-line *pieds noirs*. He received little support from the government in France, which was preoccupied with holding on to power with a slender parliamentary majority. Nevertheless, Soustelle pursued a twin-track approach of reform and fighting the war. In the spring, a new general was appointed to civilian and military command of the Aurès-Némentchas region. General Parlange had a good deal of experience in Africa and also believed in a twin-track approach: prosecuting the war vigorously and working on hearts and minds.

To serve this latter objective, he established *Sections Administratives Spécialisées* (Special Administrative Sections), known as SAS – not to be confused with the

Special Air Service. The SAS were commanded by young, talented officers with two missions: civilian administration and intelligence gathering. With them, they brought schools, pharmacies, and doctors to provide local services that had hitherto been remote from the villages. They had a complement of Muslim auxiliaries who assisted with their intelligence gathering, police, and security functions. Some 700 SAS were established across the country. They were successful administratively in bringing support to the indigenous population, and a growing flow of intelligence was the result. Naturally, this flew in the face of the objectives of the FLN, and the SAS became targets: 73 French officers lost their lives as a consequence.

From the end of 1954, three Legion units arrived from Indochina as reinforcements, including Tony Hunter-Choat's future regiment, the 1st BEP subsequently reconstituted in Algeria as the 1st REP.[4] Further troops arrived in 1955. First were an infantry division from Tunisia and Moroccan troops well suited to the type of war to be fought in Algeria. These men were followed by a division of mechanised infantry. The war through the summer of 1955 continued at a low intensity, with the focus on trying to hunt down isolated rebel groups and seize arms. Between May and August, 211 weapons were seized with 62 lost to the rebels. The French lost 43 killed in the same period and the ALN lost 332.

On 20 August 1955, there was an explosion of violence in Philippeville (now Skikda). Incited by the FLN, large numbers of Muslims from the countryside descended on the town. They converged on the European quarters – destroying, burning, and killing as they went. Troops under training and *légionnaires* on leave took up arms at the barracks and drove the rioters back. The European and army retaliation was ferocious, with possibly as many as 12,000 indigenous people killed. Seventy-one Europeans and around 100 loyal Muslims also lost their lives. The FLN had achieved their objective. They had created fear amongst the Europeans: this could happen anywhere. For the Muslims, the French presence was identified with violence and repression. A blow had been struck against the prospect of the two communities living together. Recruits flowed into the arms of the rebels, both to fight in the countryside and to join the growing resistance in the towns. This situation also caused serious problems within the French Army's regiments of *Tirailleurs Algériens* – Muslim infantry commanded by European officers. Many of these men had fought with distinction for France in Indochina, but here they were faced with fighting their co-religionists in their own country. Individual desertions increased, and, in some cases, complete detachments went over to the ALN taking with them their weapons. Among these men were experienced and competent

---

4   See Chapter 6, for the composition of 1st REP when Tony joined the regiment.

NCOs. Many Algerian regiments were transferred to serve in Germany, and the worst of the problem of desertions was stemmed. However, one regiment remained and fought loyally for France throughout the war, being commanded from 1960 by an Algerian Muslim officer.

1956

More problems were to follow in 1956 following Moroccan independence in March, when Moroccan units refused to fight for the French and were repatriated, thus depriving the French of experienced men well adapted to the fighting in Algeria. Tunisian independence followed that of Morocco some weeks later. Now the rebels could expect support across the borders from their neighbours to the east and west.

In sum, the rebels had gathered strength in numbers through desertions and now exerted increased influence over the native and European populations alike through the threat of terrorism. The French government responded to events by mobilising 57,000 reservists, but not without problems from the French Communist Party and left-leaning labour union the *Confédération Générale du Travail* (General Confederation of Labour), which disrupted movement of troop trains and called for insubordination by the reservists.

However, by early 1956, there were 186,000 French troops in Algeria. For the French, a serious problem was that the replacements for the lost Algerian and Moroccan units were largely inexperienced and poorly trained. The rebels were quick to take advantage of this situation with frequent ambushes against French columns. With their newly acquired and experienced NCOs, they became bolder, not shying away from direct combat with French patrols. To the east of the country in the region of Constantine, a report by the divisional commander of activity in January 1956 gives an idea of the scale of the problem the French faced: 112 pro-French Muslims killed; 42 schools, 58 farms, and 42 habitations burned down; 34 cases of railway sabotage; 53 bridges sabotaged; and 172 cases of telephone lines cut. Worryingly, in early 1956, the French were losing more weapons to the rebels, including machine guns and mortars, than they were capturing.

The governor-general, Jacques Soustelle, was in a difficult position. How could he continue to push the case for liberal reform in the face of such violence? Following the events at Philippeville, Soustelle moved towards the camp of the supporters of *Algérie Française* (French Algeria). However, a new government in Paris brought changes: first of all, Soustelle was replaced by a retired general, Georges Catroux, at the beginning of February 1956. However – after a violent *pied noir* reaction to his appointment during a visit to Algiers a few days later by the new head of government, Guy Mollet – Catroux resigned before even reaching Algiers. The new governor-general was Robert Lacoste. Mollet took away from a disastrous visit to Algiers a strong impression of the deep-seated commitment among the European population to French Algeria. Conscripts had not been sent to fight in Indochina because it was legally a colonial theatre, but now Mollet decided to send national service troops to Algeria. Unwittingly, he sowed the seeds for the end of French Algeria, as opposition to the war grew in Metropolitan France over the death of conscripted sons and husbands in combat and accidents.

As 1956 progressed, the rebels were engaging in combat more frequently, inflicting casualties and seizing weapons, often in ambushes, but equally the French were learning how to fight this new war. Armoured vehicles served little purpose: the key was rapid mobility. Helicopters and fixed-wing aircraft were integrated with operations by troops on the ground. Reconnaissance was provided by Piper fixed-wing observation aircraft and Alouette helicopters. As we shall see later, Tony Hunter-Choat's commanding officer flew with the observation aircraft, directing movement of his men on the ground. Airlift was provided by either Sikorsky S-58 or Piasecki H-21 helicopters. The S-58, a piston-engine predecessor of the turbine-powered Westland Wessex, could carry at best only four or five men, and its performance was poor in the higher ground and hot temperatures. The H-21, or 'flying banana' as it was popularly known, was a twin-rotor helicopter that could carry at least 20 men and was more capable than the S-58 in high and hot conditions. It became the helicopter of choice and was deployed in sections of six aircraft, capable of lifting together a half-company of men. North American T-6 piston-engine training aircraft, known in RAF service as the Harvard, were armed with machine guns, bombs, and rockets to provide air cover for the deploying troops. Jet Mistral aircraft fulfilled the same role. The French Navy also used Vought F-4U Corsairs, Second World War piston-engine aircraft, disembarked from their carriers for close air support. Artillery support was provided by 105mm guns.

The greatest challenge for the ALN was to procure weapons. Money was raised, often through collections from Algerian expatriate workers in France, and arms were purchased from Eastern European countries. The problem, then, was getting them to Algeria. French intelligence focused on tracking shipping for interception by the French Navy. Significant stocks of small arms, mortars, and heavy machine guns were seized, but nevertheless weapons were getting through to Tunisia and Morocco for onward shipment over land. The Egyptian President, Abdul Nasser, promised support with armaments, but, to the frustration of the ALN, this was not forthcoming.

On 24 November 1956, the war took on a new dimension when substantial numbers of rebels coming from Tunisia attempted to seize the town of Tebessa. French intelligence had failed to detect the preparations for the attack, but, by good fortune, a small patrol of paratroopers spotted a column of men some 400 strong on the move and were able to raise the alarm. Troops from two parachute regiments were deployed to the town. After 48 hours of fierce fighting, the rebels withdrew to Tunisia. A new phase of the war had started: the Battle of the Borders, with operations focusing on intercepting insurgent groups launching raids from Tunisia and Morocco.

In November 1956, French and British forces were engaged in operations to seize the Suez Canal. A French belief that Nasser's Egypt was the source of arms for the ALN was to be one of the motives, on the French side, for the ill-fated intervention. Among the units deployed from Algeria was Tony's future regiment 1st REP. After the cease-fire in Egypt, the regiment returned to Algeria, to play a crucial part in what became known as the Battle of Algiers.

The Battle of Algiers

During the latter part of 1956, a series of increasingly violent terrorist attacks was launched by the ALN in Algiers. Bombs placed in bars, cafés, shops, and stations caused numerous casualties, and a mayor of one of the quarters of the town was assassinated. Reprisals were taken by *pied noir* vigilante groups. By early January 1957, the situation had deteriorated to such an extent that full powers for resolving the problem were delegated by the governor-general to General Massu.[5] He deployed the 10th DP (Parachute Division), consisting of four parachute regiments including the 1st REP. He also had at his disposal a further parachute regiment, a regiment of Zouave infantry, detachments from cavalry regiments,

---

5 Commanding a battalion of Tirailleurs Sénégalais in Chad, Jacques Massu had rallied to de Gaulle in August 1940. He went on to distinguish himself in command of a battlegroup of General Leclerc's 2nd Armoured Division in north-west Europe in 1944–45 and served in Indochina between October 1945 and November 1946. As the two-star general commanding 10th DP in 1957, before sanctioning torture with electrodes in the Battle of Algiers, he reportedly submitted to it himself. He would be transferred from Algeria in January 1960 after an outspoken statement of the Army's attitude, but, by 1966, he would be a five-star general commanding French forces in Germany. It is widely believed that, in return for supporting President de Gaulle in 1968, he secured early release or amnesties for soldiers condemned after the 1961 Generals' Putsch. He retired in 1969 and died aged 94 in 2002.

intelligence units, and territorial units drawn from the European population. A ferocious campaign was launched to hunt down and eliminate the terrorist network active in the city.

Tony's future regiment played an important role in the Battle of Algiers, which started just as he arrived in Algeria to begin his training. The end of the engagement of 1st REP in Algiers more or less coincided with the end of his training and his posting to join the regiment at Zeralda in November 1957. The regiment was largely instrumental in destroying the terrorist network in Algiers. It was to become Tony's home until its disbandment on 1 May 1961 after its participation in the Generals' Putsch against General de Gaulle in the preceding month. We will now look at the battle from the perspective of the 1st REP. A number of names will appear that will recur later in Tony's story.

During the battle, Tony's future commanding officer, Lieutenant Colonel Pierre Jeanpierre, played an important part. As we shall see, Jeanpierre was a man who earned Tony's undying respect and admiration as a soldier and commanding officer. Born in 1912, he initially enlisted in the ranks before being selected for officer training. After commissioning, he joined the Foreign Legion and, at the start of the Second World War, was in Syria. After the signing of the armistice with Germany in 1940, he opted to remain with the Legion in Marseille rather than join the embryonic Free French Forces. When German forces occupied the free zone in the south of France, he joined the Resistance. Captured in 1944, he was sent to Mauthausen concentration camp until he was liberated at the end of the war. Thereafter, despite being very weak and suffering from pleurisy, he rejoined the Legion, later becoming second-in-command of the newly formed 1st BEP in 1948. Jeanpierre fought with great distinction in Indochina, being one of the few survivors when 1st BEP was wiped out in October 1950. In May 1954, Major Jeanpierre was commanding a battalion of 1st REI in Algeria when his old unit was almost annihilated for a second time at Dien Bien Phu. He commanded the rebuilt 1st BEP in South Vietnam between October 1954 and February 1955, and he thereafter led it on operations in Algeria in the Aurès and Némentcha highlands until 1 September 1955. On that day the unit became the 1st REP, command was passed to Lieutenant Colonel Brothier, and Jeanpierre became his second-in-command. This did not make for a promising relationship: the two men were of different temperaments and Jeanpierre regarded the regiment as his own. It was for Brothier to lance the boil:

> Jeanpierre, since I took command I have been content to watch you and let you work in your own way. I understand your feelings. I know that you moulded the 1st BEP to your ideas. Since my arrival you have persisted

in doing things your way. This situation cannot continue. Your dream is to command 1st REP. OK, here is what I propose. You can bend and play the game and we form a team. In this case, I will do all that I can to see that you succeed me. Or else you can continue as you have done so far. In this case I give you my word that you will never command the regiment. Am I clear?[6]

Jeanpierre replied, 'Yes, colonel', and Brothier invited him to choose. Jeanpierre said that he had done so. It says much for the two men that they were both as good as their word. They formed a good team, and Jeanpierre succeeded to command of the regiment in the midst of the Battle of Algiers in March 1957.

The FLN had decided, in part in reprisal for perceived atrocities in the countryside, to take the war to the Europeans in Algiers. Its strength was in numbers: perhaps 1,200 armed activists, including women, able to blend into the background, particularly in the Muslim quarters. They also had a small number of European supporters, largely drawn from the ranks of the Communist Party of Algeria, and had the complicit support of the bulk of the Muslim population. The web of narrow streets in the Muslim quarters, particularly the Casbah and the slums in the suburbs, provided refuges for the terrorists that were difficult to penetrate and control. However, the terrorist organization had its weaknesses. The militants were courageous and well aware of the risks that they were taking, but few had the strength of character or skills to undertake terrorist operations. In particular, there was a lack of expertise in the use of explosives, and devices were generally unsophisticated.

The operations that followed were distasteful to many of the officers: this was not their idea of soldiering. As Lieutenant Colonel Brothier said:

> For months they have made us scale the chalky heights of the Némentchas [eastern Algeria]. By day it was thirty degrees in the shade. At night we froze from the cold. Then they sent us to land on the coast of Asia [the Suez operation] in old wrecks which risked sinking before we landed. Now we legionnaires are to be cops.[7]

Jeanpierre was clear about what lay ahead and told his officers, 'The mission that we have been given is not one that that is normal for us. But orders are made to be obeyed. Nevertheless, those that do not agree may withdraw.'[8] In the Legion,

---

6   Montagnon, *Les parachutistes de la Légion*, p.164. (Author's translation).
7   Montagnon, *Les parachutistes de la Légion*, p.177. (Author's translation).
8   Montagnon, *La Guerre d'Algérie*, p.206. (Author's translation).

however, discipline was all, and the Jesuit creed was apt: *Perinde ac Cadaver* (obey like a corpse). To refuse the mission, however distasteful, was unthinkable to all the officers. Torture was widely used by the French to extract intelligence. Jeanpierre, although not eschewing the use of torture by his officers, gave orders that neither non-commissioned officers nor *légionnaires* under his command were to be asked to carry out such acts. Captain Estoup, a company commander with 1st REP, did not mince his words in giving evidence at a court martial in 1962: 'In military language, it's called intelligence gathering. In French it's called torture.'[9] At the end of the battle, Colonel Bigeard, commanding officer of 3rd RPC (Colonial Parachute Regiment), also involved in Algiers, summed things up succinctly: 'La bataille d'Alger, c'est de la merde et du sang.'[10] (The Battle of Algiers, it's shit and blood.)

Eradicating terrorism in Algiers would not be achieved overnight. Numerous IEDs (Improvised Explosive Devices) were detonated in the city on 26 January and 10 February. The challenge was not just to find the perpetrators, who were known to include women, but to root out and destroy the leadership. The 1st REP, along with the other regiments, was engaged in night raids and arrests of those found outside after curfew. Interrogations followed. On 25 March, Brothier left the regiment to become chief-of-staff to General Massu, and command of 1st REP passed to Jeanpierre. This coincided with a period of rest for the regiment at Zeralda. The first two months had not been without success, with bombers arrested and networks dismantled. However, the task was exhausting physically and psychologically, and the regiment had suffered casualties.

In May, the regiment returned to the Algiers area, being deployed about 30 miles south in an area known to be used as a refuge by terrorists from the city. The Legion's reputation had been established early during the war and was exemplified by the quote from a captured rebel: 'We heard the enemy speaking many languages. We said to ourselves: it's the Legion. We're screwed!'[11] For this deployment, the regiment, knowing their reputation with the rebels, opted to forsake their distinctive camouflage uniforms and coveted green berets and wore the khaki uniform and headgear of the French Army. The subterfuge gave the rebels confidence, believing that they were engaging inexperienced Metropolitan troops. It quickly bore results. On 17 May, a company of 1st REP destroyed a detachment of rebels, killing 87 and taking three prisoners. The cost, however, was

---

9   Montagnon, *La Guerre d'Algérie*, p.206. (Author's translation).
10 Montagnon, *La Guerre d'Algérie*, p.207. (Author's translation).
11 Montagnon, *Les parachutistes de la Légion*, p.170. (Author's translation).

five *légionnaires* killed and nine wounded. It was not always so easy. On 26 July, an isolated company was caught in the open by a superior force, suffering 13 men killed and a dozen weapons lost to the enemy. Jeanpierre drew the appropriate conclusions: he increased the emphasis on rigorous training, not least with incessant practice on the firing ranges.

By the end of the summer, many of the terrorist leaders in Algiers had fled the city, but a hard core remained. On 1 September, the 1st REP returned to the city. They took over from a colonial parachute regiment who handed them a golden opportunity: a former rebel leader, Ghandriche, had been turned and was acting as a double agent. He was in contact with Yacef Saadi, one of the principal rebel leaders in the city, who was known to be living in the Casbah. But this old Turkish part of the city was a warren of narrow climbing streets, cul-de-sacs, and terraces of houses. A successful operation here would require a precise location. On 23 September, a rebel called Kamal was picked up by chance during a routine patrol. He revealed, without recourse to torture, where Yacef Saadi was living. That night a company of 1st REP commanded by Captain Ysquierdo (who we shall meet again later) was deployed. The area was sealed off by colonial troops, police, and gendarmes. At 0250 hours on 24 September, Ysquierdo's men launched their operation to seize Yacef Saadi. On the first floor, they found bedrooms and a corridor leading to a kitchen opening onto a patio with a staircase. The double agent Ghandriche had been brought on the raid and revealed a concealed trap door in the wall about six feet above floor level. A *légionnaire* attacked the wall with a pick and the trap was pushed ajar – there was a burst of automatic fire from within and a grenade thrown out, which rolled on the floor before exploding, wounding Jeanpierre amongst others. The temptation was to return a grenade, but better to take the fugitive alive. After negotiations, which included a promise to treat Yacef Saadi as a prisoner of war, he and his female accomplice came out and surrendered.

Yacef Saadi was cooperative and revealed vital intelligence. Most importantly, he gave the address of another principal leader. Ali Ammar (known as Ali la Pointe for his skill with knives) was holed up in the Casbah with three other men. It was well chosen as a refuge. It would be impossible to approach in vehicles, but the regiment was familiar with the area after countless foot patrols. After curfew on 7 October, the area was sealed off by the Legion. They waited until the curfew was raised at 0500 hours, and then began evacuating neighbours to avoid civilian casualties. At 0600 hours, Ysquierdo's men entered the house. Two women present protested but confirmed the presence of four men in hiding. Yacef Saadi was brought in, and he revealed the door to the hiding place behind a divan. Ali la Pointe was called upon to surrender. However, he was made of sterner stuff than his chief Yacef

Saadi and remained in hiding. Jeanpierre was still in hospital recovering from his wounds received two weeks before.

Major Guiraud, Jeanpierre's second-in-command, did not want to take unnecessary risks. He evacuated most of his men until only Ysquierdo, two *légionnaires*, and an engineer sergeant remained. Explosive charges were placed against the wall with the objective of blowing a hole to give access to the fugitives. The result was not as anticipated. Explosives within the hiding place were detonated, and the whole house and adjoining dwellings collapsed in a huge explosion. Miraculously, the regiment suffered no casualties, despite some men deployed on adjacent roofs finding that all collapsed below them and one officer being left clinging to a chimney. Unfortunately, 17 evacuated civilians who had returned to their houses were killed. It took 48 hours to dig Ali la Pointe and his companions out of the rubble. A few days later, 1st REP tracked down the political leader of the movement in Algiers. The Battle of Algiers and the campaign of bombing were, to all intents and purposes, over. The regiment was withdrawn from the city and returned to its barracks at Zeralda.

5

Basic Training: May–October 1957

Tony had arrived at Zeralda in mid-October to join 1st REP, who had returned to their barracks at the base at the end of the month. Let us now return to Tony's account of his training before joining his regiment.

Oran

Tony and his contingent disembarked and boarded the now familiar trucks for the journey to the Petit Depot in Oran. The Petit Depot was the Legion's transit camp for those arriving in or leaving Algeria. It was a quiet and pleasant backwater. There were ochre-washed, red-tiled, single-storey accommodation blocks built around a square with a canteen and dining room at one end. For Tony, it had a Parisian air, though, thankfully, it was warmer than the capital in March. The depot was run by junior-in-rank but elderly NCOs, with an ancient regimental sergeant major and an officer commissioned from the ranks, who seemed to the young Tony to have 'about a million years of service behind him', in charge. If required urgently, this officer could be found without fail in a nearby bar. There was a certain familiarity again: bunk beds, a straw palliasse, a pillow, a blanket, the ever-present bed bugs, cigarettes, wine, and beer. Once again, Tony and his companions had to wait the arrival of the next batch of recruits. Tony described the new and strange environment in which these young men from across Europe found themselves:

> Looking out through the iron railings surrounding our courtyard, we saw the world of Oran going by; Algerian Arabs, Algerian Berbers, Algerian Jews, Algerian Europeans, Algerians in heavy djellabas and shady straw hats over their turbans, passing by our barracks with their donkeys or donkey carts, the sound of the muezzin, the calls of traders, the smell, of warmth.

Much of the recruits' time was taken up sweeping the immaculate courtyard with palm-frond brooms or cleaning the canteen and dining room. Free time was spent sitting in the April sun talking and awaiting the next batch of recruits. When sufficient men had arrived from Marseille to fill a train, it was time to move on to the Legion central depot at Sidi Bel Abbès. The familiar trucks took the men to the station at Oran where they embarked in cattle trucks, which Tony recalls were clearly marked, '*eight chevaux ou 40 hommes*' (eight horses or forty men). The little steam train wound its way south for the 35-mile journey to the base. This took the unarmed, unequipped, untrained recruits through dangerous hills with the ever-present threat of ambush by the rebels: the *fellagha* (the Arabic word, literally 'bandit', used to describe rebels in Tunisia, Algeria, and Morocco), *fellouzes* in the pejorative vernacular, or simply 'fell' to the *légionnaires*. Protection was limited to a couple of corporals with sub-machine guns. As Tony remembered, 'On we chuffed through warm, arid hills with tidy farms here and there, smelling the smells of the Maghreb, and seeing the olive trees, the orange groves, pomegranates, the watermelons and the extensive vineyards.'

Sidi Bel Abbès

Sidi Bel Abbès had first been established as a French camp more than 100 years before in 1843. By the time of Tony's arrival, it was home to a large military base surrounded by an extensive and well-developed town. Although he did not know it then, the base and town would feature frequently in Tony's five years with the Legion. On arrival, Tony and his companions were marched 'more or less' to *Compagnie de Passage N°3* (3rd Transit Company), a small enclave among the large three- and four-storeyed nineteenth-century barrack blocks of the Legion depot. The company buildings were single storey, similar to those at Oran. The neat, clean, well-maintained accommodation could house 200 recruits. There were hot showers and plenty of water, but, since the ablution block could only provide for 80 men, it was essential to be up and about quickly in the morning to get a space. Tony, along with the other non-French recruits, found the squat toilets took some time to get used to, but at least they were 'clean and functioned well'. The food was good, and now the recruits had a postal address (SP87 581 – Secteur Postale – equivalent to the British Forces Post Office or BFPO), so Tony was able to write his first letter home.

The routine was much as before but with reveille at 0530 hours. It was time to wait again until there were enough men to constitute basic training companies, to be despatched to bases in the north of Algeria, at Saïda, Aïn Sefra, and Mascara. Tony's claim to have been an architectural student was put to the test: he was tasked to prepare measured drawings of the company buildings – his work passed muster. The recruits were not allowed out on their own but, from time to time, went into town on *corvée* (work parties). These duties included the collection of bread, wine, beer, and mail or taking bedding to and from the laundry. The recruits were accompanied by old sweats. The goods were carried in First World War-vintage carts with four huge wheels and pulled by four mules. The carts were driven by 'a positively ancient, and usually full of rough red wine and fast asleep, heavily bearded private soldier with no rank and about twenty-years' service. It didn't matter that he was fast asleep, as the mules knew where they were going anyway.'

These journeys into town gave the recruits another view of their new world as they went past the Arab quarter full of new smells and sights, as well as a welcome glimpse of 'very pretty Algerian girls.' From their company, they could see through the railings the Legion HQ, the commander's office, and the administration buildings, as well as smart *légionnaires* with their coveted white *képis*.

The recruits were now better dressed than hitherto. Their battledress now had buttons and a belt, and they had laces for their boots. As Tony pointed out, they had to go through town from time to time and had an image to maintain. With their pay, they could buy shoe polish, razor blades, toothpaste, and other essentials. Beer and wine came free in 'sensible' quantities. For head gear, they still wore their red and green forage caps. The *képi blanc* had to be earned the hard way.

Mascara

By the beginning of May, there were enough recruits to form two training companies. One company went to Saïda, and Tony's went to Mascara to the east of Sidi Bel Abbès. They moved the 45 miles to their new destination by truck on 4 May. There were two Legion training companies at Mascara: one at the top of the town in the Quartier Ben Daoud, which included the headquarters, and Tony's company at the bottom of the town in the Quartier Soyer. They were accommodated in a three-storey mid-nineteenth century barrack block, identical to those at Sidi Bel Abbès and common throughout French North Africa. High ceilings and yard-thick walls kept the buildings cool. The barracks included a neat guardroom, an armoury, administrative buildings, NCO accommodation, a canteen, open-sided sheds for shade, a parade ground, a large toilet block, and a vehicle compound with open-sided workshops. The complex was completed by a row of small, single bedrooms for the use of the visiting military brothel. The officers were accommodated away from the barracks.

BASIC TRAINING: MAY–OCTOBER 1957

One new arrival with Tony's company was a British ex-officer who had been cashiered from the King's African Rifles. Tony found him pleasant enough company but preferred that of the friends he had made amongst the German and Hungarian recruits.

On arrival, the men were issued with equipment and uniform. The uniform was now grey-green fatigues consisting of a shirt with epaulettes and breast pockets and trousers with patch pockets. They also received sand-coloured shirts and shorts, a leather belt, socks, underpants, boots, and US Army-pattern Second World War gaiters. For headgear, there was the familiar red and green forage cap and a bush hat, which was worn for most of the initial phase of training. There was also a greatcoat for cold nights on guard duty, a US Army folding shovel, and a water bottle.

Now that the men were equipped, training started in earnest. Reveille was at 0500 hours, announced with whistle blasts and shouts of 'Debout, debout, debout!' (Up, up, up!). Anyone slow to rise was tipped out of bed by the duty corporal. The next hour was spent making beds, folding blankets and the sheet sleeping bag, ensuring kit was properly stored and had not managed to move all by itself since the previous night's inspection, dusting, and polishing: polishing boots including the soles and polishing the flag-stone floors with neutral shoe polish. Thereafter, movement was by skating on felt pads to heighten the shine and avoid scratching the surface. Finally, the men dressed in shirt, shorts, long socks, boots, gaiters, bush hat, and leather belt. The shovel and water bottle were carried, and a ballpoint pen, notebook, and knife stuffed in a pocket, all ready for the 0600 hours parade.

The pattern for training was similar on most days. The parade was followed by a quick march out to the training ground, invariably outside the barracks. Normally, it started with PT (physical training), followed by the assault course and then more PT. When classroom training was entailed, blackboards and easels would be carried by the trainees. Usually, but not always, the men marched back to barracks for lunch and a welcome siesta in total silence in the cool barrack block between 1230 hours and 1430 hours, before afternoon training in the barrack area.

Trainees carried arms, but, until they had received weapon training, they were not issued with ammunition. However, they were accompanied by experienced armed NCOs. Tony recounts how, in the hands of seasoned NCOs even unarmed, raw *légionnaires* could be a formidable bunch to meet:

> In the training company following ours the recruits, equipped with the MAS36 model 7.5mm bolt-action rifle, with its long cruciform bayonet housed in the stock, but no ammunition, and accompanied by a handful

of armed NCOs, were ambushed by a group of fellagha armed with a light machine gun, a couple of sub-machine guns, and rifles. Instead of dying or running away as the fellagha had planned, the NCOs gave the order 'fix bayonets, right turn, charge!', which they did – suffering some minor wounds, killing all the fellagha ambush party and recovering all the enemy weapons. Two of the recruits received bravery awards for this action: not a bad way to start one's career.

Tony describes discipline as strict and relentless and punishments hard. The aim throughout the early months of training was to break down the *légionnaires* so that they became dependent on each other for survival. The aim was not to extinguish individual character but to emphasise that all *légionnaires* were solidly bound by interdependence and to develop the trust that comrades will act in your and the common interest. As Tony wrote, 'The results and the effects of this character forming, this forming of légionnaires, as opposed to just "soldiers", lasted throughout one's time in the Legion, and through life thereafter.'

There were individual punishments, but the majority were collective. If one bed space in the barrack room was below standard, everyone's kit went out the window, to be recovered and reinspected at 0300 hours. If the standard still was not met, the routine was repeated, accompanied by crawling around a rough gravel track on elbows and knees. All this was because one man had not met the required standard. Tony and his comrades quickly learned the lesson that the standard of the company was a collective responsibility. It was up to the rest to support those struggling to meet the standard. Though, as Tony pointed out, 'As often as not we couldn't win anyway, because the inspecting NCOs would import cigarette ash, old razor blades, dust and other odds and ends to be dropped and "found" in great shock and horror, to be followed by the inevitable punishment. Good for our souls.'

However, there were individual punishments for faults committed in the barracks. One man was found to have dust on his bed. For this 'outrageous failure to reach the required standard', the man was ordered out of bed and down from the third floor and across the parade ground and back – all on his stomach! Minor infringements during training were usually punished by push-ups, in increasing numbers as the men became fitter and fitter. Basic training lasted six-and-a-half months, so they had plenty of time to become extremely fit. An alternative to push-ups was 'a solid smack with a fist or rifle butt, neither of which did much harm but had a very positive effect on one's memory!' The command '*à gauche, gauche!*' (Left turn!) that resulted in a right turn would inevitably be quickly followed by a smack round the head or a kick in the backside, which served well to reinforce the memory.

The key to survival was to find your way through the system and not to fight it. The early, uncomfortable months taught Tony one really useful lesson: '… that it was better to be a corporal than a légionnaire, and that it followed that to be a sergeant was better than being a corporal. I decided that I would absolutely not remain a légionnaire. This period also taught me not to be caught.'

After the 0600 hours parade, the first task was to collect MAS36 1936 pattern rifles from the armoury. At 0630 hours, the trainees marched out of barracks with rifles carried over their shoulders with the sling. They marched in two columns, five paces between each man to avoid all being taken out by a burst of machine gun fire. One of those who marched close to Tony was an ex-Afrika Korps German tank commander who had served in the Western Desert under Rommel. He was described by Tony as lean, taciturn, and self-contained. They marched out of Mascara, passing Arabs sweeping the streets, encouraging donkeys, living their lives, and past olive groves and orderly fields, heading for their usual training areas. They were accompanied by their instructors, usually a sergeant and a few corporals. Tony and his comrades 'hated them all with equal venom.' Initially, the men had yet to learn the Legion marching songs, but these would come soon, and thereafter they would never march without them.

After hours of tough PT and a short pause for a bite of bread, they got down to the hard bit, the assault course:

> The huge assault course was gaunt and black against the low morning sun looming over a red sandy plateau some way from the barracks, but not far from our usual training patch in the shade of a few trees. It was very challenging, far more so than its British Army equivalent. It had rope ladders, railway lines, deep trenches, trip wires, barbed wire to crawl under, seven-foot walls, a very high beam with a long jump into space to a rope at the end, and no safety nets! It was also very hot and dusty. D'Allesandro (who despite his name was a German), and I were always the fastest round it and there was a fierce competition between us; over time we came out about even. I loved it, and I loved the feeling of being supremely fit.

Once the assault course was over, it was back to basic training: 'outstandingly and very patiently given by our hated instructors.' It was essential that by the end of training the recruits knew enough French not to get themselves killed and, more importantly, not to put their comrades at risk. Tony recalls how a small, dark, lean, and very experienced corporal gave patient instruction, sitting in the shade of the dry trees teaching the parts of the rifle and the names of the essential parts of the countryside. The parts of weapons were taught with a common approach. The instructor would hold up a rifle and say 'fusil, fusil' (rifle); the men replied in unison 'fusil, fusil'. The process continued with the barrel, stock, bolt, and so forth until eventually they knew the name and function of every part of the rifle down to the smallest spring. In many instances, Tony did not know the names in English. Once the rifle had been mastered, other weapons were taught in the same depth and the same fashion: the MAS49 7.5mm semi-automatic rifle, the MAT49 9mm sub-machine gun, the 1924 vintage FM24/29 7.5mm light machine gun (similar to the British Bren gun), the American .30 calibre M1919 machine gun, the 73mm LRAC (lance-roquettes antichar) anti-tank rocket launcher, and the automatic pistol. The drilling continued until all the parts and their function were known and the men knew what to do when things went wrong. Next came detailed understanding of how the weapons functioned:

> A shot has just been fired; the bullet is in the barrel, the gases are compressed between the bullet and face of the breech block; the firing pin protrudes from the face of the breech block, the extractor is engaged in the rim of the cartridge case; the main hammer spring is decompressed, the trigger return spring is compressed …

And so it went on, day after day after day, until all the names and functions were thoroughly known.

Next came the names of topographical features: crest, hill, mountain, bushy-topped tree, poplar tree, bush, gully, saddle, house, marabout,[1] town, village, track, road, railway line, north, south, east, and west. Again, the same drumming in of French vocabulary, day after day.

After the end of morning training at 1130 hours, it was time to march back to barracks for lunch and siesta. At the end of the afternoon's training, the men returned to their dormitory until summoned with a whistle blast to run at the double to the dining room for the evening meal. Then the men went back to their dormitory to clean and polish until the evening roll call. The day ended with the bugler sounding lights out in the quiet African night, but the pleasure of sleep was disrupted by bed bugs: 'One's waist at the top of the pyjamas was ringed with itching bites. The bed bugs when not busy biting us lived in the seams of the

---

1   A small, domed Muslim shrine.

mattresses; painting them with paraffin slowed them down a bit. Eventually one became immune and the bites no longer itched.'

Sundays were generally free, but as Tony recounts, '... not free to do anything, as we were not allowed out of barracks for the first three months, but free to do nothing.' However, some Sundays Tony's platoon was on duty, and then the day was spent peeling potatoes and cleaning the barracks, the ablutions, and the cookhouse. On Thursdays, time was allotted for washing clothes in a great trough with concrete slabs and Marseille soap. Not a chance of a laundry for the *légionnaires*! The Legion was very self-sufficient for food, particularly for vegetables, and from time to time the recruits were sent to work on the Legion's extensive and well-irrigated farm on the Mascara plain. It was overseen by an older sergeant no longer suited to active service. He was very typically German: blonde and very bronzed. He had a set of gold teeth, which shone in the sun when he smiled: '... which was not very often. He carried a long horse whip just in case we got out of hand.'

On 17 May 1957, Tony had his first attack of malaria. He found it a terrible and debilitating illness, but it offered him no respite from training. Only three days later, he had to undergo the first serious assessment of physical fitness. Despite his malaria, he managed 90 pull-ups, chin to the bar, in 3 minutes. Over the next six days, he had two more severe bouts of malaria, the third accompanied by extreme dysentery. Nevertheless, Tony came through this, and the pace of training accelerated.

The trainees marched more, spoke more French, and started to learn the Legion's marching songs. They were now expected to have higher and higher standards of turnout. Late evenings and nights were spent in the attic after lights-out pressing uniforms. Tony found that he had an aptitude for this task, which he enjoyed, and he started to earn money from his comrades pressing their kit.

From early June 1957, the men marched faster and further each day – an essential element of their training in view of the Legion's reputation for marching fast over long distances in all weather and all types of terrain. On 10 June, they marched five miles to their training area in full kit, trained, and slept the night in six-man tents. The following day, they marched 18 miles over the hills and through soft, ploughed fields in very hot weather (average temperatures in June in Mascara are around 30°C (86°F) with 40°C (104°F) not unusual).

It was around this time that the *légionnaires* in Tony's companies received their prized *képis*. 'Unlike today's Legion there was no great Teutonic ceremony, no torchlight parade, no swearing allegiance, no singing.' The men were simply paraded and received their *képis*. They were black, with one white cover for parade and one in khaki if the *képi* were to be worn in combat. The white cover was washed every day to keep it gleaming. Now wearing his *képi*, Tony had his first spell of guard duty on the main gate at the Quartier Soyer barracks from the evening of 9 June 1957 until the following day: 'My kit was beautifully pressed, my boots shone, and I took the very serious duty very seriously; and I did well.'

With the increased pace of training came the introduction to live firing. This started with .22 calibre rifles at an indoor 10m range. Tony shot well and was very pleased with himself when rewarded with a packet of cigarettes. They then moved on to larger calibre weapons. Tony found that he had an aptitude for firing the FM24/29 light machine gun. The weapon was very reliable, and Tony only once experienced a jam in all his time with the Legion. It was fed with 25-round magazines and had a rate of fire of 500 rounds per minute. (In comparison, the rebels had Second World War German MG42 light machine guns, which were belt fed, with a rate of fire of 1,200 rounds per minute.) On 2 July, Tony won more cigarettes, this time for his skill with the FM24/29. Long, hot days were spent on the El Keurt ranges at the foot of the mountains, three miles west of the barracks. The ranges were absolutely flat apart from the humps of the range butts: there were no trees and there was no shade. Tony continued to shoot well with the FM and became competent with other weapons. Training also included firing the Browning M1919 machine gun. Tony describes it as being:

> … an extremely heavy gun (31 lbs), on a heavy tripod, fed by 250-round cloth belts. To look at it resembled the famous .50 calibre Browning's baby sister. Its heavy stability gave it considerable accuracy, but it was cumbersome and complicated. To dismantle the gun for maintenance and cleaning it was necessary to lock the recoil spring; this was done by giving a quarter-turn to the right to a screw in the back plate. However, a quarter-turn to the left released the tightly compressed spring, which either disappeared off into space or embedded itself in your stomach, depending on where you were sitting when performing the operation. One of its many shortcomings was that if the cloth feed belt became wet it swelled and jammed. Thank heavens I never had to fight with it.

Once a shoot was over, the men were ordered to the target: 'au résultat!' The results were discussed with the range NCO. An inadequate performance would lead to being required to leopard-crawl back to the firing point with the rifle balanced on the back of the hands: 'which was a bit of a bugger if it was a 300 m shoot!' Tony was very pleased with his competence with the FM24/29, but there was a sting in the tail. As Tony recounts:

BASIC TRAINING: MAY–OCTOBER 1957

Silly me. How clever I thought myself to do so well; however, I had not thought this through properly: my ability with the light machine gun followed me into the regiment, and for a long time I was stuck with carrying this heavy 21 lb weapon while everyone else skipped about with their light sub-machine guns and rifles [roughly 8lb each].

As their skill with weapons improved, so did their French. Tony had the advantage of school and holiday French, and he progressed rapidly. Life continued to be hard, and not everyone was keeping up with the pace of training. Some who could not cope deserted. In mid-July 1957, two deserters from Tony's company were caught and brought back to the barracks. The next morning the entire company was paraded in an open square:

> The two deserters were marched in, heads shaved, hands tied behind their backs. We were brought to attention. The two men were strapped to 6-foot trestle tables and whipped, by the prison NCO, with a long-plaited whip. I don't know how many strokes they were given, but it went on for a long time. Pour encourager les autres!

One of these deserters had taken his weapon with him and was sent to the Legion disciplinary company for four years. This did not count towards his service, and after his sentence, he would complete his contracted five years. The disciplinary company was near Colomb-Béchar (now simply Béchar), 300 miles south-west of Mascara on the edge of the Sahara in one of the hottest parts of Algeria. The camp was divided into two parts by a wire mesh fence. On one side were the prisoners shovelling sand from one end of the camp to the other and then back again, for however many years they were in for, 'eating by numbers, doing everything by numbers'. On the other side of the fence, clearly visible to the prisoners, were the staff with their swimming pool, a luxurious, long open-sided bar, and comfortable accommodation. Tony's view on Legion discipline was:

> Much nonsense has been written about Legion discipline. The rules were simple and easily understood; there were things you should do, there were things you could do and get away with, and there were things you must not do. If one chose the latter and were caught one was in trouble; but the choice was yours. If caught, a harsh beating was the norm. My friend … who taught me to play poker (though ensuring he only taught me enough to allow me to lose to him) was a Neapolitan thief, which really was why he was keeping out of the way in the Legion where, mostly, he was good as gold. One day, however, his natural inclination to thievery led him to steal some personal

property from a fellow légionnaire; he was caught, and disappeared off to the disciplinary company for six months.

As training progressed, Tony and his comrades learned to march at the Legion's pace of 82 steps to the minute: the British Army pace is 120, with 140 for the light infantry. The Legion's pace was designed to allow men to keep going steadily day and night through the most atrocious conditions of heat and cold, for 'Algeria is, as the Algerians will tell you, "a cold country where the sun is hot". Very, very hot during the day, very cold at night.' They learned to sing as well: 'beautiful slow, solemn marching songs.' They sang as they marched out of barracks and when they returned. On returning, they took pride in timing the song to finish the final word as they came to a halt at the right spot on the parade ground. Tony took pleasure in listening in the darkening evening to returning platoons, each singing its chosen song in bass, baritone, and tenor harmony, very faint at first and growing in volume and emotion the closer they came. Tony recalls that it was particularly emotional in Sidi Bel Abbès, where the corporals' and sergeants' courses competed to out-sing each other.

One of the regular training areas for tactical exercises was the Forêt de Saint André not far from Mascara. In the hottest part of the day, the pine needles under the shade of the trees provided welcome relief from the rigours of training. The men passed their lunch break eating bread with cheese or pâté and talking or dozing. By now, it was late June, and the summer was hot. Tony recalls a march towards the end of the month of 25 miles before lunch without pause, followed by 10-minutes' rest, and a forced march for the five miles back to barracks. As he observed, 'We were getting fitter'.

During Tony's time with the Legion, it had a strength of around 26,000, with some 20,000 in Algeria. The Legion was famously international, with men from many nations. Tony recounts how it was natural for national groups to stick together, but that this was not noticeable. The Legion had become very selective with British volunteers after a series of prominent desertions and associated books in previous years, and, since there were only about 20 Britons in the whole Legion, Tony had little choice but to mix with the other nationalities, which he did easily and willingly. There were many Germans in the Legion, 46 percent of its strength in 1955. Some had fought in the Second World War and in Indochina. They were good soldiers and hard men, but '… kind too. They instructed well, and later in my regiment, when in contact with the enemy in a fierce fire fight, they were generous with their advice and encouragement. They ensured that the rest of us stayed alive.'

Tony describes the Hungarians as very similar to the British, with a certain reserve and a super sense of humour. He considered the Belgians 'never better than mediocre'. However, the Spanish, particularly the Basques, were 'natural fighters'. The Italians, who made up, after the French (12 percent), the third largest national contingent (11 percent) were either superb or 'crap'.

It was around this time that Tony was allowed out of barracks and into town for the first time. He went with a French friend:

> We pressed out kit with great care, shone our shoes, made sure that our képis were immaculately white and presented ourselves for inspection at the Guard Room. All was well and we wandered up into the town. It felt very strange to be outside our barracks, on our own, mingling with Arab and French civilian crowds, wandering into shops and bars. The Arab [women] were charming and fascinating, with hennaed hands, thick greased-down hair and blue lines painted on their foreheads. A quite extraordinary freedom. We spent a quiet evening, didn't get drunk, didn't visit the brothels; we just enjoyed the peace and freedom of it all.

By early July, the men in Tony's company were considered sufficiently presentable to take on the formal duties of mounting guard at the Legion HQ in Mascara, the Quartier Ben Daoud, and carrying out the night patrol in the town. On 4 July, Tony took his first turn of guard at Ben Daoud. In preparation, kit was pressed and polished again. The preparation of the sand-coloured shirt was a work of art: three vertical creases above each pocket, two creases the length of each sleeve, three horizontal creases across the top of the back with three vertical below. The dress was completed by the white *képi* with chin strap, dark green tie, red and green epaulettes, polished leather ammunition pouches, belt and shoulder braces, a dark blue cummerbund folded three times to a width of 14cm wound tightly around the waste, US gaiters, and highly polished boots. In Tony's words, 'smart as a carrot.'

Guard duty on the main gate had its challenges. Guards had to present arms to every approaching officer, starting the movement when they were about 10m away. Colonels with five shoulder bars, majors with four, captains three, and lieutenants with two were easy to recognise. The problem came with second lieutenants and sergeants major. Second lieutenants had a single gold bar if infantry or a silver bar in other arms. Sergeants major and regimental sergeants major also wore a single bar, silver for the former and gold for the latter, but distinguished by a thin red line down the centre off the bar. The difference between second lieutenants and sergeants major was indistinguishable at a distance. It was a particularly heinous crime to fail to present arms to an officer, but it was nevertheless also a serious offence to present arms to a sergeant major. Tony found this '… all very difficult and worrying.' He presented arms to two sergeants major, both of whom were forgiving and understanding. He was reprimanded but, much to his relief, not reported.

Despite guard duties, training continued apace, with the men becoming more and more fit and resilient through PT and the assault course. In mid-July, unarmed combat and more complex exercises with weapons were added to the training. To further strengthen arms and shoulders, the trainees were frequently required to stand for long periods with rifles held at arms' length until the pain became too much to bear. Life was governed by whistle blasts: up, down, crawl … forward roll, forward roll at absolutely flat-out speed carrying a rifle, forward rolls over a trestle table with and without a rifle. To toughen the men up further:

> … we lay on our backs while the training NCO stamped on our stomachs with studded boots. We were made to kneel, leaning back and clasping our ankles, stretching the stomach tight. The PT instructor (moniteur de sport) walked down the line kicking us as hard as he could in the stomach. The trick, and it worked well, was to tense the stomach muscles and give a great yell as the boot arrived; the result was painless and apart from some bruising there was no after-effect. Failure to tense the muscles at the right moment and to give a great yell produced a considerable effect! My friend Mario, a little, funny Italian was next to me; Mario was about 5 ft 6 in and his stomach, therefore, when kneeling, was not far off the ground. The moniteur kicked him hard, Mario did all the right things and was fine. Then it was my turn and the moniteur kicked me equally hard. Unfortunately he kicked at the same level as for Mario, but as I was a good six inches taller my stomach was much further off the ground. So he kicked me in the testicles. Which hurt. No amount of yelling or tensing of muscles made any difference. They swelled impressively to the size of small melons. The medic applied masses of Stockholm Tar – a thick black paste usually used for reducing swelling in horses' fetlocks but also, apparently, good for *légionnaires*' testicles. Recruits were not given time off or excused anything for so minor an injury, and the next day I was painfully back on the assault course. I made makeshift slings for my unaccustomed burdens, and after about a week of Stockholm Tar everything was back to normal.

In August 1957, the fourth month of training, the trainees had their examinations: physical, tactical, and language. Marks were added for general attitude, and these counted for more than any subject. All of a sudden, like a turned-off tap, the pressure was off. All of those who were left were considered fully fledged *légionnaires* and were treated as such. From dire enemies, the instructors became human, understanding, and helpful, meeting the successful trainees in the canteen for a beer in the evening. Those whom Tony had sworn to hate forever were now good friends, who 'probably knew us better than we knew ourselves'.

No sooner was the trial of the examinations over than the *fellagha* made their presence known in Babuli, a suburb of Mascara. Tony and his comrades were called out for their first military operation. There was some shooting on both sides before all went quiet:

> The captain said: 'To hell with it, let's all go to bed and sort it out in the morning.' A good decision. On the next day, Sunday 25 August, we mounted an attack against a village just outside Mascara, straight up a cliff. One fellagha was killed and a Hotchkiss machine gun recovered, so it wasn't a waste of time and gave us a taste of things to come.

Having completed the first phase of training, the men now moved on to Part 2 Infantry Specialisation in early September. This was carried out in abnormal weather, very hot one minute, then very cold, then pouring with rain, which lasted throughout the month of this phase of training. In view of Tony's skill with the light machine gun, he was trained as a light machine gun group commander (*chef de pièce*). The group consisted of the commander, the gunner supported by his loader (who always stayed at his side, supplying magazines or belts of ammunition depending on the weapon), and ammunition humpers, who remained within easy reach but away from the gun to reduce the size of a potential target for the enemy. The test for this phase required Tony to fire 20 rounds at 400m, give all the necessary commands, bring the gun into action, and carry out a dry firing run. Tony passed the test on 3 October, receiving his *Certificat de Spécialité* as a *Tireur de Précision FM* (LMG precision shot) dated 14 October 1957 issued by the Oran Army Corps. Tony had passed well: '… reinforcing the inevitability of the fate of carrying the damn thing to which I had condemned myself.'

Now came the time for postings. Those who were to join the Legion's two armoured regiments left for specialist training, as did the drivers signallers, cooks, clerks, and so on. Tony applied for the parachute regiments of the Legion. A very hectic few days were spent cleaning the barracks from top to bottom in preparation for the arrival of the next batch of trainees. On 12 October, the men who had not already left for their further training returned to Sidi Bel Abbès to await their postings. Tony's application for parachute training was accepted, and, on 17 October 1957, he was sent to Zeralda about 30 miles west of Algiers, the home of 1st REP.

6

Parachute Training

Zeralda Camp was a 'lovely camp' about half a mile from the sea. It was built on a slight, wooded rise and had been an American Army camp with Nissen huts during the latter years of the Second World War. It had been completely rebuilt by the *légionnaires* of 1st REP, with single-storey platoon barrack blocks, a canteen, dining facilities, officers' and sergeants' messes, a large HQ complex, stores, and an MT (motor transport) compound. A chapel was under construction when Tony arrived. In sum, there were all the trappings of a major unit. The streets were wide, and there were plenty of trees. The camp was large but almost empty when Tony arrived since the regiment was still deployed for the Battle of Algiers.

The 1st REP had a regimental HQ and, later, two smaller battalion HQs at Guelma near the Tunisian border. Its combat units consisted of four rifle companies (*compagnies de combat*); a support company (previously equipped with mortars, heavy machine guns, and anti-tank weapons but now transformed into a standard rifle company while keeping its title of *Compagnie d'Appui*); a light armoured squadron (formerly with light tanks but now also transformed into a rifle company while retaining its title of *Escadron des Chars*); and a mechanised company (formerly with lorries for transport, which had also been converted to a rifle company while keeping its name *Compagnie Portée*). Thus, there were seven rifle companies. There was also a command company – which included the HQ staff, the cooks, and mechanics – and a transport company equipped with American Second World War-vintage trucks and jeeps. The CO, Lieutenant Colonel Jeanpierre, drove around in an Austin Champ that his driver had stolen from the British at Suez.

Tony was posted to 4th Platoon, 2nd Company, known as Rouge Quatre after its company colour. Until he left for parachute training, he spent his time on fatigues and getting fitter and fitter in preparation for his course. He did not yet have his paratrooper pay and, consequently, visits to the canteen were few and far between. One day, while he was sweeping outside the regimental offices with a palm-frond broom, a window opened and an officer looked out with a friendly smile. Tony sprang to his feet and presented brooms! 'I don't know you', said Lieutenant Bonelli.[1] Tony yelled out his service number, rank, and name: 'Cent seize mille sept cent quatre-vingts dix-huit, Légionnaire Choat A. H. à vos ordres mon lieutenant!' (116,798, Legionnaire Choat at your command, lieutenant!) 'Well done, carry on.' It is illustrative of the camaraderie of the Legion across the divide of rank that the two became firm friends, and, 44 years later, Bonelli was present at the ceremony for Tony's investiture as an Officer of the Legion of Honour. At the ceremony, Bonelli had a gift for Tony: a broom in memory of their first meeting. This meeting was typical of Tony's experience with the regiment. He found his treatment wonderful: '… no screaming and shouting, no working to the whistle, kind and generous fellow-soldiers.' The small number of men at the camp was composed of those like Tony waiting to go on their parachute course and others on leave from Algiers or returning from France. Tony found Zeralda to be '… a very happy camp'.

On 7 November 1957, with the regiment still absent on operations in Algiers, Tony and his fellow *légionnaires* on 66 Parachute Course set out by truck for the journey of 20 miles to the French Army airborne training base at Blida at the foot of the Ouarsenis mountains, passing through small villages, farmland, and the large town of Boufarik. The camp was well equipped, and the canteens and dining facilities were 'just perfect'. 'Everything worked, except the lights in the barracks, and they continued not to work for the duration of the course.'

Tony found the instructors to be superb, but they would not tolerate any slacking. However, this was not a problem for the extremely fit *légionnaires* fresh from basic training, and they sailed through the preliminary tests.

Training began with the practice of landing positions and the associated parachute roll on contact with terra firma. They jumped from ever increasing heights until they could leap nimbly from a 10-foot wall and execute perfect rolls on landing. They then moved on to an apparatus to simulate a parachute descent. The trainee donned a parachute harness and jumped from a high platform, the fall being braked by a large fan, which allowed descent at the normal speed of a parachute jump. The height was sufficient to give time to adjust to the correct

---

1   Bonelli subsequently commanded 4th Company, 1st REP with the rank of captain. Along with other company commanders, he was given a two-year suspended prison sentence for his part in the putsch against de Gaulle in April 1961. He was amnestied in due course and went on to build a successful career at a senior level in the electronics industry.

landing position before hitting the ground. The training also included climbing onto mock-up aircraft. On board, they practised the routine of hooking up the static lines – which would extract the parachute from its pack as the paratrooper jumped from the aircraft – checking each other's equipment, and then jumping from the mock-up aircraft. They also trained to pack equipment to be carried on the chest or a bag attached to a leg. When they were not training, they were ripping up angle-iron pickets and vines along the edge of the DZ (drop zone). On previous courses, some trainees had been impaled on the pickets in drops in high winds, and '… it was thought a good idea that they should be removed. We agreed, but wondered why it had not been done before.'

The day of Tony's first jump came. He did not sleep at all the night before. He did not show it, but he admits that he was feeling extremely nervous, although '… I knew not of what. The unknown probably. The fear of failure? For some unfathomable reason parachuting always takes place at some unearthly hour in the morning, so by 0430 hours we were up dressed and heading for the airfield. So at least I didn't lose much sleep.'

They disembarked from the trucks at the airfield in the cold light of dawn:

> … all quiet, all empty, planes all asleep. We were issued our parachutes and strapped ourselves into the harness, adjusting the straps until it was a really tight fit with no possibility of sliding out of the thing by mistake at 1,200 feet. Not that one could, the harness is designed so that you don't; it's just that it feels more reassuring when pulled tight.

Weapons were not carried on the first few jumps, so the next task was to clip the reserve parachute onto the clips on the front of the harness. Finally came the steel helmet, rammed onto the head and secured by a chin strap pulled tight to prevent it flying off during the descent. Unlike modern paratroopers' helmets, the type then in use did not have extra webbing either at the back, to stop it smashing forward onto the face when the parachute opened, or under the chin for stability.

Now fully prepared, the men lay back on their parachutes and pretended to snooze nonchalantly, awaiting their aircraft. At long last, they heard the Noratlas twin piston-engine transport aircraft bursting into life and taxying across the airfield to collect them. The dumpy twin-boomed aircraft could carry 36 fully equipped paratroopers; it had two side doors, but only one would be used for this first jump. The men got to their feet and walked clumsily across and boarded the aircraft. Tony recalled that:

PARACHUTE TRAINING 67

Trainee Legion parachutists emplane on a Noratlas transport at Blida air base. The Noratlas could carry 36 paratroopers, and, on later operations, the rear doors on either side allowed two sticks to jump simultaneously, which greatly speeded up their exit (the rear clamshell doors were used for dropping cargo only). The trainees are wearing standard infantry helmets without extra strapping and what appear to be French TAP 660 parachute rigs; later, Tony would jump with the American T10. He qualified for his 'wings' after seven jumps from 1,200 feet, including one while deploying the chest emergency parachute, one by night, and the last heavily loaded with full combat kit. (Linda Hunter-Choat).

The racket was incredible, the aluminium shaking and rattling, the engines roaring, the jump masters pushing us into place. We all sat down and the Noratlas taxied for take-off, holding on its brakes at the end of the runway until the revs were right and then leaping, rattling forward, accelerating down the runway until suddenly we were airborne and all the noise abated to the steady hum of the two engines. We could see out of the windows and out of the open door the ground drop even further below as we flew up and away from Blida to enable the plane to make a long and straight run in for our first jump, to give the instructors all the time they needed to check our equipment while at the same time reassuring us all with the normality of it. We reached 1,200 feet, the standard French jump height, and the plane quietened down to a cruise. 'Debout, accrochez!' (Stand up, hook up!); we struggled to our feet against the weight of the parachute and the rocking of the plane. We took the clasps from where we had tucked them in the elastic bands of our harness shoulder straps and pulled them forward to release several feet of strop from its bag on the parachute; we hooked them onto the steel wire static line running the length of the plane at roof level, inserted the pin to lock the clasp, and gave it a tug to make sure it really was properly locked on. The instructors pushed past us, checking every clasp and safety pin. They checked all our parachute harnesses too, although they had already done this on the ground. 'Equipment check!'; every man checked the parachute pack of the man in front to ensure that there were no loose bits hanging out, or tears or holes. The last man turned round and the penultimate man checked him. Then came the shuffle forward towards the open door with nothing but space beyond. The first man to jump stood in the door, one foot forward on the edge of the sill, the other braced back ready to push off, one hand on each side of the door. Looking up, straight ahead. Into the distance. As we ran in to the DZ in a long steady run the red light came on to warn us we had two minutes to go. The heart-stopping 'GREEN ON!', and the raucous buzzer. The despatcher slapped the first man hard on the back of his chute and bellowed 'GO'. And he went, kicking forward and out and away. We shuffled forward. The next man turned to the door, hand either side, foot forward. 'GO' slap. And he went. I was too anxious (frightened?) to be fully aware what was happening, simply that it was my turn, that I was at the door, that my hands were each side of it, my foot forward on the sill, looking into space, conscious of how far down the ground was and buffeted by the roaring slipstream and the racket of the engines. 'GO' slap. And I went kicking out into space. The slipstream took me, whipping my legs to the horizontal as I hurtled away from the plane, from the noise. The strop raced out of its bag pulling the parachute from its pack; I seemed to free fall for an age, but it was only the length of the strop and of the as yet uninflated chute. The parachute inflated immediately, bringing my flight to a sudden stop, whipping me back into a vertical position, the risers catching the back of my helmet and smashing it forward onto my nose. Total lovely silence, disturbed only by the soft hiss of the wind in the rigging lines. I opened my eyes. I was parachuting! I looked up and checked the proper deployment of my canopy, and grasping the rigging lines I levered myself round to make a 360-degree check for other paratroopers in my vicinity and liable to collide with me, ready to pull away. 'Vérification de la coupole; tour d'horizon'. (Check the canopy, look around you). Voices floated up to me from megaphones below: 'Serrez les jambes, pliez les genoux, rentrez la tête, préparez vous pour l'atterrissage!' (Legs together, bend the knees, tuck your chin in, prepare for landing!). All of a sudden the ground, which had been drifting very gently up towards me, accelerated and was now rushing up at a frightening rate. Head down, chin tucked in, arms tucked in pulling the risers down, approaching the ground fast now at a slight angle to the rear right; feet touch, calf, thigh, across the buttocks, roll across the back, feet flung over in a backwards roll and straight up onto my feet pulling on the risers to deflate the chute before it drags me across the DZ. Wowee!

If a trainee paratrooper refused to jump, he was thrown bodily into the back of the aircraft as quickly as possible, to get him out of the way so that all the others could get out of the door and before his weakness could infect others. The shame of refusal was unimaginable to most, far worse than the fear of jumping. One *légionnaire* in Tony's group refused; he did not get a second chance. The first jump behind them, the men repaired to the canteen to consume copious quantities of Kronenbourg beer, '… recounting their many stories of parachuting – one jump!'

Seven jumps were required to qualify as fully fledged paratroopers, and the remainder were no less terrifying. The fifth jump required the men to pull their reserve parachute, to practise gathering it into their hands and throwing it well out beyond the periphery of the main canopy. The sixth was at night, and the final jump on 18 November 1957 was with full kit, weapons, back packs, and radios. The men held a joyful and proud parade for the 'wings' ceremony and then retired to the canteen to consume a huge quantity of beer. Training was over at long last. Just over eight months since Tony had knocked on the gates of Fort Neuf in Vincennes, he was proudly sporting parachute brevet number 132489.

7

Operations November 1957–May 1958: The Sahara and Guelma

The Nature of the Algerian War

Having completed his parachute training, Tony returned to Zeralda barracks to join his regiment, which had recently returned from the Battle of Algiers. He was now known as 'Johnny', being English, which was '… a friendly change from Choat.' He was known as such to his Legion friends for the rest of his life. Only a few days later, the regiment having had little rest, 1st REP moved out for Mrhaïer, 250 miles as the crow flies south-east from Zeralda in the Sahara Desert and 100 miles west of the Tunisian border.

Tony was now to embark on operations in a savage war that was marked by atrocities on both sides. The use of torture by the French, as discussed above, was a great concern among the military, the civil authorities, and in Metropolitan France. After the Battle of Algiers, officers in the Army, who had found their policing role distasteful, were relieved to get back to soldiering. One general and one senior administrator had resigned in protest at the use of torture. The Battle of Algiers was probably the worst episode, and when Charles de Gaulle came to power in May 1958, shortly after Tony's involvement in operations, he proscribed such methods. Their politically unauthorised use continued in some quarters, but it was no longer systematic nor officially sanctioned by the government. However, the attitude of some officers, including of general officer rank, was often ambiguous.[1]

---

1   French historian Raphaëlle Branche gives a sombre but harrowing account of the political context and military practice of torture by the police and military in *La torture et l'armée pendant la guerre d'Algérie, 1954–1962* (Paris: Gallimard, 2016).

OPERATIONS NOVEMBER 1957–MAY 1958

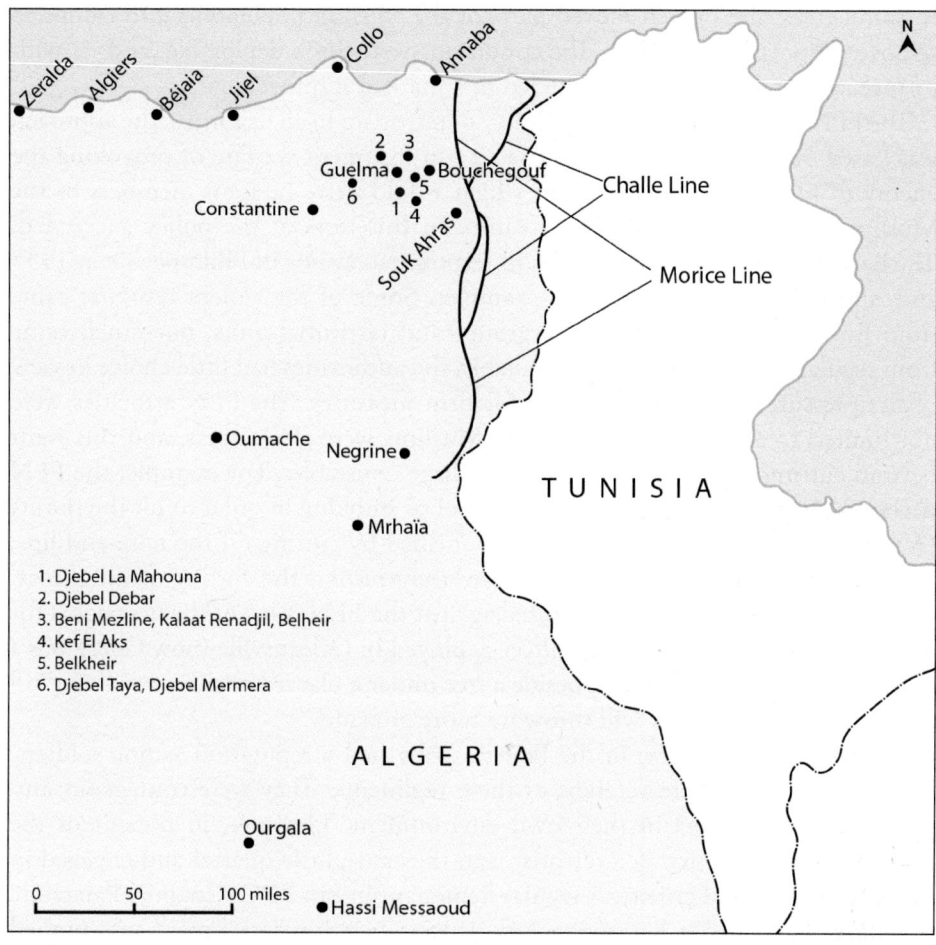

North-East Algeria: Places mentioned in Chapters 7, 9, and 11 relating to operations involving 1st REP. I have been unable to precisely locate the topographical features Kalaat Renadjil and Koudiat Megroun El Ougami. However, the former is close to Beni Mezline and the latter Guelma. (Author's illustration). (Map drawn by George Anderson)

In some areas, the French moved parts of the Muslim population into camps to remove support for the ALN. The conditions were often deplorable, and, as with torture, outrage expressed at home led to a marked improvement.

The FLN deliberately adopted a policy of terrorism in all its forms. The approach was based on the well-established practice in insurgent warfare of provoking the enemy to respond with repression, which would drive hesitant members of the Muslim population into the FLN camp. In this respect, the policy succeeded. The harsh repressive measures taken in response to events in Philippeville in 1955 and Algiers in 1957 were notable examples. Some of the violent response came from European *pied noir* vigilante groups and territorial units, but much came from regular French Army units. Arguably, the authorities had little choice in view of the pressure from the *pieds noirs* for firm measures. The FLN atrocities were not limited to Europeans. Francophile Muslims were also targets, and this went beyond cutting the throats of *caïds* and village constables. For example, the FLN declared a ban on Muslims drinking alcohol or smoking in order to hit the profits of *colon* businesses. A first offence was punished by cutting off the nose and lips; a second offence resulted in execution by *égorgement* – the cutting of the throat. However, loyal Muslims also retaliated against the FLN. One of the first sights for a young French national service officer deployed in Orléansville (now Chef) was a dead FLN combatant slumped beside a tree under a placard reading 'I will not kill my brothers any longer, I will throw no more grenades.'²

The *Tirailleurs Algériens* in the French Army had a reputation as fine soldiers. Many of the ALN were veterans of these regiments. They were courageous and often effective fighters in their own environment. However, in pursuit of the ALN policy of conducting a terrorist war, they gave little quarter and engaged in many horrific acts of cruelty. A regular lieutenant in 8th BPC (Colonial Parachute Battalion) described a harrowing experience when his detachment was pinned down with two wounded paratroopers lying 200 yards in front of them. Three men had crawled out under fire to try to rescue them. All had been wounded, and the company commander forbade any further attempts as the detachment awaited relief. In the lieutenant's words:

    She also gives an account of the impact of the experiences of French conscripts during the war in «.*Papa, qu'as-tu fait en Algérie ?* » (Paris: La Découverte, 2020).

2   Alistair Horne, *A Savage War of Peace, Algeria 1954–1962* (New York Review of Books: New York, 2006), p.172.

My poor friend V lay howling on his bed of stones till morning. He suffered unimaginably, both physically and mentally, a prey to mortal terror. He only really stopped at dawn, when we could perhaps have saved him. For several hours a rebel had been slithering towards him; [V] could have seen him all that while. ... The rebel ... took away his weapons. He gouged out his eyes. Then he slashed his Achilles tendons – afraid, perhaps, that he might still come back and die with us. But he didn't finish him off, merely wanting him to have to lie still and suffer. His friend T, the staff sergeant, also died shortly afterwards, 100 yards away, his eyes gouged and his tendons slashed, a slow death, while we were waiting for the dawn.[3]

A further FLN practice was to cut off the genitals of the dead and wounded and stuff them in the mouth. The French journalist and politician Jean-Jacques Servan-Schreiber, called up as a reservist at the age of 33, served as a lieutenant in Algeria; he recalled that soldiers accustomed themselves never to say, '"Watch out, you're going to get yourselves killed" but one repeats several times a day, "make a mistake and you have your balls cut off."'[4] It was what the soldiers expected, and, not surprisingly, there were also cases of brutality by French soldiers. After an incident where a unit of *pied noir* territorials opened fire on a truck full of Muslim miners going to work, a newly arrived officer opined that it was bad practice to kill possible innocents. A seasoned campaigner replied:

Either you consider a priori that every Arab, in the country, in the street, in a passing truck is innocent until he's proved the contrary; and permit me to tell you that if that is your attitude ... you will immediately be posted, because the parents of reservists one has had killed don't like it, and will write to their deputies that you are a butcher ... Or you will ... consider that every Arab is a suspect, a possible fellagha ... because that, my dear fellow, is the truth ... But once you're here, to pose yourself problems of conscience and treat possible assassins as presumed innocents – that's a luxury that costs dear, and costs men, dear sir, young men themselves innocent, and our own ...[5]

As Alistair Horne points out in his magisterial history of the war:

---

3   Horne, *A Savage War of Peace*, p.171.
4   Horne, *A Savage War of Peace*, p.171.
5   Horne, *A Savage War of Peace*, p.174.

The choice posed was a hard one for any young soldier to have to face, and in Algeria by no means all – or even a majority – opted for the alternative of suppressing the 'problems of conscience'. But … indiscriminate injustice *did* take place on the French side – as indeed they take place in every similar war. What is equally sure is that such acts … usually militated against French interests.[6]

As a member of the FLN said after a particularly brutal French reprisal in which women were killed, 'Voilà, we've won another battle. They hate the French a little more now. The stupid bastards are winning the war for us.'[7]

Naturally, there are no statistics about the use of torture, but it seems predominantly to have been used to try to prevent terrorist outrages in towns, notably during the Battle of Algiers. As we shall see as Tony's story unfolds, 1st REP was not involved in reprisals or operations, which led them to be involved in urban warfare after its part in the Battle of Algiers. Perhaps because of its nature as an elite unit of professional soldiers, it was much more useful to employ 1st REP in key military operations against rebel combat groups in the bled. It is notable that few prisoners were taken after engagements. This should not necessarily be construed as meaning that prisoners were killed but more as a reflection of the nature of the rebels' approach to combat and of the terrain. If the situation were unfavourable, they would simply slip away using the countryside that they knew so well as cover. They were also courageous fighters to the death. Furthermore, much as the Legion would not abandon its wounded, the *fellagha* took their wounded with them and made every effort to recover weapons from their dead. Those French prisoners who were taken by the ALN were effectively held as hostages and risked suffering extra-judicial execution in reprisal for executions of rebels found guilty of terrorist acts by French courts. As we shall see later, an event of this type served as a trigger for the events in Algiers in May 1958 that brought General de Gaulle to power once again.

It is worth noting at this point that many Muslims fought for the French: one source estimates that, by 1961, some 210,000 Algerian Muslims had fought loyally in regular French units, tracking commandos, and local defence units. They and their families were particular targets for the ALN. Those who fought in irregular units were known as Harkis, although this term is sometimes used more widely to include all who remained loyal to France. They suffered severe and savage reprisals

6   Horne, *A Savage War of Peace*, p.174.
7   Horne, *A Savage War of Peace*, p.174.

along with four other *légionnaires*, discovered a magnificent FLN flag hidden in a cache. It belonged to an ALN leader: '... Si Saleh [Salah] ready for use in a future victory parade. By the time victory had come for the ALN, I had the flag and Si Salah was dead. I still have the flag. However, I had still not been in contact.'[10]

Early 1958: Tony (left) and his comrade Ray Palin (right) among paras posing with an ALN flag captured by Tony and Ray during operations. Palin had suffered an eye injury during the climax of the urban Battle of Algiers in October 1957, before Tony joined 1st REP. Though by then half-blind, he was still serving in the Legion, as a caporal-chef with 1st REC, in December 1982. In Tony's day, there were only three British volunteers in 1st REP and about 20 in the whole Legion. (Linda Hunter-Choat).

Many of the friends who Tony made at the time remained so throughout his life. Friendships in the Legion were formed across barriers of rank or grade. This reflected the respect that the *légionnaires* had for the experienced and competent officers and NCOs with whom they served and, in turn, the respect that those

---

10   Si Saleh, the renowned commander of Wilaya 4, would controversially take part in fruitless negotiations with the French government in June 1960. He did so without the approval of the FLN and was subsequently held in Algeria for some months by the ALN. He was killed in an ambush by French special forces while on his way to Tunisia for trial in the summer of 1961.

crossing from Tunisia. It was at the southern extremity and about 100 miles to the west of the line that 1st REP was deployed from late November 1957 until late January 1958. Groups of rebels occasionally attempted to pass into Algeria from Tunisia by cutting south of the Morice Line, but the conditions were unfavourable due to the lack of cover and the long distances to be covered. The presence of the Legion would be a further deterrent.

However, the principal mission of the regiment was to ensure the security of the recently completed oil pipeline between Hassi Messaoud and Biskra. Exploration for oil in the Sahara had started in 1945, and oil was due to flow from the newly exploited reserves on 7 January 1958. When Tony's company arrived at Mrhaïer, they found a company of the French Army in residence. This unit and the local headquarters maintained that the whole area was quiet and that there were no rebels present. 1st REP had a reputation for surpassing any other major unit in operational efficiency and intelligence management – which was precisely why they had been deployed to the area – and they had nothing to do with the unit already there. They were soon to prove the resident company wrong by making contact with rebel groups, killing and capturing *fellagha* and seizing weapons.

Tony's company commander, Captain Antoine Ysquierdo, had outstanding tactical skills.[8] He was ably assisted by Corporal Soler Oviedo. Soler was an illiterate Spanish peasant, but 'being a country hill man he was a wonderful tracker with a superb sense of ground'. He was also 'remarkably good at finding well-hidden chickens'! Over the coming months, Tony spent much time with Soler, teaching him to read and write. Tony also remarks that their competence as a combat unit owed much to the leadership skills of his platoon commander, Lieutenant Ghislain Gillet,[9] and of Staff Sergeant Wallisch.

Much of Tony's time was spent patrolling at night through Saharan villages. Such patrols were invariably frustrated by barking dogs. An order was issued to the local population that all dogs were to be kept indoors during hours of darkness; those that were not locked in were shot. A reputation for success was established, with *fellagha* captured and weapons and documents seized. On one occasion, Tony,

---

8   We have already seen the part played by Ysquierdo in the Battle of Algiers. He had started his career as a *légionnaire* and been commissioned in 1950. He fought with distinction with 1st BEP in Indochina. After the Generals' Putsch against de Gaulle in 1961, he was given a one-year suspended prison sentence. His career was at an end.

9   Lieutenant Gillet left 1st REP around the end of 1959 on promotion to captain and returned to France as an instructor for two years. He returned to Algeria in 1962 with a Legion infantry regiment and finished his career as a general.

stationed at Hassi Messaoud and Ouargla. The company set up camp in 20-man tents on the outskirts of the town. Mrhaïer was a large and magnificent palm grove sunk into the Saharan sands so that, from afar, only the very tops of the date palms were visible. Some 30 to 40 feet below the level of the desert was the thriving town. There were running water ducts everywhere and a maze of tiny lanes between high, mud-brick walls. It was '… a veritable Garden of Eden hidden deep in a bleak, and cold, landscape'. Tony was now a *voltigeur* (scout) armed with a sub-machine gun, 'the splendid and reliable MAT49'. Tony carried eight or more magazines, each with thirty-two 9mm rounds, and as many grenades as he could manage. A good friend of Tony's – a quiet, amusing Yugoslav – marched with the platoon headquarters and carried a MAS51 rifle designed to fire rifle grenades. He carried several, but, because they were heavy, others were shared out among the rest of the platoon.

The *légionnaires* wore their green Legion para berets in combat, unlike their sister regiment 2nd REP, who nearly always wore a steel helmet that 'must have been quite awful at the height of summer'. The paras also wore a cheich, a very light muslin scarf that could be wound round the stomach to keep off the cold at night, round the head to keep off the sand by day, or round the neck the rest of the time. Since the Sahara is cold by day in winter and very cold at night, a balaclava helmet was also worn. The *légionnaires*' dress was completed by grey-green combat kit and boots: either heavy leather Rangers, shin high and, once broken in, very comfortable, or canvas desert boots with soft rubber soles.

By September 1957, the French had completed constructing the Morice Line, named after the defence minister of the time, to try to cut off arms and men from crossing the frontier from ALN bases in Tunisia. This stretched from near Bône (now Annaba) on the Mediterranean coast for almost 300 miles south into the Sahara, stopping just south of Negrine. It consisted of a 5,000-volt electrified fence, barbed wire entanglements, anti-personnel mines, and surveillance radars. Incursions were detected by motorised patrols, breaks in the electric current, and radar. The line was later doubled over roughly the northern half by the Challe Line, named after the then commander-in-chief, who conceived and instigated an aggressive plan against the ALN. Its historical and infamous predecessor on the French frontier with Germany, the Maginot Line, had failed because the mechanised divisions required to manoeuvre behind the fixed defences had never been provided. In contrast, the Morice Line was to prove a success because of the deployment of highly mobile forces using helicopters, and with air support to rapidly counter rebels crossing the line, detected either by the surveillance systems or by the efficient French intelligence services, it was to prove the key factor in bringing military success against the ALN, reducing to a trickle the arms and men

after independence. As we shall see from Tony's experiences, there were often good relations between the Arab and Berber Muslims and the Legion.

1st REP Operations

Mrhaïer – November 1957 to January 1958

A week after gaining his parachute brevet, Tony was on his way east through the Saharan Atlas Mountains and then down into the fringe of the Sahara to guard an oil pipeline between Biskra and Toggourt in the Far South. This view of the El Kantara gorge in the mountains shows typical scenery: dry, naked crags overlooking an isolated fertile oasis, with walled vegetable gardens crammed into the shade of date palms, surrounded by arid, stony ground that supports only prickly pears and dwarf palms. (Linda Hunter-Choat).

On 25 November 1957, the regiment set out in an unending convoy of trucks for the three-day journey to Mrhaïer, across the Atlas Mountains through the magnificent Gorges d'El Kantara, and paused at Biskra airfield before carrying on down the Touggourt road. Tony's company was based at Mrhaïer, with others in command had for their men. We have already seen how Lieutenant Bonelli became a life-long friend. The qualities that Tony demonstrated as he gained experience quickly earned the lasting friendship of his platoon commander and his staff sergeant. As Tony recounts:

> Our platoon commander, Lieutenant Gillet, was an extremely brave man and also a very kind man. He made sure that I was made to feel at home in Rouge 4, [as] the brand-new boy among many who had been through the Second World War, Indochina, Suez in 1956, and now through the intense and exciting Battle of Algiers. Gillet was quite keen to improve his English, which his wife, Marlène, already spoke well. He and I would lie on the sand in the evening cool as I taught him English and he would tell me about life in the Legion. One night as we lay on our backs looking up at the absolutely clear, star-speckled Saharan sky, we watched the first space object, the Russian Sputnik, a tiny brilliant silver dot, travel steadily from horizon

December 1957: a small family tented encampment near Mrhaïer, where 2nd Company, 1st REP was based in November–December 1957 while mounting patrols in the edge of the Sahara. The villagers were friendly: headmen would often greet patrols with offers of sweet mint tea, in accordance with the Muslim tradition of hospitality, and even provided the occasional sheep for a mechoui feast. (Linda Hunter-Choat).

to horizon.¹¹ [They were still good friends 51 years later]. It was he who presented me with my Legion of Honour in Paris in 2001; the day I received my broom from Bonelli; the day Wallisch was my accompanying officer ... Staff Sergeant Johann Wallisch was outstanding, and finished his career as one of the most highly decorated NCOs in the Legion.¹²

One of Tony's comrades at this time was a Liverpudlian *légionnaire* called Ray Palin. As a batman to Lieutenant Simonot, one of the platoon commanders in the company, he served both the lieutenant and the Legion well. He had had an extraordinary experience, and miraculous escape, during the raid in the Battle of Algiers – which, as we have seen, resulted in the death of Ali la Pointe (see above, Chapter 4). Ray Palin had been placed on the roof of the house to prevent any movement between the buildings by terrorists trying to escape the encirclement. When the building collapsed after the explosion following the attempt to blow a hole to allow access to Ali la Pointe's hiding place, he fell through two floors and damaged his right eye, which many years later went blind. Apart from Tony and Ray, there was only one other Briton in the regiment. Tony and Ray went out together from time to time: '... it always ended in disaster.'

By mid-December 1957, Tony's para pay had still not come through, and he was broke. However, even if short of cash, the approach of Christmas brought material improvements. They moved from their tents to vacant single-storey houses, each built around its own courtyard, on the edge of town. It had long been Legion tradition that Christmas cribs were made by each company, and Tony's company put a great deal of hard work and loving care into the manger scene. It was another, but more recent, tradition in the Legion that:

---

11 Sputnik 1 was launched on 4 October 1957 and remained in orbit for three months until 4 January 1958.
12 Johann Wallisch was an Austrian who enlisted as a paratrooper in the German Army in 1943 at 17 years of age, after having been imprisoned for anti-Nazi sentiments. He subsequently fought in the Battle of Normandy and was taken prisoner by the French when his unit surrendered in May 1945. He was transferred to a POW camp near Carcassonne; in December 1945, a Legion recruiting officer offered him the chance to enlist in the Legion. He, along with other Germans and some French and Belgians who had fought for the Germans, took the opportunity to build a new life. He subsequently served with the Legion in Indochina, was captured at Dien Bien Phu, and after his release served with 1st REP in Algeria. He left the Legion in 1962.

... *légionnaires*, having no family but the Legion, should each receive a Christmas present from her. I was given an excellent track suit; over the years I was given sleeping bags, electric razor, a watch. For all of which I was very grateful. Legio Patria Nostra, La Légion est notre Patrie, Der Legion ist mein Heimat. The Legion is our Fatherland. How very true. Particularly at Christmas.

However, the comfort of the houses was short lived. On Christmas Day 1957, the company broke camp, and the regiment moved 50 miles or so north to the ancient village of Oumache, near the old Legion fort of Bordj d'Oumache. They continued to patrol, but there was little enemy activity in their new sector. The local population was particularly friendly and gave the *légionnaires* a couple of sheep for 'that outstanding Algerian meal, the mechoui.' In the morning, they dug two large pits about three feet deep, six feet long, and three feet wide. In each hole, they lit a mass of wood, topping it up as it burnt away until, by late afternoon, there was just a mass of red-hot embers. The sheep were spitted and turned over the charcoal. Around the edges were pots cooking vegetables, chicken, and couscous. The meal, 'accompanied by Kronenbourg, was quite outstanding.'

Guelma, January 1958: Tony with his FM24/29 before first seeing combat as a member of 1st REP. He is wearing a zipped sweater, the olive-drab trousers of the all-arms M1947 combat fatigues, and the short canvas-and-rubber tropical boots known as Pataugas. During his second engagement, on 14 February 1958, Tony's No.2 on the LMG would be mortally wounded beside him. Tony was cited for his first Cross of Military Valour for his conduct that day, and his second award would be gazetted only 11 days later (that citation recorded that he had been wounded, but not the fact that it was by an over-shot French 105mm shell).
(Linda Hunter-Choat).

Relations between the regiment and the local population continued to be good. As the *légionnaires* patrolled the local villages, the elders often set up a 'pretty little Arab table' in the middle of the road, from which was served 'wonderfully refreshing mint tea.'

On 16 January 1958, the inevitable happened, and Tony stopped being a *voltigeur* and became a light machine gunner. There were two light machine gun teams in Tony's platoon, and the other gunner was a German friend of Tony's, an ex-member of the Hitler Youth, Otto Behrendt. Otto had a more modern gun, the AA52 belt-fed weapon introduced into service in 1952. Tony preferred his magazine-fed FM24/29.

Guelma

Shortly thereafter, in mid-January 1958, the regiment changed into camouflage combat kit and moved 160 miles north-east to Guelma, joining four other parachute regiments for what was to become known as the Battle of the Borders. The journey took three days in trucks. On the journey south, they paused at Biskra airfield and then drove past 'wonderful Roman ruins' as they approached their destination. Guelma was 'a delightful market town' about 20 miles west of the Morice Line. Nearby were the hot springs of Hammam Meskoutine and the old Roman town of Heliopolis. The position at Guelma was chosen because of its proximity to known passages of the barrier. The frontier between Algeria and Tunisia projects a deep salient into Algerian territory about 40 miles east of Guelma. Within this salient, there were a large number of ALN camps. From there, the rebels were known to cross the barrier between Duvivier (now Bouchegouf), 15 miles east of Guelma, and Souk Ahras.

Not only did the salient thrust deep into Algeria, but the terrain in this area was also more suitable for infiltration than further north or south. To the north was the coastal plain of Annaba, to the south a barren high plateau. In between was a band of about 20 miles in width with Mediterranean vegetation, often exceeding the height of a man, which provided excellent cover. Guelma is about 1,000 feet above sea level, but the plain is dominated to the north-west by the Djebel Debar and to the south by the Djebel La Mahouna, both rising to an altitude of around 3,300 feet, Beni Mezline to the north-east rose to around 2,800 feet. Djebel Debar, Djebel La Mahouna, and Beni Mezline were all covered by dense vegetation – although La Mahouna less than the others – and provided secure staging places for rebel bands that successfully crossed the Morice Line. It was in this terrain that Tony's regiment was to fight, having installed itself in several camps with the command element and two companies, including Tony's, at a farm, other units

January 1958: paras of 1st REP on their way north to Guelma to take part in the Battle of the Borders. They wear the REPs' green beret, camouflage-printed, many-pocketed jump smocks and trousers of one of the many variants of the long-lasting M1947 series, and ranger boots with buckled ankle flaps. Visible on the TAP1950 webbing equipment are a five-magazine pouch for the MAT49 sub-machine gun, a fighting knife, and a US-type canteen and cup in its cloth carrier. Company-coloured neckerchiefs might be worn for quick recognition – Tony's 2nd Company wore them in red. (Linda Hunter-Choat).

at the sports stadium, a further farm, and at Heliopolis. In addition to his own regiment with seven rifle companies, the commanding officer, Lieutenant Colonel Jeanpierre, had under command an artillery battery, a helicopter detachment with six 'Bananas', and the *Commando Extrême-Orient* of around 400 men.[13] He also

---

13   The Far East Commando (*Commando d'Extrême-Orient*) was a unit that had come to Algeria at the end of the Indochina War. Under the command of Captain (later

Operations on the Morice Line defending the Tunisian frontier near Guelma, spring 1958. Below the paras on the brush-covered hilltop, dust is thrown up by a Piasecki H-21 Shawnee helicopter delivering supplies or reinforcements in the field. The deployment of separate para companies around the battlefield by helicopter was a major tactical advance perfected by the French forces in Algeria. These 'flying bananas' had a payload of 2.8 tons; they could carry up to at least 20 fully equipped infantrymen. This machine appears to be unarmed; the H-21 was unsuitable for ground-attack work, but most of them eventually mounted 12.7mm (.50 calibre) door-guns for use when landing troops under fire. (Linda Hunter-Choat).

had on call air support and the sector reserves, a remarkable force for a lieutenant colonel's command.

The primary mission of the regiment was to contain the movement of ALN reinforcements and arms from Tunisia across the Morice Line to wage war further west in Algeria. However, the *fellagha* were also burning settlements and farms and killing Europeans and Arabs alike. A secondary role of 1st REP was to prevent such attacks. The specific orders given to Lieutenant Colonel Jeanpierre were '… acting

General) Simon, it comprised experienced soldiers drawn primarily from Vietnam but also from Cambodia, Laos, China, and even one ex-Japanese Imperial Army soldier who had fought in the Second World War. They were often simply called 'the Vietnamese'.

independently to the west of the barrier and in liaison with the central sector: prevent the passage of outlaws and intercept the traffic in armaments; destroy local bands. By applying your effort in particular in the zones of refuge of Djebel Debar, Beni Mezline, Djebel La Mahouna and Kef El Aks.'[14]

There were insufficient troops to patrol the fence line in strong enough numbers to stop the rebels crossing, although there were sufficient troops to aid the detection of breaks in the wire. When incursions were detected, preregistered artillery fire would often be brought down on the location, but that alone could not stop the crossing: infantry were required for that task. The operational concept was for incursions to be signalled to the nearest units. The rebels invariably crossed at last light to give them the maximum time to reach the relative safety of high ground or forests before sunrise. It was winter, so the nights were long. Units would be given the time and place of the incursion together with an assessment of direction of movement and the likely route to be taken. Well-trained rebels, even fully loaded, could move at up to five miles per hour, and their likely daylight refuge area could be calculated. The regiment was on permanent instant standby. All equipment, weapons, ammunition, and grenades were ready to hand; the only thing to be issued at the last minute was rations.

Nearly all the regiment's operations over the next months, until they returned to barracks at Zeralda on 11 June 1958, started just after last light. The men quickly embarked on American Second World War-vintage GMC trucks to drive towards the mountainous frontier region. They drove with lights out up rough, narrow, steep tracks flanked by precipitous drops. Once disembarked, they marched, usually at the run, to get above the anticipated *fellagha* location at very first light: 'The first shots nearly always rang out just as day was breaking. It was good that we were fit; always heavy loads of ammunition and grenades, always marching or running in the pitch black as fast as possible, always up and up. And lugging my machine gun. Oh, how proud I had been of my expertise!'

Things did not get off to a promising start. On 21 and 22 January 1958, three companies of the regiment and the Vietnamese Commando suffered four killed, two wounded, and a sub-machine gun lost to the enemy. For this, the rebels had lost two men killed and a rifle.[15] Jeanpierre was a demanding commander. He

---

14 Montagnon, *Les parachutistes de la Légion*, p.209. (Author's translation).
15 Sometimes the figures for casualties and weapons captured vary between those given in Tony's account and other sources. In general, I have taken Tony's numbers as being contemporary evidence. Where there is a figure in an official document, such as an award citation, I have used that number since it will have been drawn

was not the kind of CO to accept the results of the 21 and 22 January; he let his subordinates know in no uncertain terms that the enemy must pay a heavy price in blood and that the loss of weapons must not happen again. His officers knew that he had no difficulty getting rid of men who were not up to his exacting standards. (One officer had been immediately posted from the regiment during the Battle of Algiers for visiting his wife at Zeralda.)

However, it was not in Jeanpierre's nature to place the blame on his men, and he rapidly rethought his approach to operations. He concluded that he needed a more flexible organisation. He established two battalion tactical HQs, Command Post *Blanc* (white) and Command Post *Lilas* (lilac), under two captains from the HQ Company, Morin and Verguet.[16] The units under command of the two HQs were not fixed but allocated as the situation demanded. This structure allowed Jeanpierre to deploy forces flexibly to approach the assessed location of the enemy from a number of directions simultaneously. He could leave the immediate conduct of contact with the enemy on the ground to Morin and Verguet. This left him free to plan his next move, coordinating the activities of his regiment and that of supporting units while maintaining contact with the upper command chain.

On 23 January, the regiment had a much more successful day. Tony's company was rapidly deployed to the Djebel La Mahouna, along with other elements of the force, to counter a reported band of approximately 150 rebels with at least six machine guns. At 0730 hours the next morning, as the mist lifted, the first shots were exchanged. The 1st Company, supported by tanks and the Vietnamese Commando, was heavily engaged. By the end of the day, 92 rebels had been killed and five medium machine guns, 32 rifles, and eight automatic pistols captured.

The following day, an attack was launched against two rebel command posts on the heights of the Djebel La Mahouna. To date, the other French units had been reluctant to venture into this area of steep slopes and gorges. Perhaps they were influenced by the memory of an ambush in 1955 in the same region when a section had been annihilated and all its weapons captured. If so, Jeanpierre

---

from a regimental operations record. In any case, precise figures are not essential to understand the success or otherwise of particular operations: it was the balance between relative losses that was important.

16　Captain, later Major, Morin had been with 1st BEP fighting throughout the Indochina War, and then fought with 1st REP throughout the war in Algeria. He resigned his commission after the disbandment of the regiment in protest at the prison sentences given to a number of his fellow officers. Captain Verguet finished the war in Algeria as a major. He remained in the army and ended his career as a four-star general.

was unimpressed. During the night, a battalion command post, the Vietnamese Commando, and a rifle company deployed by truck and then on foot to gain the heights. At 0950 hours the following morning, they were all deployed at their start points. The weather was not auspicious, with snow and visibility of a few tens of yards hiding the mountaintops, so air support was out of the question. Nevertheless, the rifle company and the commandos were soon in contact. Despite the appalling weather, Tony's company, held in reserve, was deployed by helicopter between 0900 hours and 1000 hours to cut off any rebel flight to the north-east. Contacts and searches continued throughout the day. By nightfall it was over: Jeanpierre had lost three men killed, but the rebels had lost 67 killed and eight prisoners. Six machine guns, one sub-machine gun, eight machine-pistols, and 32 rifles had been captured. Jeanpierre was satisfied with the results and the conduct of his men.

A photo taken from a *fellagha* casualty: 'Trained in Tunisia, killed in Algeria. Poor brave bastards ... they didn't have a chance.' These rebels wear the usual motley assortment of civilian and military clothing; one man carries a German MP40 sub-machine gun, another a green-and-white ALN flag bearing a red crescent and star. (Linda Hunter-Choat).

Further operations took place on 28 and 29 January in the forest of Fedj Zezoua on the high ground of Beni Mezline and Kalaat Renadjil. The Support Company, relieved by 1st Company, killed 44 of the enemy, took 10 prisoners, and seized a light machine gun, two sub-machine guns, nine rifles, and 11 shotguns. Shotguns were not weapons to be taken lightly in this form of often close-quarters combat. They were generally loaded with solid shot used to hunt wild boar. As Tony recounts, 'The rebels had a trick of loading their shotgun cartridges with two solid shot tied together by a length of very fine wire. Over short range this could cut off a leg. Or a head.'

The nights were spent marching fast in the pitch black, and the days in blocking any escape from the contact:

> There was little sleep at night as we lay in the cold and the wet, freezing, ambushing the tracks nearest the latest contact, listening for the sound of careful enemy movement. It was often not possible to heat coffee or any food as the smell of the hexamine blocks carried too far. I always had a small plastic water bottle full of methylated spirits and an empty shoe-polish tin. The tin full of methylated spirits was exactly the right amount to boil a metal cup (un quart) of coffee, and made much less smell. If we did manage to get any sleep it was in a cold and sodden sleeping bag, boots on, weapon under one's head so that there was no need to fumble for it in the dark. I was learning.

By the end of January, Tony's 2nd Company had deployed rapidly several times. While other companies had been in contact with the enemy, they had not, other than killing the occasional escaping rebel, despite Captain Ysquierdo's skill and deep tactical sense. Then, on 2 February, it was their turn. They climbed into trucks late in the evening of 1 February and drove, as always, out of town east along the N20 road through Millésimo (now called Belkheir) and Bouchegouf into the mountains, debussed, and marched quickly until dawn. A Piper spotter aircraft found a group of the enemy. The 1st Company was immediately in contact, and Tony's 2nd Company linked up with them and the Support Company. The 3rd and 4th Companies were deployed to block the *fellagha's* most likely routes. By the end of the day, the 1st Company, with the cooperation of Tony's company, had killed 47 rebels including a regional commander. They had captured a Bren gun with a spare barrel, five sub-machine guns, four US M1 carbines, 16 rifles, and binoculars. Tony's 2nd Company encircled the area with ambushes all night on 2 February. The next day, they pushed up on a ridge line where, on Hill 652, they met a hail of fire from a strong *fellagha* group, with the fire intensifying as they identified the whereabouts of the main party, numbering about 20 men. Fighting was raging throughout the sector. The Piper continued to orbit above the battle, trying to pinpoint the enemy to guide T-6, Corsair, and Mistral air support aircraft. Tony gives a graphic account of his first action:

> I didn't shoot much at first as I couldn't see any worthwhile targets; we moved forward driving the enemy back into a steep, rocky, wooded outcrop and a serious fire fight began; they had a number of light and medium machine guns as well as sub-machine guns and rifles. When fighting in thick scrub we developed the rouleau compresseur (steamroller) tactic; advancing in line and knowing roughly the whereabouts of the enemy, whose escape was prevented by blocking forces, we would throw a grenade, fire a burst from our sub-machine guns, move forward and repeat the action until we were in actual close physical contact with them. Today the last stretch up to the rocks and trees was over relatively open ground. Artillery fire had been brought down on the hill not far ahead of us and we could see the heavy crashes of the American 105s [M2A1 105mm howitzer], see the flash and smoke and the shower of debris, and smell the cordite. As we broke cover from the tree line the order 'charge' was given, and we ran as fast as we could over a couple of hundred metres of open ground firing as we went to keep their heads down. Heinz Kalble, my loader, ran beside me passing me fresh magazines as fast as I emptied them. 'Magazine.' – 'Thanks. You OK?' – 'Yes' – 'Magazine'. A lot of bullets were going in the opposite direction. The smoke from the artillery and from our rifle grenades was drifting between the rocks and trees; the last artillery rounds were arriving some 75 meters ahead of us. I saw the head blown off a fellagha, by the artillery, just as he stood up to fire. The body, in perfect balance, stood there for a few seconds blood shooting skywards; then it fell. The firing became intense. I wasn't frightened; I wasn't really anything, not even particularly consciously trying to stay alive – just firing, reloading, running. Now we are up in among the rocks and trees where the stench of cordite from the artillery and from our and their grenades and weapons was thick. The artillery had done good work. I saw a leg with apparently no body from which it had become detached. Two other legs side by side with a spare foot between them. Part of a head in a tree. Bodies everywhere. In the distance we could hear desultory firing as the fleeing rebels ran into the blocking forces and were eliminated one by one.

They had killed about 20 rebels and captured two. Weapons had also been captured together with ammunition destined for groups already in Algeria, along with important documents and letters from the HQ in Tunisia to ALN commanders in

Algeria. Many of the dead carried photographs of themselves and their fellow rebels taken in the Tunisian training camps carrying the very weapons that had just been captured. They also found in the packs of the rebels brand new lightweight ankle boots (known as Pataugas) with canvas uppers and rubber soles. The *légionnaires* treasured them, but not '… the French manufacturers who were selling them to Tunisia.' Tony had survived his first contact, his first moment of danger:

> I had felt nothing; perhaps I had yet to understand how dangerous it all was. We wearily wound our way back down the hill, happy to be still alive, happy to have done extremely well that which we had been trained to do, happy in the congratulations of our officers and NCOs: 'Well done Johnny, good shooting, good operation, well done.'

The pace of operations for the regiment picked up, with other companies in action the following day and on 6 and 9 February. Days without operations often involved funeral ceremonies for comrades killed in action – it was rare for a company to return from such combat without having lost a man. Wounded were evacuated to hospitals in Bône and Constantine, but evacuation to Constantine overland was not without its risks – the 80-mile journey was through terrain ideal for ambushes.

On 12 February, Tony's 2nd Company was brought to immediate readiness as part of Captain Verguet's Battalion Group *Lilas* to track down a rebel group that had crossed the border. They waited but were then stood down as the band had moved out of the regiment's sector. Two days later again an alert, but this time the rebels were in the 1st REP sector. The men grabbed their kit, collected their rations, climbed into the GMC trucks, and went to sleep. They moved out at about 0400 hours heading for the Beni Mezline by a long, looping route to reduce the risk of alerting the enemy to their arrival. Through the night, they climbed up the mountains towards the Fedj Zezoua, leaving the main road and following roughly bulldozed tracks hacked into the mountain side. Cliffs rose on one side, and, on the other, there was a sheer drop. The tracks were barely wider than the trucks, which struggled and skidded round the tight bends, all lights out in the pitch-black darkness:

> It was cold and nerve wracking; but it beat marching. We smoked surreptitiously, lighting them under a poncho and cupping our cigarettes in our hands. Up and up we drove, with engines roaring and gears crashing. Suddenly, in the pitch dark we stopped and silence fell. No crashing of tailgates being lowered, no shouting or swearing. Everyone disembarked quietly and immediately began the long single-file march, sometimes

running to keep up, occasionally bunching as the leader checked the map, up and up into the dark hills, seeing nothing, hearing only the soft thump and scrabble of Ranger boots on the path, and smelling the distant smoky smell tinged with excreta of invisible Arab villages. Very dark. Whenever we stopped we could hear in the distance other companies making their way up the mountains, only the sounds of their feet to be heard; no clashing of weapon or sound of voices. We moved fast into the Fedj Zezoua.

The first shots rang out at first light while we were in fairly open country, a long wide slope stretching down before us with the occasional clump of bushes or little rocky outcrops. There was automatic fire everywhere as other companies were already in contact, the sounds of the bursts distorted by the rocks and valleys and bushes; long bursts across the hill, hollow and distant-sounding, [from] our FMs [light machine guns] and their MG42s. A continuous racket of sub-machine guns, on and on. Captain Ysquierdo had manoeuvred us to exactly the right spot, we were, as he had planned, on the ridge above them. We put our yellow and black air identification panels on the top of our packs to avoid being strafed by our own Air Force. At the first contact the fellagha came under heavy fire from the T-6s and Corsairs overhead and had retrenched themselves in a large rock outcrop on the flank of the hill from which they had excellent fields of fire, plenty of cover against the aircraft fire and ours, among the rocks and little limestone caves; but no escape. We advanced under heavy fire, the sound of the 1,000 rounds-a-minute MG34s and MG42s sounding like tearing paper as the rounds swished overhead. The superb 7.92 rifle the K98 [Second World War German Mauser K98] sounded hard and sharp as the bullet passed, followed by the softer boom of the gun firing – it made a noise something like Tac-Koom. And as Tac-Koom we always knew it.

My light machine gun group commander, Caporal-chef Couannet, headed off to the right looking for a good position for the light machine gun.[17] Heinz Kalble and I followed, looking not only for good cover but also for a spot from where we would have a good field of fire. The rest of the group carrying the ammunition trailed along behind dodging from cover to cover. Heinz and I lost sight of the group commander but found a good group of rocks from which we would have a perfect view of the enemy positions. We crawled as flat as possible forwards, with the MG42 persisting in trying to get us. We reached our rock and I set up the gun; Heinz put the magazines

---

17   I have in general used British Army equivalent ranks. An exception is the rank of caporal-chef, which has no direct equivalent in the British Army. It is, in effect, a rank of senior corporal coming between corporal and sergeant.

ready for quick changes and looked round to see where the ammunition-humpers were. They weren't far away, and if they became pinned down and couldn't move they could probably throw their magazines and loose rounds to us.

I could see where one of the rebel machine guns was firing and opened up on him. My fire was more accurate than his and his gun stopped. I looked for and found the next one and opened up on that; he saw me, and I saw him seeing me. He moved his gun round and opened fire. A long stream of bullets hammered into our rock, thwack, thwack, thwack, thwack, thwack, thud, thud. The two that went thud, thud were the ones which went into Heinz's head, together with a scattering of stone chippings knocked off our rock. He fell back, then got to his feet. The enemy guns opened up again. I dragged him down and made him lay beside me in relative safety where I bandaged up his head; he was dying anyway, and no amount of bandages were going to change two bullets in the head. He got up again and wandered off, undoing the bandage I had so carefully put on him. Amazingly he wasn't hit again, but eventually just dropped dead.

The ammunition-humpers were either wounded or had withdrawn to better cover, so I was on my own. I still had some of my magazines and all of Heinz's, so I carried on firing. Eventually the enemy fire was sufficiently suppressed for an assault on the rocks to be made, to which I continued to give covering fire until our own men were too close to the enemy for me to be able to fire without putting them at risk. A small group led by one of our sergeant majors, Sergeant Major Herrera, managed to get on top of the rock complex vertically above the enemy; they called for an airstrike from the T-6s and Mistrals on a cave below the summit. Unfortunately the grid reference of the cave was the same as that of the sergeant major's party directly above it, and the first rockets wiped out the group, cutting Sergeant Major Herrera in half, amputating both legs of Kumbartzki and of Lieutenant Lesort, killing légionnaires Abels and Kugel and wounding Captain Hautechaud and Medical Captain Palu, who lost half a foot.

Our company's 57mm recoilless rifle firer raised himself above the bushes to get a clear shot to blast a rebel gun, and was promptly shot. The remainder had reached the rocks and were attacking the rebels with their sub-machine guns and dozens of grenades. The rebels replied with their own and a fierce exchange of grenades took place. The battle lasted six hours, during which we had three helicopter ammunition resupplies. Fresh grenades were thrown from hand to hand to those well placed to throw them at the enemy. We stayed the night on the ridge line, the other companies encircling the whole area of the contacts, and continued to sweep the terrain the next morning, when we found and killed a few more enemy and recovered their weapons. Of this contact, and of all the others before and after, the things I remember most are the incessant crashing noise of small arms fire, theirs and ours, the incessant thunder of grenades, the smells of cordite and burning undergrowth and of burnt bodies, and the smell of death. Noise, noise, noise.

Sixty-nine enemy had been killed by Tony's company, and the weapons captured comprised five heavy machine guns, one light machine gun, 16 sub-machine guns, numerous Second World War Schmeisser MP38 machine-pistols, some Beretta 38/42 9mm sub-machine guns, and 34 rifles. The total enemy killed by the regiment over the two days of combat amounted to 139, plus three prisoners taken. A large haul of weapons and munitions had been captured, including mortar and PIAT (a British Second World War man-portable anti-tank weapon) rounds and more than 60,000 rounds of ammunition. The regiment had suffered 14 killed and 36 wounded. Of these, six of the killed and a dozen of the wounded were in Tony's company. Among the wounded was Tony's platoon commander Lieutenant Gillet. Lieutenant Lesort, who had been hit by the air-support rockets, remained an invalid for the rest of his life. 'The usual burial service in Guelma cemetery followed. I still wasn't afraid. That would come later.'

For this action, Tony was awarded his first decoration, the Cross of Military Valour with Silver Star:[18]

> Young light machine gunner who has just shown himself to be a courageous and calm combatant. On 14 February 1958 in the Fedj Zezoua, caught under rebel fire at close range, he reacted with coolness even though he remained alone serving his weapon. By the precision of his fire he neutralised an element solidly entrenched. He thus contributed efficiently to an action where the rebels lost 69 men killed, five machine guns, one light machine gun, 16 machine-pistols and 34 rifles.

Tony had the utmost respect and admiration for the commander of the regiment, Lieutenant Colonel Jeanpierre: 'He was a good commander, and his photo sits above my desk as a reminder of one of the military men I most admire. He had

---

18   *La Croix de la Valeur Militaire* was created in 1956 as a quirk of the war in Algeria. Since Algeria was part of France then, by definition, the fighting could not be considered a war but rather 'operations for the maintenance of order'. By extension of this logic, the *Croix de Guerre* could not be awarded for exceptional service in Algeria.

a powerful presence and was extremely tough both physically and mentally, an outstanding tactician, and smart enough to avoid the perpetual political pitfalls of the French military.'

When the regiment arrived in Guelma, Tony's company had reasonable accommodation in a group of solid and clean wooden huts. They were absolutely forbidden to take anything from the local farms and other buildings, including stealing fruit. Punishments in the Legion were harsh, and the most common for a relatively minor misdemeanour, apart from a solid beating, was the *tombeau* (grave). The guilty culprit was made to dig a pit about six feet long by two-and-a-half feet wide and five feet deep. Therein, he stayed day and night for as long as the punishment lasted, being allowed out only to relieve himself. His only cover, and that at night only, was a ground sheet stretched over the top of the grave. So Tony was taking a serious risk when he was up a tree scrumping. Suddenly he saw, some way away coming down the path, Colonel Jeanpierre:

> It was too late to drop down and run and anyway there was nowhere to hide, so I sat perfectly still. He came closer and closer and eventually passed right under my tree. As he did so, and without raising his head he called out 'Bonjour Johnny'. And that was that. He mentioned it to no one, there was no punishment. I had been in his regiment for just over two months and yet already he had taken the trouble to know who I was, me and the other 1,600. I worshipped him thereafter.

At about this time, Tony experienced the delights of the Legion's field medicine. He developed masses of large and very painful boils on his backside and the back of his neck. The medical officer's senior medic, Sergeant Schüller, sorted them out by the simple expedient of slashing them open with a scalpel and scooping out the pustulent contents with an old spoon. He then threw in some antibiotic powder, and that was that.

Operations continued at a great pace and at a great physical cost of fatigue and casualties. Jeanpierre drove his regiment hard, particularly the officers. About halfway through the battles of the Tunisian frontiers, while 1st REP was deployed at Guelma, some officers told Jeanpierre in the mess that the regiment was tired and that the *légionnaires* needed rest. 'Tired' was perhaps not a word to use to a man who had walked out of the Tonkin jungle in Indochina after the massacres of October 1950. His reply was to the point: 'Je vous fabrique de la gloire, de quoi vous plaignez-vous!'[19] (I'm giving you glory, what are you complaining about!) But if the costs to the regiment were great, they were 10 times greater for the enemy.

Every spare moment back in Guelma was spent sleeping, eating, changing kit, restocking ammunition and grenades, and 'cleaning, cleaning, cleaning our weapons, for the day that they jammed we would be dead. I loved my FM and it never left my side.' The N20 road east out of Guelma became very familiar to the *légionnaires*, and they knew that, once out of the trucks, they had a long, hard night and a long, hard day in front of them.

Legion paras snatching an opportunity for rest during an operation. The long radio antenna seems to identify this as a company headquarters group, in which case the junior officer on the left, wearing a dark forage cap and olive-drab fatigues, is presumably an attached artillery or Air Force forward observer. (Linda Hunter-Choat).

Around this time, a new man arrived in the company as a casualty replacement. He did not take to combat at all, and, in one particularly vigorous contact, he held well back. As the *rouleau compresseur* tactic required all the men to move more or less in line with only the heavier supporting weapons behind, having a man

---

19   Montagnon, *Les parachutistes de la Légion*, p.215. (Author's translation).

shooting away from behind the rest was both distracting and dangerous: 'He was shot and died. By the enemy? Maybe.'

The helicopter tactics developed by the French armed forces during the Algerian War were revolutionary and owed much to the innovation of the parachute forces, including 1st REP under Jeanpierre's command. No standard operating procedures existed, and these were worked out as experience was gained: seating arrangements, safety, security, embarking, and disembarking. Jeanpierre developed and refined the helicopter tactics to a fine art. When the alert occurred during daylight hours, or just before dawn, he would drive out of Guelma as fast as he could go. There were insufficient helicopters to lift more than half a company and some HQ elements at a time, so the tail company would peel off into a suitable LZ (landing zone) and be lifted off while the rest of the force drove on. The new tail company would repeat the process, and so on. Each time, the turnaround distance for the helicopters was reduced by the distance travelled to the target area by the ever-shortening convoy. Once deployed, rapid helicopter moves around the sector of operations, as enemy movement was detected or became clearer, allowed the regiment to dominate far more ground than would otherwise have been possible. As the men were flown into the LZ, an armed version of the Sikorsky S-58, known as the Pirate, equipped with a Mauser 20mm cannon and a .50 calibre Browning heavy machine gun, circled the area firing at any likely rebel hiding places until the *légionnaires* were safely on the ground and deployed in all-round defence. The Pirate 'was always welcomed by us. One thought always occurred to us as we flew over the ever higher ever more rugged mountains, flying over vertically sided gorges, and that was that we would, inevitably, be marching out at the end of it all.'

Often, when the terrain did not permit landing, the *légionnaires* had to jump from a considerable height: 'The pilots were superb, flying steadily through heavy small arms fire, hovering with great care while we disembarked, poised with one wheel on a steep hillside where no LZ was available. We owed them a good deal.'

Operations continued apace during February and March 1958. On 20 February, the fighting was high in the snow-bound Djebel La Mahouna. Thirty-two rebels were killed, and three MG42s, one Bren gun, three sub-machineguns, and 18 rifles were captured. The difference between the numbers of rebels killed and weapons captured was because often a number of the men in rebel bands were there solely to carry munitions and stores to resupply groups operating elsewhere in Algeria.

Wounded

On the night of 25 and 26 February, the regiment was stood to and deployed to the Koudiat Megroum El Ougami on a ridge line above a large, open-ended bowl with two enemy companies climbing towards them. Tanks and regular troops from the local sector blocked off the open end of the bowl, about three miles from the *légionnaires* on the ridge. The ridge lines on the flanks of the bowl were held by other companies while Tony's company faced the advancing enemy. They hadn't seen the *légionnaires*, but, when they did, a battle ensued that lasted 10 hours. In order to ensure that the enemy continued to climb to where Tony's company was waiting for them, the artillery liaison team:

> … called for their American 105s to fire behind the enemy, advancing the fire to push them forwards up the hill. A fierce fire fight was already taking place with those enemy who had already reached our level and I had been firing my FM continually for a couple of hours as the enemy came into view. The artillery linear barrage continued to mount the hill towards us, pushing the enemy ahead of it. Soon it was quite close and the boom of the distant guns [the howitzers had a range of about seven miles] followed by the shrieking whistle and huge crash of arriving shells was constant. Bushes, rocks, earth and bits of enemy were thrown into the air with each barrage. We thought it a brilliant tactic and it worked exactly as planned, achieving the desired result.
>
> Unfortunately, the artillery Forward Observation Officer (FOO) was backed up by a more senior artillery officer flying in a Piper as an aerial OP [observation post]. Our FOO could see that the barrage was getting too close and called the guns to stop firing. He was overridden by the air OP officer who transmitted: 'Taisez-vous, je prends le commandment!' (Shut up, I'm taking command!) The next several barrages landed on us, even more impressive than their predecessors. My lovely FM was seriously damaged by shrapnel and a smallish piece of shell traversed my hand. Staff Sergeant Wallisch bellowed at the artillery officer, and, since there was no apparent reaction opened fire on him with his M1 carbine. This produced a reaction and the fire stopped. Wallisch's radio operator had lost the best part of a leg and the pain was so bad that he tried to shoot himself with his automatic pistol – only to find that the splinter had cut it in half, and that the missing bit was somewhere in the remains of his leg.

Tony's 'Emma' – his FM24/29 light machine gun: 'I loved it … it never left my side'. The standard French squad LMG from the mid-1920s to the late 1950s, it took the same 7.5mm ammunition as the MAS36 and MAS49 rifles. With its pistol-grip, 30-round top-feeding magazine, and folding bipod under the muzzle, it bore a superficial resemblance to the later Czech-British Bren gun, but at 24.5lbs it was a pound or two heavier. It also differed in lacking the Bren's quick-change barrel and in having two triggers – the front one was used for single shots, the rear for firing bursts. (Linda Hunter-Choat).

By the end of the operation, 197 rebels had been killed, seven prisoners taken, and eight MG42 machine guns, one PIAT, 46 sub-machine guns, 116 rifles, 13 pistols, 24 PIAT rounds, 28 anti-tank rounds, and 60,000 rounds of ammunition captured. However, 1st REP had lost an officer and an NCO killed in action and had suffered more than 100 wounded. The regiment was already distinguishing itself in the operations on the frontier and was described by General Vanuxem as the most elite regiment in the French Army in an order of the day issued around the end of February: [20]

---

20   General Paul Vanuxem had himself established a fine reputation as a determined and courageous soldier. Starting life as a schoolteacher, he had joined the army in his 30s at the approach of the Second World War. He served with the Free French, including in the Battle of Monte Casino, and subsequently with great distinction in Indochina and then in Tunisia before taking command in the Constantine area in Algeria in

I congratulate Lieutenant Colonel Jeanpierre, commanding 1st REP for his exceptional promotion to the rank of Commander of the Legion of Honour. In this circumstance I address my admiration to the commander, officers, NCOs and légionnaires of 1st REP who, by their valour, their spirit of sacrifice, their incomparable ardour in the assault, their ferocious determination to win, have caused to the enemy, in less than five weeks, losses of 600 killed, have amassed 447 captured weapons, including 29 machine guns and 13 sub-machine guns, beating all the records during the fighting in Algeria and placing their regiment in the first rank of the assault troops of the French Army.[21]

For Tony's performance in the action up to the time that he was wounded, he was awarded his second decoration, the Cross of Military Valour with Gilt Star:

A light machine gunner, courageous, particularly calm and efficient in combat. He distinguished himself on 25 February 1958 at Koudiat Megroum el Ougami during combat against a strong rebel band equipped with numerous automatic weapons. After having succeeded in pinning down by his fire a group which was trying to infiltrate, he was at the front of the assault against this element which was annihilated, leaving on the battlefield a machine gun and 10 individual arms. He was wounded during the action.

Tony had a long and increasingly painful wait behind the ridge line, out of enemy fire, during which the many more seriously wounded were evacuated. He was feeling more and more sorry for himself, but at long last he was airlifted by Alouette helicopter with several other wounded, two of them in side stretchers, to Guelma hospital. Lieutenant Gillet, already back on operations after his wound only 10 days before, was there to see his men on their way. The facility at Guelma was a small hospital for a small town; suddenly, it was flooded with more than 100 wounded. Some had minor wounds, but others had lost limbs or had head, stomach, and chest wounds. The regiment's own doctors and medics were in the thick of battle, and the town's few surgeons and doctors were very hard pressed. The casualties were triaged to establish priorities for treatment. The triage was

---

1957. He was accused of being involved in the OAS and arrested in 1961. He always denied the charge and was acquitted at his trial after having spent two years in prison on remand.

21 Bénédicte Helcégé, *Capitaine Bonelli, L'arbre à papillons* (Sceaux: L'Esprit du Livre Editions, 2009), p.169. (Author's translation).

revised each time more casualties arrived, and Tony was towards the bottom of the pile. As they waited, townspeople, grateful for what the *légionnaires* were doing to keep them safe from the rebels, arrived with quantities of food and drink:

> I will never forget the absolutely delicious fresh ham baguette with lashings of butter, which was my first taste of food since the day before. Wonderful. My wound was hastily dressed with lots of mercurochrome and bandaged; the excitement of the day, the shock of the artillery and the pain of the wound made me very tired and I was allocated a bunk bed in the hospital dormitory, where I fell immediately asleep.
>
> When I woke in the morning to coffee and more wonderful baguette the légionnaire in the next bed was nearly dead and there was a large puddle of blood under his bed; his simple bullet wound through the flesh of his upper arm had not required urgent treatment and, like mine, had simply been bandaged. Unlike mine, his had bled steadily all night as there was not a single member of the hospital staff not involved in the operating theatre. He was caught just in time, given a huge transfusion and soon recovered. Throughout the next morning wounded continued to be brought in, and I stayed in the Guelma hospital until the end of the month with the pain in my hand increasing; by now it was starting to smell pretty bad. On 1 March a number of us were casevac'd to the main military hospital in Constantine, a huge place high above the Constantine ravine with views far out over the plain below to the distant hills. We had been flown from Bône in an old DC-3 Dakota with half the windows missing; it was the middle of winter and extremely cold; then by a fleet of ambulances to the hospital. The hospital was large, bright and airy, the beds comfortable, my hand painful and the food awful. Bed 209, Surgery Ward 1.
>
> On the second day, now nearly four days since I had been wounded I was taken into surgery; the surgeon could not have been kinder or more gentle, despite having been working pretty well non-stop for days. 'Well, this looks a real mess', he said as he unwrapped the dirty and disgusting dressing to reveal a swollen, discoloured and stinking hand, 'it is gangrenous and I think it will be better off'. I couldn't have cared less, and would have been glad to get rid of the damn thing, and said so. I awoke the next morning from the general anaesthetic to find on the end of my right arm a huge plaster with the tips of my fingers poking out the end. So all was well, and although it still hurt it was much better than it had been. He had worked carefully, picking out any splintered bits and cutting away any rotten flesh, then whanged me full of penicillin.

There was little enough to do in hospital, but there was plenty to read, and the *légionnaires* had their wine ration and some beer. In addition:

> There were two really high class, and expensive, prostitutes in town who came in every day with cigarettes and other gifts, bought from their own money, for the wounded troops. We had more gifts and kindness from them than we ever did from all the charitable or religious organisations of Constantine, and we were extremely grateful to them both. The man in the next bad to me had lost a great deal of blood when he was wounded, and to build him up again he was prescribed a bottle of good Bordeaux every day. I wished that I had lost a lot of blood.

On 10 March, Tony left Constantine by ambulance for the journey of 260 miles to the barracks at Zeralda. It was nice to be home, but he was missing the action. A comrade of Tony's, Fernandez, was there with his arm in plaster:

> He had been shot straight through his brand-new automatic watch which he had only just bought from the canteen. Most of the little bits of the watch had finished up in his arm. He was very cross about the whole thing, but, remembering that the watch was under guarantee, wrote to the watch company complaining that he had paid a lot of money for a watch which stopped working at the very first shot. He enclosed all the bits which had been extracted from his arm, mostly with bits of flesh attached and covered in blood, and posted the lot. They sent him a new watch.

Another comrade, also wounded on the frontier, joined the others convalescing at Zeralda. He was 'wonderful company, a good friend, undemanding and not given to excess.' On 26 March, Tony was taken to the military hospital in Algiers to have his plaster removed, some of the stitches removed, and a splint put on. Three days later, the splint and the remaining bandages were removed. Although Tony missed the action, he was glad to relax. The month's operations and the wound at Guelma had taken its toll, and Tony, along with the others, was exhausted. They stayed at Zeralda for a month recovering, working hard on the company garden. On a trip into Algiers, one of the *légionnaires* noticed a huge quantity of:

> … very nice cobble stones stacked by the side of the road … and thought that they would be good for little walls round our company garden. In the MT compound were several trucks which had been acquired from time to time, not painted in Legion sand colour but in khaki and with other unit markings. They were always useful when we needed to pick things up which

weren't exactly ours. That night, wearing French Army fatigues and berets, we picked up two truckloads of cobble stones for our garden. They looked very nice.

While Tony was recovering at Zeralda, the base was inspected one day by a senior general not from the Legion. He visited the cookhouse and asked one of the cooks what he was cooking. The cook replied that it was spaghetti. The lighting in the cookhouse gave a greenish hue to the light. 'But it looks green', said the general. The cook turned out the lights and said, 'Now it looks fucking black, general.'

The placard is dated 30 April 1958, Camerone Day. That year, 1st REP did not spend the Legion's annual feast in the traditional celebrations but on an operation near Souk Ahras (though Tony, still convalescing from his wound, missed it). That day, the regiment recorded killing 120-plus of the enemy, taking eight prisoners, and capturing six machine guns, six LMGs, 37 SMGs, and 75 rifles. The miscellany of Second World War types displayed here is typical. The rifles include many British .303in SMLEs (Short Magazine Lee-Enfield), among 7.92mm Mausers – either German Kar98s or Czech-made VZ24s. The machine guns include German MG34s (foreground) and Czech ZB30 LMGs, which the French called Skodas. The sub-machine guns include a German MP38 or MP40, but the most common type seems to be the Italian Beretta M1938a. (Linda Hunter-Choat).

On 30 April 1958, Tony and his fellow *légionnaires* recovering from wounds were at Zeralda, while the remainder of the regiment remained deployed on operations. They were, therefore, able to celebrate the most important day in the Legion calendar: Camerone Day, a battle synonymous with the courage and commitment of the Legion, which is commemorated every 30 April throughout the Legion. The battle was fought when war followed Napoleon III's attempt in 1862 to install Maximillian, Archduke of Austria, as Emperor of Mexico with the objective of Mexico becoming a French client state. On 30 April 1863, a company of three officers and 62 *légionnaires* were faced by a force of 1,200 Mexican infantry and 800 cavalry. They held out for 11 hours in a complex of farm buildings at a place whose name was recorded as Camerone, with the *légionnaires* refusing all offers to surrender despite the overwhelming odds. When the final assault came, one officer and five *légionnaires* were left in action. They charged with their bayonets, and, as they were overwhelmed, a Mexican officer intervened to prevent the last three men being killed. They surrendered on the condition that the Mexicans rescued and treated the wounded and allowed the last men to keep their weapons. When the battle closed, there were 300 dead Mexicans and as many wounded. The *légionnaires* had achieved their mission of protecting a vital convoy on its way to the French forces besieging Puebla. Napoleon III ordered that the name 'Camerone' be inscribed on the Legion standard.

For Tony's first Camerone since finishing training, the day started with wine in bed, as well as coffee, served by the officers and NCOs. This was followed by a parade of the rear party personnel and then a superb lunch. The rest of the day was free and spent by most of the *légionnaires* drinking beer in the canteen.

Tony recounts how Camerone Day was invariably a day of great festivities. On one occasion:

> … my friend Marciniak and I, having had a considerable amount of wine at lunch, moved on to Pastis which is usually cut with water. We ran out of water and mixed it with red wine, which was interesting but not delicious, so we bought a Jeroboam of champagne. Later in the afternoon we went to Algiers for an evening out. We lost touch with each other somewhere in Algiers. However, next morning I caught the truck back to camp, still neat and tidy, and presented myself to the company office. Everyone was pleased to see me though they asked me where I had been. 'To Algiers for the evening after Camerone'. 'But today is Thursday, Camerone was on Monday.' Ahh. I seemed to have lost a few days somewhere.

Return to Operations

On 3 May 1958, Tony left to rejoin his regiment, still in action in the Guelma sector. During his absence, the pattern of alerts, rapid deployments, and ferocious contacts had continued without respite. If the ALN were to continue the fight in Algeria, it was essential that reinforcements, arms, and munitions crossed from Tunisia despite the losses being suffered. The regiment was engaged at least nine times during March. There was a particularly bloody engagement on the Djebel Marioun on 18 and 19 March, when rebel losses amounted to 133 killed and captured and a large number of weapons seized. However, 1st REP's casualties were heavy with 12 men killed. The pace had continued in the early part of April, but, towards the end of the month, rebel incursions seemed to be reducing, perhaps as a result of the shorter nights giving less time to reach safe areas. As the end of the month approached, there was calm, and 1st REP started to prepare to celebrate Camerone Day. It was not to be. On the morning of 29 April, patrols discovered six trenches that had been dug under the Morice Line some three miles south of Souk Ahras.

Souk Ahras was in the sector of 9th RCP (*Régiment de Chasseurs Parachutistes*), and troops were deployed to counter the incursion before night fell in about five hours' time. It was apparent that this was a major incursion, and 1st REP was placed on alert to reinforce 9th RCP, which soon came under increasing pressure, with one company surrounded by rebels. In a manner harking back to earlier times, the company commander formed his men into a square, and the troops held on for relief despite the loss of their commander. When they were finally relieved, they had lost 28 men. In view of the scale of the incursion and the pressure on 9th RCP, largely made up of conscripts, General Vanuxem took command of the operation and deployed 1st REP on the night of 29/30 April. During the day of 30 April, the brunt of the fighting fell to 1st REP. By the end of the day, the battle fought by 9th RCP and 1st REP over the two days had resulted in 192 rebels killed and eight prisoners taken, plus a large quantity of weapons seized. Tony regretted having missed the action: 'This is a good example of why légionnaires in 1st REP were so reluctant to take leave; there was a serious risk of missing a great contact. I took no leave at all for the first three years.'

As Tony returned to the regiment by train, he passed through seemingly endless scented orange groves. He was looking forward to getting back to his company and back to a light machine gun. However, during the two months of his absence, he had been replaced on the platoon's light machine gun and now resumed his original role as a *voltigeur* armed with a MAT49 sub-machine gun. The *voltigeurs* carried at least eight 32-round magazines, eight to 10 grenades, and spare belts for the new AA52 light machine gun. The grenades the *légionnaires* carried were a mixture of defensive, offensive, and tear gas. The first two had seven-second fuses and the tear-gas grenade a two-second fuse. The defensive grenade was the heavier of the two explosive grenades, designed to break up into a mass of fragments and to kill everyone within a certain radius; it was not used in the attack, as the thrower would be charging forward into its lethal zone as it went off. The offensive grenade was designed to keep the enemies' heads down as the *légionnaires* charged. It had a light metal casing with a large explosive charge that deafened the enemy and often burst lungs with the force of the explosion. Whenever the *légionnaires* found a *fellagha* hiding place:

> … we would start by throwing in a couple of offensive grenades; because they had a seven-second fuse the fellagha was often able to catch them and throw them back out again before they exploded, causing us to dive for cover. Fortunately, the firing mechanisms were interchangeable, and we would replace the seven-second fuse in the offensive grenade with the two-second fuse from the tear-gas grenade. It would still be caught, but too late, and often the explosion was accompanied by an amputated hand flying out of the cache.

Throughout his time in the Legion, and thereafter whenever he carried a heavy load, Tony had blisters on the soles of his feet, deep under the very hard skin created by nonstop marching. The only thing to do was '… to stick a knife in them to relieve the pressure; amazingly, none of them ever became septic as a result.' Tony always hung his magazine pouches, water bottle, and grenades from his webbing shoulder-braces rather than his belt and thus took the weight on his shoulders. He found it easier going if he undid the belt to take the pressure off his stomach when climbing.

The tempo of the Battle of the Borders was slowing after the heavy fighting at the end of April. The combat on 29 and 30 April proved to be pretty much the last throw of the dice for the ALN in attempting to cross with large groups of combatants. This had really been an exceptional effort with, it was estimated by the French, 800 men having been mustered for this incursion. The intensity of operations reduced throughout Algeria as a consequence of the paras' success. Mopping-up operations continued until the end of May, and the pressure on the ALN fighting within Algeria was considerable. The ALN command in Tunisia, in due course, changed their strategy: although border incursions would continue on a small scale, they began to concentrate on building a substantial force within Tunisia while they waited for the political climate to change in their favour. The rebel groups in the interior would continue to fight to the end but were hampered by much diminished resupply in munitions and trained reinforcements.

Bône, 9 May 1958: Tony (in white-covered *képi*, left centre) is decorated with the first of his three Crosses of Military Valour by General Paul Vanuxem (saluting), the general commanding the ZEC (East Constantine Zone). General Vanuxem, a Second World War veteran of the Italian campaign, had distinguished himself in Indochina. In the ZEC, he was largely responsible for the effective deployment of French mobile units to intercept ALN incursions through the Morice Line. (Linda Hunter-Choat).

During the lull in fighting, Tony travelled to Bône on 9 May 1958 along with several other *légionnaires* who were to receive decorations. The awards were presented by General Vanuxem. Tony received his first decoration, the Cross of Military Valour with Silver Star. As Tony recounted:

> It was a wonderful day, good to be out of the mountains, good to be able to walk around a big city. At that time I also learnt about my second decoration, and the fact that I was off to join the Corporals' Course near Sidi Bel Abbès due to start on 9 June. My Legion career seemed to be set fair.

Back on operations, the regiment was deployed again on 19 and 24 May, on both occasions to the west of Guelma in the Constantine mountains. Tony describes life during this phase of the Battle of the Borders:

Marching fast at night in a long single-file column, in dense black, very tired, the fear was always of losing contact with the man marching in front and losing the track – which was often no more than a faint goat path, invisible to the eye in the dark but felt by experienced feet. From time to time my head would jerk up and my eyes snap open as I realised that I had been marching fast asleep; sometimes I crashed into the halted man in front, sometimes the man behind did the same to me. At least we were so used to marching in the pitch dark that our feet could feel that we were on or off a minute path: it felt right, or didn't. I was permanently terrified of being asleep, marching in the pitch black, when the column ahead of me changed direction, and of waking to find them gone. It happened from time to time, but not, happily, to me. We were just about worn out.

There were good moments: the first cigarette of the day, the early-morning coffee brewed on my shoe-polish tin lid cooker, something to eat. Our rations were good as far as packed army rations can be good. They came in a cardboard box and were subject to much swapping of their contents as they were stowed into our packs. They usually contained a tin of some sort of meat, described by us as monkey though it probably was zebu [a hump-backed cow]; a tin of sardines in olive oil or tomato sauce; a small block of nougat; coffee; sugar; matches; twenty Troupe cigarettes; toilet paper; and last but absolutely not least, a very small bottle of eau de vie. On short operations we had half a round of coarse bread per day.

Throughout our operations, marching with us all the time, was the wonderfully mad Captain Régis Forissier (our regimental doctor) and his team, and Père Delarue (our padre) of whom we saw a great deal, both on the ground in the mountains and at our many funerals. Père Delarue was also padre to 2nd RPIMa (Marine Infantry Parachute Regiment) and walked as many miles as we did; he was in exactly the same danger as the rest of us all the time, and was everything a padre should be. He buried lots of us too. Despite heavy incoming fire I never once saw Dr Forissier duck or hide; he moved swiftly from wounded to wounded with his medical team, as if he were out for a quiet walk. His team didn't enjoy it, but they never flinched either.

Tony also describes the hazard of losing immediate contact with others in combat:

During one particularly vicious contact I was operating with Montez-y-Acha as a pair. We were used to working together and had little need for discussion; one covered the other as he moved forward, and then the roles reversed. He and I were steamrollering forwards down a long slope, killing a number of fellagha and recuperating their arms. The scrub was particularly thick and high, and we really couldn't see very much apart from each other and, from time to time, the enemy. We fought on, and in due course the company stopped; we were now a good 150 meters ahead of the rest and tight up against the enemy. Our side assumed we were enemy, and the enemy knew exactly who we were! We lay very, very flat until our own troops caught up with us.

On 28 May, a report came in saying that one of the last rebel bands in the area, about 50 strong, was on the Djebel Taya, a heavily wooded mountain about 13 miles west of Guelma, close to the Djebel Mermera. The regiment was deployed; they debussed at about 2300 hours and headed upwards through very rough country, climbing the Djebel Mermera. As light dawned, it became apparent that the Djebel Mermera was a brush-covered, sugar-loaf-shaped mountain. Tony's company was one of two lead companies. At first light, there was initially no sign of the enemy, and then the other company received a few shots, one wounding an officer. The *légionnaires* started to find traces of the *fellagha* – sleeping areas and sentry posts. Colonel Jeanpierre wanted to helicopter the company to a nearby hill, but Captain Ysquierdo sensed that the enemy were not far away and, instead of waiting for the helicopters, continued the advance. By 1300 hours on 29 May, when they were just about ready for the next phase, bursts of automatic enemy fire came from a rocky outcrop:

> I was sitting against a tree eating my rations, and as I bent down to pick up a tin a bullet hit the tree where my head had just been. Another légionnaire wasn't so lucky. I abandoned any idea of lunch. Support Company aligned itself while preliminary artillery fire was brought down on the enemy position. Jeanpierre, call sign Jacky Soleil, decided he would come and have a look for himself, flying in low over the spur in his Alouette helicopter, trying to locate the automatic weapons which were giving us so much problem. Suddenly the engine stopped. Then a crash. And silence. Lieutenant Simonot's platoon, Rouge Trois, was the first there. Simonot and Ray Palin, his batman, undid Jeanpierre's harness and laid him on a ground sheet. But it was too late: Jeanpierre was dead. Simonot reported to the company commander 'Soleil est mort'. Captain Ysquierdo repeated on the regimental net that Soleil was dead. Major Morin, the second-in-command, flew in and took over. We assaulted the enemy position. There were no prisoners that day.

Lieutenant Colonel Pierre Jeanpierre, greatly admired by his men, including Tony. Jeanpierre was a hard-bitten veteran of the Indochina War; he was a very demanding CO but never a petty disciplinarian. Under his leadership, the regiment earned a reputation as the best of the best in General Massu's 10th DP. (Linda Hunter-Choat).

On the morning of 31 May, a crowd estimated to number 10,000 gathered in Guelma to show their respects for Jeanpierre before his coffin was flown in a DC-3 for burial in El Alia cemetery in Algiers the same day. The regiment marched past the coffin followed by the crowd. At Jeanpierre's funeral, both General Salan, commander-in-chief in Algeria, and General Massu, commanding the regiment's parent 10th DP, delivered eulogies that demonstrated the respect and high regard in which Colonel Jeanpierre was held. General Salan's remarks summed up the feelings of Jeanpierre's superior officers and subordinates alike:

> Jeanpierre, you have just departed from us. My dear old friend, I loved you very much. The Legion will ever hold you dear. I was, in any case, always with you in Indochina where you were always in the thick of it. You never once failed your motto: ever forward. In Algeria you have proved it again. Your loss is really very hard for us to bear. Our only thought is that you left

when we need you most. We know that you approved everything we are doing today. My dear Jeanpierre, all these men, your comrades, your friends will never forget the great sacrifice you have just made. From the bottom of my heart I tell you that we all miss you. I salute you, Jeanpierre.[22]

The Battle of the Borders was now at a close, and, on 5 June 1958, Tony left Guelma by train for Algiers. From there, he moved back to Zeralda, where the cantonment of 1st REP within the barracks was afterwards named Camp Jeanpierre, to prepare for his corporal's course. On 11 June, the remainder of 1st REP returned to barracks. Behind the scenes, there were manoeuvrings to find a replacement for Jeanpierre. It seemed that Major Pierre Darmuzai, serving on the staff at Algiers Army Corps HQ, was the preferred choice of the command staff. This was not well received by the officers of 1st REP, who took the extraordinary step of approaching the inspector of the Foreign Legion to express their concerns. He was not the least pleased by this breach of discipline but gave consideration to their opinion. Despite his reservations about their irregular behaviour, he decided that the efficiency of the regiment took priority over protocol.[23] Lieutenant Colonel Brothier, who had handed over command of the regiment to Jeanpierre a little over a year before, was back in command on 17 June. As Tony wrote, 'Life went on as normally as it could without Colonel Jeanpierre.'

---

22   Translated by Tony Hunter-Choat.
23   It is not clear why the officers of 1st REP took exception to the appointment of Pierre Darmuzai. He was an experienced Legion and para officer who had served in Indochina and Algeria. Indeed, he had commanded the predecessor of 1st REP, the 1st BEP, in Indochina. However, it is clear from the account of Pierre Sergent, who served in both 1st BEP and 1st REP, that Darmuzai was not a popular commander, being known as something of a martinet (Pierre Sergent, *Je ne regrette rien*, (Paris: Fayard, 1972)). He had also fought for the Free French; perhaps he was considered too much of a Gaullist for the Legion paras. This seems plausible since, during the Generals' Putsch against de Gaulle in April 1961, when he was commanding 2nd REP, he was deliberately left out of the picture by his second-in-command, who led the regiment to Algiers in support of the Putsch without Darmuzai's knowledge. He retired as a general in 1972.

The Results

The success of the Battle of the Borders was clear for all to see, forcing the above-mentioned change of strategy upon the rebel command in Tunisia. The French estimated that the percentage of ALN rebels neutralised during attempted infiltrations increased progressively from 35 percent at the start of operations to 80 percent by the end of April. Much of the success achieved was due to the new tactics developed for the use of helicopters by the French, with Jeanpierre's 1st REP at the forefront. As Jeanpierre had said when briefing the governor-general on a visit to the regiment in March, '... so that is how the operation is conceived, how it is executed, by surprise and speed. The second often delivers the first. This is the case of operations launched on the basis of fresh intelligence arriving unexpectedly. There, the helicopter is king.'[24]

During this phase of operations, 1st REP had killed 1,193 rebels and taken 82 prisoners. However, the regiment had paid a high price: 111 men killed and 278 wounded.

---

24 Montagnon, *Les parachutistes de la Légion*, p.217. (Author's translation).

8
May 1958: Turmoil and Change

While Tony's regiment was engaged in the final mopping-up fighting in the Battle of the Borders, momentous events were taking place elsewhere in Algeria, notably in Algiers, and in Metropolitan France. These would bring France to the brink of civil war and culminate in the return to power of General de Gaulle. This was to prove a critical turning point in the war, but not in the direction that the plotters hoped or wished.

A persistent worry among the *pied noir* population was that, at some point, they would be sold down the river by the French government. There had long been tension between those in France, supported by a minority of liberal European Algerians, who believed that reform was necessary and those, again both in France and Algeria, who believed firmness without compromise was the only answer to the rebellion. However, the instability of post-Second World War French governments made pursuing a programme of reform impossible. No party was able to form a majority in parliament, and the fragile coalitions frequently fell. Twenty-two governments were formed during the 12-year life of the Fourth Republic until its final collapse in 1958. In the year running up to May 1958, there had been four governments in power. It was easy in these circumstances for *pied noir* deputies sitting in parliament in Paris, with the support of some deputies from Metropolitan France, to stymie any reform programme.

Overlying this was a determination on the part of the Army that the war in Algeria must be won. There were several reasons for this: the commitment to the idea of Algeria being an integral part of France; desire to efface the defeat in Indochina; the sudden stop to the Suez intervention, which had left a bitter taste; and a belief among many officers that victory in Algeria was necessary to stop the march of communism. This latter was fuelled by the supply of weapons from Eastern Europe – despite the fact that the FLN was determined to keep communism at arm's length. This is not to say that the Army and the *pieds noirs* were as one: many in the Army believed that reform was necessary and regarded the attitudes of *colons* towards the Muslim population with distaste.

The appointment of a new commander-in-chief in December 1956 did nothing to reassure the *colons*, and subsequent events showed the lengths to which some European Algerians and senior officers in the Army were prepared to go to pursue their ends. On 14 December 1957, General Raoul Salan arrived in Algiers to take command. Salan was France's most decorated soldier; he had fought at Verdun in 1918 and, in the inter-war years, had served in the Middle East and Indochina. He commanded a Senegalese battalion during the German blitzkrieg of 1940. After the Armistice, he initially served the Vichy regime in Senegal, but, in 1943, he had joined the Free French in Algeria. He took part in the Allied landings in the south of France in 1944 and fought with distinction until the end of the war. After the end of the Second World War, he served in Indochina, becoming commander-in-chief in 1952–53 and returning to preside over the humiliating withdrawal in 1954. This latter part of his record did not endear him to the *pieds noirs*. To them, he was far from a hero but rather a left-wing general who had sold out in Indochina and was going to do the same in their beloved Algeria.

Within days of Salan's arrival, General Faure, chief-of-staff of the Algiers Army Corps, revealed to an astonished secretary-general of the Algiers Prefecture, Paul Teitgen, that there was a plot within the Army to seize Governor-General Robert Lacoste and put Salan in power. Faure admitted that Salan was not aware of the plot, but he was sure that he would join the conspirators once the coup was a *fait accompli*. Tietgen held a second meeting with Faure and recorded the proceedings. Having warned Lacoste, Tietgen was despatched to Paris to see the defence minister, who took the whole business very lightly – his main concern seems to have been that this might disrupt his skiing holiday. Shocked by this attitude, Teitgen went to see Prime Minister Guy Mollet; he took the matter much more seriously – Faure was recalled to France and sentenced to 30 days' fortress arrest. Salan was angered that Teitgen had gone over his head, but the issue was rapidly overtaken by events.

At 1840 hours on 16 January 1957, General Salan left his office for a meeting with the governor-general. Some 20 minutes later, he heard a powerful explosion: his office had been attacked. His *chef-de-cabinet* in the adjoining office had been killed, and Salan's daughter in the apartment above injured by flying glass. Two anti-tank rockets had been launched from the roof of a building opposite. A number of extreme *pieds noirs* were eventually tracked down as the perpetrators. At their trial in July 1958, one conspirator was sentenced to death in absentia after having fled to Spain, and two others to 10- and six-years' imprisonment, respectively. Both were freed by demonstrators in Algiers in January 1960. It was strongly suspected that senior politicians in France were involved in the plot, which had as its objectives the replacement of Salan by a general thought to be better disposed to the interests of the *colons* and the installation of a government of 'national unity' in Paris. No one other than the three men immediately involved was ever brought to trial. The December plot and the assassination attempt were indicative of the profound disaffection within elements of the French Army and the growing extremism among the European population of Algeria.

The early months of 1958 were marked by numerous conspiracies and counterconspiracies, divided between those who wanted to bring about de Gaulle's return to power and those who did not. Whichever side they were on concerning General de Gaulle, all had the common ground of keeping Algeria French. The government had fallen on 15 April 1958; while Pierre Pflimlin was struggling to form a replacement to fill the vacuum, an event occurred that proved the catalyst for the turmoil that erupted in Algeria and France in the last half of May. On 9 May, the FLN announced from Tunisia, 'On 25 April 1958, the special court of the ALN condemned to death for torture, rapes, and murders committed against the civilian population … the following [three] French military personnel … The sentence was carried out on the morning of 30 April. Other cases, for similar offences, are currently being investigated.'[1]

These unfortunate men had been captured in an ambush some 18 months earlier. It appears that they were selected at random to be shot as a reprisal for the execution on 24 April in Algiers of three terrorists involved in bomb attacks in the city. In advance of the executions, the FLN newspaper *El Moudjahid* had warned that '… each Algerian patriot to mount the scaffold signifies one French prisoner before the firing squad.'[2]

These killings caused outrage in Algeria and in the Army. With unfortunate timing, almost at the same time that news of the death of the three soldiers became known, Pierre Pflimlin had announced in a newspaper article in France that his government would '… seize every opportunity to engage in talks with a view to a cease-fire [and would] call on the good offices of the Tunisians and the Moroccans.'[3] In Algeria, there was incomprehension, among both the European population and the Army, that the next government could take such a step in the face of the killing of three French prisoners.

1　Montagnon, *La Guerre d'Algérie*, p.147. (Author's translation).
2　Horne, *A Savage War of Peace*, p.270.
3　Montagnon, *La Guerre d'Algérie*, p.258. (Author's translation).

MAY 1958: TURMOIL AND CHANGE

Just before the news of the killings broke, General Salan had sent a telegram to the Chief of the General Staff in Paris emphasising the gravity of the situation in Algeria due to the absence of a government committed to the maintenance of *Algérie Française*:

> The present crisis ... shows that the political parties are profoundly divided over the Algerian question. The press permits one to think that the abandonment of Algeria would be envisaged in the diplomatic processes which would begin with negotiations aiming at a 'cease-fire' ... The Army in Algeria is troubled by recognition of its responsibility towards the men who are fighting and risking a useless sacrifice if the representatives of the nation are not determined to maintain Algérie Français ... The French Army, in its unanimity, would feel outraged by the abandonment of this national patrimony. One cannot predict how it would react in its despair ... I request you bring to the attention of the President of the republic our anguish, which only a government firmly determined to maintain our flag in Algeria can efface.[4]

The message was clear: there was, for the first time since the coup of Napoleon III in 1851, the threat of army intervention in French politics.

The same evening, Salan called on the governor-general with other senior officers, including General Massu. Lacoste had come under pressure from the influential editor of the *Echo d'Alger* to sign a letter for publication in the paper calling for the formation of a 'committee of public safety'. He indicated that he might do so, but, overnight, he decided that such a declaration would be in conflict with his socialist principles and that he would not sign the letter. Promising that he would convey the request to the President of the Republic and pleading 'avoid violence', he then left Algiers. France was without a government, and Algeria without a governor-general.

Salan followed his telegram by calling for a ceremony at the Algiers war memorial to pay homage to the three soldiers executed by the FLN. Meanwhile, the prospect of Pflimlin forming a government, which looked set for 13 May, was widely seen in Algiers as potentially disastrous for the future of Algeria. On 11 May, the *Echo d'Alger* published an article under the headline, 'Speak ... speak quickly Mon Général'[5], an unambiguous call to General de Gaulle to take power. This support

---

4   Horne, *A Savage War of Peace*, p.282.
5   Horne, *A Savage War of Peace*, p.283.

for de Gaulle, coming from a former supporter of Vichy and its leader Marshal Pétain, sent a shockwave throughout Algeria.

Anti-Gaullists feared a Gaullist coup to bring de Gaulle to power on the day following the ceremony. They decided that they must get ahead of the Gaullists. The prime mover was Pierre Lagaillarde, who was, to say the least, a colourful character. He came from metropolitan France, although he had spent his childhood in Algeria, had served as a conscript second lieutenant in a parachute regiment, and had been involved in both the Suez intervention and the Battle of Algiers. After he was discharged in 1957, he became a reserve officer. He returned to his law studies at Algiers University, where he became leader of the Algerian Students' Association, leading it into fiercely ultra *Algérie Française* politics. He frequently appeared in public in his para uniform and had grandiloquent ideas of his place in the politics of Algeria. He was likened by some to Don Quixote, with another of the leaders, a bistro owner called Jo Ortiz, unwittingly playing the role of Sancho Panza. Both Lagaillarde and Ortiz were members of a conspiratorial band known as the Group of Seven. The seven had their differences, but all shared a strong antipathy for Charles de Gaulle, representative of the deep-seated *pied noir* support for Pétain and Vichy during the Second World War. They were in close contact with the chief-of-staff of 25th DAP (airborne division) based in Algiers, who sympathised with their aims if not their methods. Lagaillarde told him that on 13 May, during the planned ceremony, he was going to '… seize the radio and Gouvernement-Général [the offices of the governor-general and the administration], and I shall throw the files out of the windows. We shall perhaps be shot up, but Salan will be obliged to take power. As for me, I swear that I shall not leave the demonstration before getting into Lacoste's office.' The chief-of-staff was horrified, telling the Group of Seven that they were madmen: 'The Army will fire on you … you will lose Algeria through your folly.'[6]

The plans were not much of a secret, with the Algiers correspondent of *Le Figaro* cabling Paris on 12 May that it was probable that the next day the *Gouvernement-Général* would be stormed by the mob. Paul Teitgen warned a disbelieving Salan of the way things were going but said that the paras would not fire on the mob. He also sent a warning to the incoming prime minister in Paris, a message that arrived too late.

The ceremony at the war memorial, when Salan would lay a wreath, was scheduled for 1800 hours. By early afternoon, the area around the monument was thronged by a huge number of demonstrators, reinforced by *colons* from the

---

6   Horne, *A Savage War of Peace*, p.283.

surrounding countryside. Laigaillarde arrived in advance of Salan and harangued the crowd: 'Are you going to let Algérie Française be sold down the river? Will you allow traitors to govern us? Will you go to the end of the line to keep Algérie Française?' The crowd roared back its support, and, by the time Salan arrived, Lagaillarde had the crowd in his thrall. Salan was greeted by cries of 'Power to the Army!'[7] and also calls for Massu, the hero of the Battle of Algiers, to accede to power. Salan laid his wreath, there was a minute's silence as a mark of respect, then the crowd accompanied Salan in enthusiastic singing of the Marseillaise. Salan left, and all hell broke loose.

The mob stormed the *Gouvernement-Général*. Riot police fired a few teargas grenades and then retreated. The paras were called out but stood by and watched without intervening: as predicted by Teitgen, the Army was not going to fire on the crowd. Sheltering under his desk, the deputy governor-general called the absent Lacoste, who could offer nothing beyond an order that the mob was not to be fired upon. There was no help from France: the outgoing prime minister considered that he was no longer responsible, and Pflimlin had still not been sworn in. Lacoste's military advisor tried to pacify the crowd; unable to make himself heard, he showed a blackboard on which he had written, 'I have just telephoned Paris to call for a government of public safety'.[8] This drew applause but did not stop the rampaging mob.

Salan, hearing what was going on, went to the *Gouvernement-Général*. Massu arrived at a similar time, seething with anger at the chaos. He took strong exception to seeing Lagaillarde dressed as a para: 'What are you doing in uniform?' Shouts of 'Massu to power!' did nothing to improve his humour. When Salan stepped onto the balcony, he received a hostile reception: 'Fuck off!', 'Indochina!', and 'Vive Massu!'.[9] The support for Massu could hardly be expected to go down well with his superior commander, but neither was Massu impressed. When he was expected by the crowd to say some encouraging words about *Algérie Française*, he growled, 'All these assholes piss me off!' A conference between Salan and Massu followed rapidly, and they decided to call for names to form a committee of public safety.

A list of members was quickly drawn up for the approval of the crowd. Explaining the decision in a telephone call to Lacoste, Massu made it clear that it had been taken as an expedient to avoid troops having to be ordered to fire on the crowd rather than out of any conviction: 'There is no question of a *coup d'état* ... it's [the

---

7   Horne, *A Savage War of Peace*, p.285.
8   Horne, *A Savage War of Peace*, p.285.
9   Horne, *A Savage War of Peace*, p.286.

committee] just to confirm to parliament the will of Algeria to remain French ... I could not act otherwise. Or we would have had to fire on the mob ...'[10]

The anti-Gaullists had stolen a march on their opponents, but the advantage did not last long. Salan was persuaded to send a message to President Coty in Paris calling for a 'national arbiter' to form a government of public safety and restore calm. The message was veiled but unequivocal: General de Gaulle must take control.

In the early hours of 14 May, Pflimlin was sworn in, but in the meantime the outgoing prime minister, despite having initially washed his hands of the whole business, had delegated full powers to Salan in the area of Algiers. Massu had no taste for politics, but Salan was in his element. The fickle *colons* now acclaimed Salan with cries of 'Vive Salan!'

Ostensibly, the new prime minister was backing Salan, but he was in a dither. Playing a double game, he imposed a blockade on Algeria. His swearing-in was a blow to the conspirators. On 15 May, Salan addressed the crowd. He concluded his speech with 'Vive la France! Vive l'Algérie Française!' and then almost as an afterthought with encouragement from the Gaullists '... et vive de Gaulle!' Pflimlin was furious and demanded that Salan explain himself. He did so: '... only de Gaulle legitimately at the head of a government could save Algeria and France.'[11] This was tantamount to open rebellion. The government was in a quandary about how to deal with the crisis, balking at the thought of French troops being required to restore order. De Gaulle was at his enigmatic best, declaring that he was ready to assume power but not saying either how or when. Despite the lack of precision, this was received with great enthusiasm. On the following day, even significant numbers of the Muslim population came out onto the streets in support.

On 19 May, de Gaulle gave a press conference in Paris, at which he undertook to hold himself at the disposition of the country, and he omitted any reference to a solution for Algeria. In Algiers, his words were greeted with both satisfaction and frustration. In face of the blockade imposed by the Pflimlin government, time was running out for the revolt. Salan sent messages to both Pflimlin and de Gaulle: if General de Gaulle did not take power as soon as possible, it might be impossible to prevent a military incursion into France. Salan's power was growing.

Plans were drawn up for *Opération Résurrection*. The plan was for paras to seize key points in order to control communications, the Ministry of the Interior and the offices of the *Confédération Générale du Travail* left-wing trade union and the

---

10 Horne, *A Savage War of Peace*, p.287.
11 Horne, *A Savage War of Peace*, p.289.

Communist Party. Massu would be with them and would go to a HQ in Paris. The 2nd Armoured Task Force would bring its tanks in support. Lagaillarde, looking for a role, planned to provoke an uprising in the Latin Quarter and then seize the Assembly. Once control had been established, President Coty would be persuaded to fly by helicopter with General Massu to de Gaulle's country home to present him with a *fait accompli*. Assuming that the remaining armed forces in France were at worst passive, opposition would be limited to the gendarmerie, the CRS (*Compagnies Républicaines de Sécurité*),[12] and possibly the Communists and likeminded groups. The provisional date to launch the operation was fixed as 27/28 May. On 23 May, Salan confidently asserted in a press interview that, within a week, General de Gaulle would be in power. Surprise was clearly not going to be an element in the operation.

As an appetiser, on 24 May, a para regiment already stationed in Corsica seized power. A Gaullist deputy who took part, when asked if there had been any casualties, remarked, 'Of course not. It was a revolution, not an election!'[13] Pflimlin considered intervening, but, when he asked the Admiralty about the availability of the fleet, he was advised that it was at sea and sailing for an unknown destination. In Paris, the left-wing Minister of the Interior set about organising resistance to the planned operation: the CRS was mobilised, and trade union leaders were asked to stop the trains running in the event of a landing. However, one union leader pointed out acidly, 'The paras don't often go by train!'[14] There was talk about arming the Communists, who reckoned they could get 10,000 militants on to the streets.

On 26 May, General de Gaulle held a secret meeting with Pflimlin. There were two stumbling blocks as far as Pflimlin was concerned: he could not simply hand power to de Gaulle – President Coty would need to be involved – and he wanted General de Gaulle to repudiate the use of force by the Army. De Gaulle was clear that he would not return to power by force, but nevertheless he refused to call for restraint by the Army. The talks broke up without agreement.

The following day, the crisis reached its peak. The Minister of the Interior received intelligence that *Opération Résurrection* was ready to go the following night. The CRS was ordered to defend government buildings. Early in the afternoon, General de Gaulle issued a *communiqué* announcing that he had started the process of

---

12 The CRS is an element of the *Police Nationale* rather than the Gendarmerie. It is used for general security, although is generally known for crowd and riot control.
13 Horne, *A Savage War of Peace*, p.294.
14 Horne, *A Savage War of Peace*, p.295.

forming a government and condemning any threat to public order. He sent a message to Salan calling for him to drop *Opération Résurrection*. Salan sent his deputy to see de Gaulle, who made it clear that he wanted '... to be summoned as an arbiter coming at the demand of the whole country ... I must appear as the man of reconciliation and not as the champion of one of the factions ...'[15]

On 28 May, an ultimatum arrived from Algiers: either de Gaulle was in power by 1500 hours on 29 May or the paras would go in at 0100 hours on 30 May. On the morning of 29 May, President Coty announced that he had invited General de Gaulle to form a government; the next day, he agreed to do so.

The coming to power of General de Gaulle meant all things to all men. The *pied noir* extremists and the Army both felt that he owed his power to them and would dance to their tunes. Events would prove otherwise. He also gave hope to many Muslims, and even the FLN thought that he would bring the prospect of them achieving their aims closer. The reality was that no one knew what he was thinking. However, for de Gaulle, the priority was to restore the position of France as a great power, respected in the world and with a modern army. Although he had probably not at this stage decided how this could be achieved in detail, he seems to have been clear that this required peace in Algeria – hopefully with the country still as part of France or, at worst, in close association with the motherland.

On 4 June, de Gaulle set out for Algiers. The storm clouds were already gathering, with discontent among the ultras about the composition of de Gaulle's first cabinet. Wearing uniform, General de Gaulle addressed the crowds from the balcony of the *Gouvernement-Général*. His first sentence drove the crowd wild. With his arms above his head in a giant V-sign, he spoke the words that were to be the subject of interpretation and misinterpretation for years to come: 'Je vous ai compris!' 'I have understood you!' In the building opposite, there is said to have been an extremist *pied noir* marksman who, on hearing these first words, put down his rifle and listened to the rest of the speech, which was, as always, enigmatic. It omitted direct reference to *Algérie Française*, praised the Army, declared that all in Algeria were henceforth French (the implication that this could mean self-determination seems to have escaped most), and called for reconciliation between Europeans and Muslims. Two days later, he did pronounce the longed-for words: 'Vive Algérie Française'. He later dismissed them as having escaped from him unintentionally. It is clear that from the outset he was saying one thing in public for the benefit of the masses while another voice was speaking internally as he grappled with the realities. One of his enthusiastic aides expressing satisfaction

---

15   Horne, *A Savage War of Peace*, p.296.

over the visit received the dismissive riposte from Charles de Gaulle: 'Africa is fucked, and Algeria with it!'[16]

De Gaulle's objectives were to bring Algeria firmly under the control of the central government in Paris, to demonstrate to the FLN that France was aiming for peace (but a peace that preserved French ties with Algeria), and to reinforce military presence to ensure that nothing in the field would interfere with political decisions. In the event, due to the slow progress towards ending the war, any momentum of support within the Muslim population eroded with time, and with it the prospect of Algeria remaining French.

The practicalities of Charles de Gaulle's plan were more money for the Algerian economy and education, new efforts to win the war, a single electoral roll embracing all the adult populations, and free elections. Algeria, along with other colonies, would also be free to vote in a referendum on a new French constitution. It was not yet to be a referendum on self-determination. On 28 September, the referendum was held across the French empire. In Algeria, the support was impressive. Despite threats and pleas of the FLN, the Muslim population (including women for the first time) voted in large numbers, overwhelmingly in favour. Algerian parliamentary elections followed, with a strong turnout once again. The downside was that, faced with death threats from the FLN, few of the candidates were Muslim moderates.

Quickly following on the heels of the referendum was a speech made by General de Gaulle at Constantine on 3 October 1958. In what became known as the Constantine Plan, he set out objectives for industrial modernisation, land redistribution, expansion of schooling for Muslim children, and the opening up of posts in the administration for Muslims. De Gaulle finished with a direct appeal to the FLN to choose peace. By way of encouragement, amnesties for imprisoned rebels were accelerated. The Constantine Plan was followed on 23 October by an appeal by General de Gaulle for what became known as the 'peace of the brave'. He acknowledged the courage of the ALN and called for those who wanted peace to come forward under a flag of truce. He promised that they would be treated honourably. The proposal fell on stony ground on both sides. For the *pieds noirs*, it was a move towards premature negotiation; for the FLN, it was tantamount to a call for surrender: '… a cease-fire in Algeria is not simply a military problem. It is essentially political, and negotiation must cover the whole question of Algeria.'[17] The FLN made a renewed call for a fight to the end, and a fresh campaign of terrorism followed.

---

16   Horne, *A Savage War of Peace*, p.302. (Author's translation).
17   Horne, *A Savage War of Peace*, p.307.

Meanwhile, de Gaulle had purged the Army command. Massu was left in place (still Gaullist, as he would prove again in 1968), but Salan was recalled and given the sinecure post of Military Governor of Paris. He had hoped to be appointed as Chief of the General Staff, but instead this post was given to a trusted Gaullist. On Salan's departure, the civil and military powers were divided once again. Paul Delouvrier, a brilliant young administrator, was appointed to a new post of Delegate-General instead of Governor-General. De Gaulle made it clear to him that he was '... France in Algeria, and *not* the representative of the Algerians in France.'[18] Accompanying him, as commander-in-chief, was General Maurice Challe, an Air Force general – an appointment that caused fluttering in the Army dovecot. However, Challe was not only a highly competent airman, but he also had a profound understanding of land operations. Challe's task was to inflict a crushing defeat on the ALN with the objective of giving de Gaulle the strongest possible hand in future negotiations. He was to prove the most effective of the commanders during the war. He was also seen as a strong Gaullist, although that was not to survive the turn of events in 1961. He and Delouvrier hit it off from the start, and they got on well.

18   Horne, *A Savage War of Peace*, p.310.

9

Caporal-chef

Tony's regiment was still engaged in operations in the closing stages of the Battle of the Borders when events exploded in Algiers. By the time the regiment returned to Zeralda and Tony had started his corporal's course, de Gaulle was in power. No doubt Tony would have been aware of the events taking place. However, he had not missed out on the excitement of a possible coup in Paris since 1st REP, absent on operations, had not been earmarked for *Opération Résurrection*. With a demanding course to come, he would probably have had little time to reflect on the political turmoil or to speculate on the future.

On 7 June, he was kitted out at Zeralda for the corporals' course and, the following day, travelled by train to Sidi Bel Abbès. On arriving, Tony was assigned to one of two training platoons, each with 50 trainees. On 9 June, he moved with Platoon 1A to Khamsis, a former tuberculosis sanatorium in the cooler hills above Sidi Bel Abbès. It was here that they were to spend the first few weeks of their five-month course.

So started their new life: 'Shades of Mascara, but no cruelty. Everyone wanted to pass. Lieutenant de Haldat du Lys was the course commander, ably supported by Staff Sergeant Gschwind (Drei mal schneller als der Wind – three times faster than the wind), Sergeant Dehez and Sergeant Standfuss, all superb instructors and extremely helpful and encouraging.'

Tony considered the Legion's system of instruction to be exceptionally thorough, always training the student to function competently several ranks above. This gave the men a great deal of confidence in their abilities by the end of the course. Even with six months' basic infantry training followed by the parachute course behind him, Tony found the regime at Khamsis demanding. The days were long, with reveille at 0530 hours and evening roll call and room inspection at 2200 hours. The student corporals came from units of the Legion all over the world, but most were from Algeria. They had different backgrounds and experiences, and a common basis had to be established. They started off with a quick march to the

North-West Algeria: Places mentioned in Chapters 9, 10, and 11 relating to operations involving 1st REP and 7th Intervention Company, 1st RE. (Map drawn by George Anderson)

firing ranges to see how fit they all were. Six miles to the ranges in 59 minutes: 'A good start, though we would need to improve.' Every second night they were on guard duty, and the other nights were taken up with night ambushes and patrols until 0100 or 0200 hours. They worked every day, including Sundays, with one day off each month. Siestas were obligatory, as throughout the Legion in the hot months. Tony always took advantage of the siesta to wash the clothes he had worn for the morning's training, certain that they would be bone dry in about 20 minutes, ready for ironing and for him to appear immaculate on the afternoon parade.

There was a small swimming pool at Khamsis in which the men were trained, and sometimes punished, in river-crossing techniques. There was also:

> ... the most wonderful natural live-firing assault course; we charged down the very rough track, scattered with pop-up targets, which led steeply down a gully to a stream, which in turn led to a cave into the wet darkness of which one plunged. For safety reasons weapons were left at the cave's entrance and recovered afterwards. The cave decreased in size and increased in darkness until one was crawling absolutely flat in the stream in the pitch black, with the roof of the tunnel touching one's back. There was no light and no indication where to go when a branch was reached. All the branches led nowhere and required painstaking backing out to the main tunnel. Those suffering from claustrophobia had a hard time; I didn't, but I didn't enjoy it much the first time. Eventually after a lot of crawling one emerged into the brilliant light, grabbed one's waiting sub-machine gun and continued the course. The first obstacle after the tunnel was a 10-foot drop at the bottom of which, as one landed, a target popped up only a few feet ahead. Inevitably the last part of the obstacle course was uphill – what else! Once one had done it a couple of times and knew the tunnel it was fun. The targets changed each time, so they were always a surprise and tested one's reactions.

Tony and his fellow students were being trained both to lead and to instruct. They had to know their subjects inside out. Most of their days were spent in weapon training and in command and control of group weapons. All weapons were taught to a common pattern:

1. General characteristic: uses (one or more operators, grenade launcher, etc.), ballistic values, accuracy, power (for example, armour piercing), and maximum and effective ranges.
2. Ammunition: the different types of munitions, their weights, the different metals used in their manufacture, the weight of the charge, constitution of the charge, the numbers of rounds in the various packaging (boxes, bandoliers, belts, etc.) and their weights.
3. Design qualities: ease of use, ease of handling (weight and length), safety, and visibility (that is, an anti-tank rocket launcher is visible because of smoke and dust, a pistol is not).
4. Detailed design: the barrel (calibre, length, weight, and rifling), sighting systems, functioning (how it worked), accessories, and maintenance.

All this the students had learnt, in less detail, as recruits, but now they were being taught how to teach it themselves, in more depth. They were also instructed in how to teach recruits to shoot. The system was simple and productive. The weapon, usually a rifle, was clamped horizontally onto a tripod that could be adjusted horizontally and vertically by turning a couple of wheels. Some distance away stood a target. The student corporal was required to sight the rifle and adjust it accurately onto the centre of the bull. The instructor would then look through the sights to see whether the student had understood the alignment of the back sight and the foresight necessary to hit the target.

Much of the time was taken up with drill, combat tactics, and – since they were *légionnaires* – singing! Combat tactics were well taught by staff with considerable experience. Many of the instructors had fought in the Second World War, including on the Eastern Front, in Indochina, and in Algeria since the start of the war in 1954. However, what they taught was doctrine and theory, and '… many brand-new corporals and sergeants returned to their units full of knowledge and pride from their courses at Sidi Bel Abbès, crammed with theory – only to be killed on the first contact when theory failed to match reality.'

After the first few weeks spent at the idyllic Khamsis, where the students and their instructors were very much on their own and away from the formality of the depot, they returned to Sidi Bel Abbès for the remainder of the course. The student corporals continued to study hard with '… drill, lots and lots of drill, weapons, shooting, communications, tactics, teaching skills. Every day we marched out to our training areas and to the ranges; every evening we marched back singing.'

They also visited the Legion museum with its Salle d'Honneur and Crypte. The crypt contained the names of Legion officers killed in combat, the battle honours and standards of disbanded regiments, and the wooden hand of Captain Danjou. Danjou was in command of the *légionnaires* who had fought the legendary action at Camerone. He had lost his hand in 1853 when a signal gun exploded and had it replaced with an articulated hand. After the Battle of Camerone, his hand was taken when the bodies of the dead were robbed. It was subsequently recovered and returned to the Legion, and it became a symbol of the corps' values, almost a sacred relic. It is paraded every year at the Legion's HQ – in Tony's time at Sidi Bel Abbès and now at Aubagne near Marseille – by an old ex-Legion officer, NCO, or *légionnaire* chosen for his contribution to the Legion. It has been carried by two friends of Tony: Staff Sergeant Johann Wallisch and General Jean-Claude Coullon.

On 15 October 1958, Tony's course came to an end, and he was promoted to the rank of caporal-chef. He returned to 1st REP at Zeralda. In his absence, Colonel Brothier and the regimental colour party had taken part in the annual

14 July Bastille Day parade in Paris in recognition of the regiment's success in the Battle of the Borders. They had subsequently spent time in the Algiers region assisting with the referendum. The FLN had threatened those Muslims who voted with death and the *légionnaires'* role was to encourage them to vote, escort them to the polling stations, and patrol the streets on polling day. Since many of the Muslim population were illiterate, the voting papers were coloured white for 'yes' and chocolate for 'no'. It is said that Muslims were encouraged by the *légionnaires* with the advice, 'Ne prends pas celui-ci. Tu vois sa couleur. C'est de la m ...' (Don't take that one. You can see its colour. It's shit).[1]

No sooner had Tony returned to 1st REP at Zeralda than the regiment was deployed to the region near Mascara and Saïda. A tented camp was established outside Mascara, and, on 24 October 1958, sweep and search operations began in the hills. The *légionnaires* were out every day and most nights until, the operations having brought very little result, they returned to Zeralda on 26 November. Much of the time they had been wet and cold and living in tents that leaked. However, Tony took some comfort from the fact that, as a caporal-chef, his pay had shot up to the equivalent of about £60 a month – a great deal more than he was to earn as a second lieutenant in the British Army a few years later.

Two days later, they were redeployed again; this time, the regiment was sent to the region between Aïn Sefra and Béchar. The *légionnaires* were on the move frequently and set up temporary camps with two-man tents from place to place as their operations took them through a wide expanse of desert terrain: '... a vast area in which to roam ... with here and there blocks of square mountains in every colour; many were pale yellow from the sand carried up on to them by the hot winds. There were mushroom shaped rocks carved by the sand and wind, and a few stultified, twisted trees and a little alfa grass [alfalfa].' Sitting still and hidden, looking over these vast expanses taught Tony to see things a long way off and to spot the slightest movement half a mile away. Despite the lateness of the year, it was still hot and there was no water:

> I normally carried two US Army aluminium water bottles which I could make last for four days. I drank no more than a sip at a time and swilled a little round my mouth without swallowing, before spitting it onto a handkerchief which I then hung on the back of my neck. The evaporating water created a cool zone which was bliss – for about five minutes. In the white rock wadis the reflected heat beat in from the sides and from below as

---

1   Montagnon, *La Guerre d'Algérie*, p.281, n.5. (Author's translation).

much as from above, and you could feel it hitting you under the chin with as much force as on the top of your head. A cold country where the sun is hot; when the sun was hot in Algeria it was very hot! The wasps were thirsty too and could smell the water in our water bottles, which were always covered in swarms of them. One had to be particularly careful when opening the water bottle as the wasps would fight to get in, and swallowing a live stinging wasp was not good. Heaven knows where they all came from; there was nothing there, just desert.

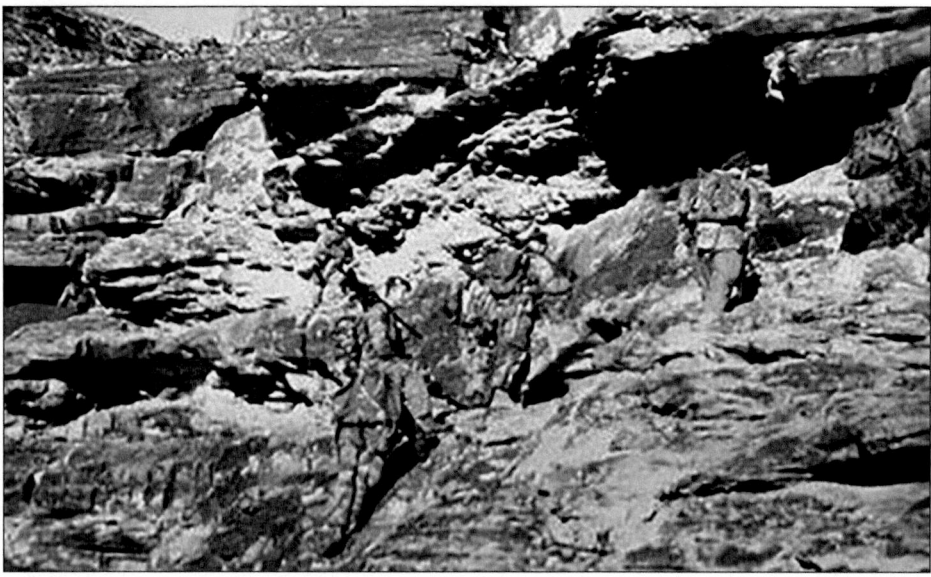

Paras of 1st REP on operations during 1958–59, probably in the Aurès mountains of Kabylia. Traditionally, Algeria's hinterland is referred to as the *djebel* (mountain) and the *bled* (desert). The regiment did occasionally operate in the Far South, including between Ain Sefra and Colomb Bechar on the Moroccan border in December 1958, but usually they spent a great deal more time in the highlands. Typically, exhausting approach marches were made by night, blacked-out and in silence, on vestigial goat-tracks over the most difficult terrain imaginable. During such operations, Tony was constantly nervous about losing contact with the single-file column in the darkness. (Linda Hunter-Choat).

Water, or rather a lack of it, was an ever-present preoccupation. On one operation in the foothills, they came across a small stream. Having had no water for some time, the *légionnaires* gratefully filled their water bottles. They moved on following the water course upstream only to find 300 yards farther on that the stream was full of the dead bodies of *fellagha* killed a few days before: 'The water tasted fine!'

On a later operation, they were seriously short of water on a high plateau, miles from any roads or tracks. They had set out on a two-day operation with two water bottles per man, but they were now on day four. Tony pointed out that the British Army specified the daily requirement as five gallons per man per day but unhelpfully did not say how it should be carried. By the end of the third day, a capful of water was going for the equivalent of a pound, but there were few willing to sell. Tony still had enough, but many did not, and the situation was about to become serious. An air drop of water was planned for the morning of the fourth day. The aircraft duly arrived, to the relief of all. The crew lobbed out the five-litre cans of water – which promptly, without exception, burst on impact with the ground. Tony unfortunately does not relate how the problem was resolved.

Tony recounts how flies were also a dreadfully irritating nuisance. Sleeping during the day in the meagre shade of a rock or a bush would inevitably mean awaking with lips thick with flies looking for moisture. However, flies were not the only irritant in the desert. One day when '… it was just too hot to chase around the desert …', Tony was sleeping in the heat of the day, in the partial shade of a rock with his head on a stone for comfort: 'The scorpion whose stone it was did

Tony is armed here with a MAS49 semi-automatic rifle fitted with a telescopic sight. Because the airborne infantry squad was equipped with a number of small-calibre, short-barrel sub-machine guns and carbines, it was normal to issue one marksman with this 7.5mm rifle for longer-range engagements. (Linda Hunter-Choat).

not approve of my presence and stung me on the back of the neck, which gave me a headache for two days.'

Tony recalls two extraordinary experiences during this period of operations in the desert. The first was when they were pinned down by very heavy enemy fire and were finding it difficult to move: '… all of a sudden a whole squadron of Algerian mounted troops, riding beautiful grey Arab horses, dressed in Saharan uniforms with crossed red Moroccan leather bandoliers and armed with short carbines, sub-machine guns and swords, charged through us at full gallop and routed the enemy.'

Later on the same day, during an extension of the same contact, the *légionnaires* were on fairly high ground when a strong group of *fellagha* attacked them up-hill: 'My FM jammed for the first time and towards me was charging a fellagha firing a Thompson .45 sub-machine gun. I unjammed the FM and shot the fellagha, now only a matter of yards from me. It was a woman, in combat kit, her breasts strapped down, and carrying a great quantity of very heavy Thompson magazines.'

The regiment returned to barracks at Zeralda for Christmas 1958. However, the return was not without incident, which demonstrated the ever-present hazards of driving on the Algerian roads. Returning to base in heavy rain, one of the trucks skidded and fell into a ravine killing an officer and six *légionnaires*.

Tony's lifestyle was changing with promotion. As a *légionnaire* he had had a single bed, a locker, and a bedside table. His weapon had been kept in the armoury, but all his ammunition and equipment were under his bed ready to go. At the end of the platoon's single-storey building was a wash and ironing room and at the other end a room for the *chef de chambre*. Now as a caporal-chef, he had his own room – which had belonged to a caporal-chef killed in the fighting at Guelma – complete with a stove, cupboards, a shelf, and a couple of chairs. In the winter, 'I would have the stove going all evening, heating up our saved wine rations, adding sugar and oranges, making a wonderful warming drink to share with friends.'

Tony was good friends with a Polish-French *légionnaire* from near Lille, François Marciniak. Since they were in different platoons, they saw little of each other at other times, but they made the most of the time when they were back in barracks together at Zeralda. It was their habit when they had evening passes to go out to Algiers. They put on their smartest, pressed kit, with their gleaming white *kepis* (and when Tony became a caporal-chef his black *kepi*), and presented themselves at the guard room to pass the guard commander's inspection, without which they could not leave the camp. They then boarded trucks for the 15-mile journey to the main square at the entry to Algiers. They would start their evening with:

... a long relaxing Turkish bath in a building which was a hundred years old, at the bottom of the Casbah. Old cannon balls were heated to red hot in a brazier and then thrown into a trough of water to generate steam; the steam room was a large dome, and we reclined round the wall on brick benches, sweating and being fiercely massaged by Algerian masseurs pulling, cracking and pummelling. After about an hour of that we were wrapped in huge, soft white towels and lay in the cool, drinking mint tea to relax. Then back into uniform, feeling absolutely terrific, out of the Casbah and into town to tackle a crate of Kronenbourg or '33' beer. We usually ate at the same restaurant in the Rue d'Isly, starting with bread, olive oil and Maggi [a concentrated vegetable-base sauce used to season food and soups], followed by steak and chips or steak tartare, and a bottle or two of the most marvellous rosé, Pelure d'Oignon from Domaine de la Trappe, or the strong robust red Mascara.[2] If we were very hungry we sometimes had an omelette as well.

Marciniak had lost the forefinger of his right hand and all that was left was a stump about half an inch long. It amused us greatly while eating in our very respectable restaurant, and when someone was looking our way, for François to stick the stump in his eye, his ear or up his nose so that it appeared as though a good two-and-a-half inches had been jammed into his head. Then on with the beer, up and down the length of Rue d'Isly in and out of the bars, playing poker dice or 421 [a dice game] at the bar counter, meeting other légionnaires, mostly ignoring non-légionnaires, with the exception perhaps of those from [Colonel] Bigeard's 3rd RPC [Colonial Parachute Regiment], with whom we got on well and whose fighting ability we admired. Probably the most interesting drink was the képi blanc: a standard légionnaire's white kepi was filled with a measure from every bottle in the bar, and in French bars there are plenty. As a kepi holds about three or four pints it was normally shared with one's friends. At the end of the evening we made our way back to the main square at the foot of the Casbah to take the trucks back to Zeralda. If we had the whole day there we would buy absolutely fresh shrimps and beautiful aioli mayonnaise on the Algiers docks.

With his new-found wealth, Tony bought a 'superb little steel-bodied 35mm camera, a Ricoh Caddy', in Algiers. It was strong and very robust, ideal for operations and

---

2 According to a French friend of the author, Pelure d'Oignon is not a rosé of the finest quality but has the advantage of being cheap. A case here, perhaps, of the expression variously attributed to Stalin, Lenin, and Trotsky, that 'quantity has a quality all of its own'.

parachuting. Some days Tony would spend alone in Algiers taking photographs. When doing so, he would sometimes visit the British Seamen's Mission on the docks where '… the beer was cheap and the atmosphere pleasant.' On one such visit, Tony met a visiting American with whom he stayed in desultory contact for many years. There was a particularly pleasant small bar at Bains Romains, just outside Algiers on the coast road to Zeralda, where Tony often spent entire days playing *pétanque* (boules) for an anisette per game. In the evening, they would eat in a *vivier* restaurant at Bains Romains where they could choose their fish live from the tank.

Tony had fond memories of these '… lovely, lazy days, but they were very rare', and, in January 1959, they were back on operations. This time they were operating from their home barracks at Zeralda, which felt very odd to Tony. The weather was very cold, and high in the hills there was deep snow. On one occasion, they were out on patrol and saw, well over half a mile away, a column of black dots moving across an open plateau. Certain that it was a band of rebels, the patrol forced their way through the snow as fast as they could go to approach the supposed *fellagha*. Once they were within binocular range, they stopped to assess the situation. Things were not as expected: a dozen monkeys were on the move. They were allowed to go on their way quite unperturbed and unaware of their lucky escape.

One of Tony's hardest operations during his time in the Legion took place during this period in the hills south of Koléa, about eight miles south-west of Zeralda. Many of the regiment had had passes for Algiers, enjoyed themselves, come back, and gone to bed. The *légionnaires* were woken at about 0130 hours and, by 0430 hours, had debussed. Intelligence believed that there was a strong enemy group present:

> It was our misfortune first that there was a great deal of urgency, second that the hills behind Koléa were nearly vertical, and third that we were carrying a full load of ammunition and rations. We forced our way up the mountain at the double, on and on and on, up the steepest and most indistinct of tracks, ever onwards, up and up. For those who had had a heavy evening in Algiers the task was too much. Many vomited, some collapsed, and five died of heart failure. We found no enemy. On the way down next day we were attacked by monkeys charging down the mountain and grabbing the first thing they saw on the way past and disappearing into the forest with it. There was no point in chasing them.

The Zeralda-based operations lasted until the end of January 1959. On 3 February, the regiment deployed rapidly to Jijel, 150 miles to the east of Algiers. The *légionnaires* had just enough time to check weapons, restock with ammunition, and replace clothing and equipment. The country was tough, but Tony did not find the operations very rewarding, resulting in '… some fellagha, some weapons and papers, but nothing like the fun we had at Guelma.'

Meanwhile, the new commander-in-chief, General Challe, had been considering how best to prosecute the war. The result became known as the Challe Plan, which was to start on 6 February 1959 and run until April 1961. The barriers on the Tunisian and Moroccan frontiers had proved very effective. Nevertheless, there were still numerous groups operating in the interior, and the barriers could not be entirely leak-proof. Challe's objective was to destroy what remained of the ALN active within Algeria. To do this, he reinforced the barrier along a length of the northern frontier with Tunisia. He created forbidden zones in the more remote country regions, where the Muslim population were grouped in protected areas; this was to deny the ALN bands support and access to food. Operationally, the plan was to roll up ALN groups starting in the west and moving progressively to the east. Challe appreciated that his strength lay in his regular parachute and Legion regiments. Many of his other units did not have the capability to carry out highly mobile and aggressive operations. He would use his elite regiments in the way developed by men such as Jeanpierre and Bigeard, with strong air and artillery support. To chase down small groups, he created small commandos and employed Muslim trackers.

On 21 February, 1st REP, as part of the Challe Plan, moved to Ténès, a small port 100 miles west of Algiers. The town was almost isolated from the rest of the country by the fearsome hills to the south. A regimental tented camp was established on a wide, flat area on the beach: '… perfect to return to after days in the hills'. The regiment's operations, interspersed with reasonable periods of rest, were not very fruitful. Time was found to fit some parachuting at Orléansville (now called Chlef) into the schedule. One jump on 6 March ended with Tony landing with one foot on a rock; he broke his leg and sprained his ankle, which swelled up hugely a full third of the way up the shin. He was taken to the French Army military infirmary in Chlef, where his foot and shin were put in a soft splint:

> After a couple of days I was made to get out of bed and start exercising my foot. The problem was, as far as I was concerned, that I had broken a leg, which none of the medical staff had identified, hidden as it was under the swelling of the ankle. Broken it nonetheless was and extremely painful to walk on. This continued, showing no sign of improvement, until 11 March when I was sent to the military hospital at Blida, where I had done my para course. Here they x-rayed my leg and established that it was, indeed,

broken. I was in big trouble, berated on and on for being so stupid as to continue to walk on a broken leg. Self-inflicted injury. They plastered it up and sent me back to Zeralda on 13 March. On the way, at a roadworks, the ambulance had a head-on crash, breaking two of my ribs. It was good to be home again. Here I was bollocked again for walking on a broken leg, and given the automatic punishment, broken leg or no broken leg, of fifty push-ups. It would probably have been the same if I had had two broken arms.

Nevertheless, Tony was glad to be back at Zeralda. Two of his friends were there on leave: 'To accelerate the cure of my leg we drank a great deal of Kronenbourg, which did the trick'. On 12 April, he went to hospital in Algiers, and the plaster was removed. Tony was not yet fit enough to participate in operations, which the regiment continued to mount from Zeralda until 28 April. During the pause that followed, the regiment prepared for the annual Camerone celebrations on 30 April. There was '… a huge parade and a wonderful lunch. The colonel was still paying for beer for everyone at 0200 hours the next morning. We were still drinking on 2 May.' However, it all came to a sudden stop at 0500 hours when the regiment was on the move again to take part in *Opération Courroie*. They were deployed near Cherchell (ancient Caesarea) to operate in the Ouarsenis mountains alongside two Legion infantry regiments. The camp was once again on a wide, flat strip next to the sea, cooled by a sea breeze and with 'lovely swimming'. Tony, still exempt from full duties, remained at base camp and was responsible for the administration of the company area, taking over the role of the company quartermaster sergeant who took Tony's place in the platoon.

Somehow, during all the celebrations for Camerone, the regiment found time to for the hand-over of command on 1 May 1959 from Colonel Brothier, who was posted to take command of 1st REI (Legion Infantry Regiment), to Lieutenant Colonel Henri Dufour. Dufour was an experienced Legion officer with a reputation for being a difficult character as far as his superiors were concerned. He had fought in the Second World War in North Africa and Europe, and then in Indochina. He had been in Algeria at the start of the war but, from 1955, had served in Germany before returning to join 1st REP in late 1958.

One of Tony's self-appointed duties was to draw the company's wine ration each day while they were out in the mountains. They had large 10-gallon thermos containers in each company, and he managed to '… steal quite a few more'. Every day, he filled the containers with the wine ration and then poured a thin film of olive oil on top, which sealed it hermetically and kept the wine fresh. When the company returned from operations, he took a wad of cotton wool and swept it quickly across the surface, lifting all the olive oil and '… voilà – 10 gallons of

Zeralda, Camerone Day 1959: Tony in parade uniform. Since he was now a caporal-chef, the white *képi*-cover was discarded to show the NCOs' red-topped black *képi* with gold grenade badge. For this order of dress, his M1949 wool battledress uniform is adorned with the Legion's green, red-fringed epaulettes with NCOs' gold threads in the red crescents, and the blue waist sash wound and folded under his web belt. On his right breast are his parachute wings, above 1st REP's regimental badge; on his left, his Cross of Military Valour with stars for two awards, the Algeria service medal, and a wound medal. From behind his left shoulder to the top buttonhole, he displays the regiment's lanyard in the green-flecked yellow of the Military Medal ribbon, marking 1st BEP's fourth collective citation in Indochina on 17 December 1953. Hidden here by the shadow, he wears on his upper left sleeve the Legion's black diamond-shaped *écusson* edged with three green pipings and bearing a gold grenade, with one gold and two green points-up rank chevrons above it; the chevrons alone are also worn on the right sleeve. (Linda Hunter-Choat).

wine'. For once, Tony had time to explore a little and was able to visit the Roman ruins. He also ate well. Every mid-morning, he made himself '… a little snack of the best part of one pound of raw steak, a complete head of garlic, a whole camembert and some good bread. And a bottle of wine. Then a nice little siesta, followed by a walk to the port to eat shrimps and mussels. No wonder my leg recovered quickly.'

Tony was not free to idle all the time, and, having a strong sense of responsibility, he had the bright idea along with a few others to give the company's camp cookers a thorough clean. They procured some strong caustic acid in Cherchell to shift the worst of the grease and grime. It worked well but '… also took my fingernails off; they simply dissolved in the acid'.

During the operations from Cherchell, '… one of the great Legion figures', Warrant Officer Laszlo Tasnady, was killed in action on 14 May 1959. Tasnady was a Hungarian, and two other Hungarian warrant officers serving with other regiments of the Legion in Algeria were also killed in action within a few days of each other. All were highly decorated, and all had joined the Legion in the immediate aftermath of the Second World War. Tony recalls that Tasnady had been shot in the back of the head. The death of these three men in such a short period of time seemed too much of a coincidence. A rumour circulated that they had fought for Germany in the Second World War and that the Hungarian communist government had infiltrated men into the Legion to hunt down and kill them.[3]

On 8 June, the regiment returned to Zeralda. There was a pause before they were deployed again, and Tony was able to attend the reception at the British Consulate in Algiers in honour of the birthday of the Queen: 'It was very strange to be in other than Legion surroundings and with other than légionnaires. It was certainly very enjoyable, though not a lifestyle I hankered after.'

The next deployment for the regiment was to Algiers on 3 July. For accommodation, they took over a large and beautiful three-storey house in the Casbah, built around an open atrium with a fountain in the centre. They were employed on peacekeeping duties, patrolling the Casbah and streets of the city. This was not to be for long, and, by late July, 1st REP was participating in General Challe's *Opération Jumelles* in the east of the country. However, no sooner had Tony got to Algiers than he was told that he was to attend the Sergeants' Course starting at Sidi Bel Abbès on 11 July. For the few days left in Algiers, Tony's time was split between patrolling and company administration. This latter duty included going by jeep to the Army barracks, the *Caserne d'Orléans*, above the Casbah to collect the company's coffee and bread. For this, Tony had to be up and on his way by no later than 0530 hours. Therefore, he bought '… a huge alarm clock and balanced on top of it my mess tins and knife, fork and spoon so that when it went off the whole lot fell to the tiled floor with a huge crash, ensuring that I woke up'.

---

3   The account by Pierre Montagnon in *Les parachutistes de la Légion*, p.247, is more prosaic. He recounts that Tasnady, identified by his radio as the section commander, was shot at close range by two *fellagha* who had been chased to ground. According to this account, he was killed by a shotgun loaded with solid shot designed for hunting large game. The true circumstances remain unknown.

While patrolling in Algiers, before leaving for his course, Tony came across a group of visiting NATO officers. Noticing a British general, Tony wished him '… "Good morning", but he took absolutely no notice of me whatsoever. Screw him.' With that as a send-off, Tony left for Sidi Bel Abbès. It is testimony to his ability and the mark that he had already made in the Legion that Tony was starting his sergeant's training at only 23 years of age, just over two years after joining the legion and nine months since being promoted to caporal-chef.

10

Sergeant

Tony arrived at Sidi Bel Abbès by train at 2130 hours on 10 July 1959, having passed through Zeralda to collect his kit. Tony liked Sidi Bel Abbès and was pleased to be there again, now in the capacity of *Elève Sous-Officier Choat A H, Peleton 2B, Compagnie de Perfectionnement de Cadres et Instruction Parachutistes* (student NCO, Platoon 2B, Training Company for NCOs and paratroopers). They moved to Sully (now Douar Djebairia) – an old, requisitioned farm – commanded by Captain Glasser about 10 miles from Sidi Bel Abbès. Michel Glasser[1] was '… an exceptionally good officer' and son-in-law of General Paul Gardy,[2] inspector of the Foreign Legion at the time. Glasser had lost three fingers on his right hand and saluted with only the thumb and little finger. The course itself was commanded by Captain Bachus, with a Vietnamese lieutenant as his second-in-command. Tony liked Sully, although another British *légionnaire* described it as 'an absolute shithouse'. Tony's view was that this '… says more about …. [his] delicate sensibilities than it does about Sully.'

'Every single day started with an eight-to-10-mile forced march; we were all keen, all either caporaux-chef or corporals, all already experienced in Legion life and habits and in combat; we knew the rules and the bounds of behaviour. We were all determined to succeed, and the atmosphere was super.'

---

1   Captain Glasser deserted after the failed Generals' Putsch in 1961 and became an active member of the OAS. He was arrested in Paris in June 1962. Tried in October 1963, he was sentenced to seven-years' imprisonment but was freed at the end of 1965.
2   General Paul Gardy had a distinguished military career. His last post was as inspector of the Foreign Legion. He retired in 1959 but returned secretly to Algeria in April 1961 to join the Generals' Putsch. He became a leader of the OAS. In 1963, he went into exile in Argentina. Although amnestied in 1968, he remained in Argentina until his death in a road accident in 1975.

Tony teamed up with Stanislaus Krol, and they marched together when they could, egging each other on. The course followed very much the same pattern as had that for corporals but at several levels up and much more demanding. At the end of the course, the graduate sergeants were expected, *in extremis*, to be capable of commanding not just a platoon but even a company, both in the field and in barracks.

On one long and tiring tactical exercise, during which the course members were issued with Benzedrine to keep them going:

> I suddenly collapsed. Pneumonia. I woke up in the Sidi Bel Abbès infirmary a day later; I was to stay there for the next 24 days being given injections in the morning to keep me awake and injections in the evening to make me sleep, and antibiotic injections. Every morning suction cups were applied to my chest and back to suck the fluid from my lungs … While in the Legion hospital I was under the care of a young doctor doing his national service. He was not yet fully qualified. He decided that I had some difficulty in breathing through my nose; he was correct, and his diagnosis of the cause was also right – that my nose had been broken a couple of times and internal deformity prevented me from breathing easily. He could sort it out by removing some of the damaged tissue blocking my nose. On the day of the operation I was strapped by my arms and legs to an operating table, my head covered by a cowl with just my nose appearing, and given a local anaesthetic. He started by inserting expanders into my nostrils and ratcheting them ever wider, stretching my nose so that he could easily gain access to the offending area. He started to cut, saw and chip with a little hammer and chisel. The racket in my head was enormous. Even more enormous was the pain as the anaesthetic wore off after about half an hour, since the operation went on for an hour. I tried to point out, politely, that the anaesthetic was no longer working but was told to shut up – which, being a para caporal-chef of 1st REP, I did. At the end of the operation both nostrils were packed with yards of fine paraffin gauze designed not to stick to the cut area, and the nasal stretchers were removed.
>
> About two weeks later the same doctor came in, out of hours, dressed in civilian clothes rather than his normal white coat. He decided to remove the gauze strips which went from the opening of my nostrils to the back of my throat. Being the fucking idiot he was he yanked them out. They had stuck fast to the wound, and their removal was followed by about half a pint of blood rushing into the back of my throat; I was choking. I coughed and a half-pint of blood liberally sprayed his beautiful brand-new cardigan, a gift from his wife. I was much happier now.

For the first 10 days or so, Tony was very weak and all was a dream, but then he started to recover quickly and was able to rejoin the course. There were several diversions from the rigorous training, including parades, a demonstration para drop, and participation in a film as extras.

On 9 September 1959, there was a parade in the Quartier Prudon for the decoration of Captain Bachus, the course commander, as *Chevalier de la Légion d'Honneur*. The *légionnaires* wore their standard sand-coloured shirt and trousers, ranger boots, their three-metre-long blue cummerbund, epaulettes, webbing, and *kepi*. This was an exception since, as they were at a para centre, for all other parades in Sidi Bel Abbès they wore their para camouflage uniforms and green berets, the latter at that time worn only by Legion paras. Tony recalls that:

> ... during one enormous parade in the Grand Quartier we had to fix bayonets before presenting arms. The bayonet of the MAS36 rifle had a long thin cruciform blade, like a seventeen-inch needle. It lived when not in use in a housing in the stock, under the barrel. To put it into use it was extracted from the stock and its end reinserted in the socket so that the blade now stuck out in front of the rifle. The drill movement for all this must have dated from the 1800s, but looked good. On the command 'Bayonets!' the rifle was placed, butt on the ground, in front of you, held in the left hand; the right hand went to the end of the bayonet and pushed the release catch. On the command 'Fix Bayonets!' the bayonet was pulled out of its housing and raised with the arm stretched straight out and up at an angle of 45 degrees. Several hundred bayonets flashed in the Algerian sun. It was then brought down to be housed, point out, in its socket, and the rifle returned to the side ready for presenting arms. At this particular parade all went well until I whisked the bayonet high – and lost it! This extremely sharp and dangerous object disappeared high in the air behind me and into the crowd. I did all my present arms bit without the bayonet, was inspected by generals, and no-one noticed that my bayonet was missing. Thank heavens, some kind soul returned it after the parade.

In October, the trainees travelled to Oran airfield to take part in a massed demonstration jump as the finale to the National Air Meeting. The weather was awful and blowing a gale, and the jump was repeatedly delayed. Being a non-Legion affair, the organisers had not taken the usual precautions:

> ... all the canteens on the airfield were open, and we spent our time in them drinking huge quantities of beer while waiting to go. By the time we did jump, late in the day and in very high winds, most of the Legion paras

were pretty well incapable of doing anything really sensible. Some dozed off on the way down. Having landed all over the place – I landed on the concrete runway, which was uncomfortable – we gathered up our chutes, handed them in to the ground staff, and formed up to march past the main saluting base, packed with French Air Force and French Army generals and visiting dignitaries. Being légionnaires: we sang as we marched. There was a small snag: those at the front were singing one Legion marching song, those in the middle another, and those bringing up the year yet another. All with great gusto. It was a complete and utter shambles. Not our fault though, they should have closed the bars.

Three days later, they were back in Oran again. This time they were to be extras in '… a very silly film, with a very silly title, *Sergent X*.' They did not jump from aircraft but simply simulated jumping from parked aircraft. Tony was not impressed by Christian Marquand, the star of the film, whom he considered to be '… a complete prat and very twee. Anything less like a para sergeant it would be difficult to imagine.' Tony viewed the whole episode as a complete waste of time, its only redeeming feature being a break from training.

Parachuting could also have its costs. Most of the parachutes were olive green, but the odd one was white. Alas, on one training jump, Tony had the misfortune to be assigned a white canopy: as was the custom, he was required to pay for a case of Kronenbourg beer.

As the end of the course approached, the trainees took part in a large amphibious landing exercise on the beaches near Arzew, 20 miles north-east of Oran. Tony and his fellow paras found it very strange to be in a landing ship, echoing with the creaks and groans of its progress. The troops landed in a mixture of Sherman tanks with floatation screens, DUKW amphibious vehicles and LCTs (Landing Craft Tank). 'It wasn't very exciting; we landed, and that was that.'

After the exercise, they returned to Sully for their final examinations, which lasted from 29 October to 3 November and culminated in end-of-course drinks. The evening's festivities clearly had an effect on the judgment of the course members. In the centre of the crossroads next to Quartier Prudon was '… a flat, circular cat's-eye thing which, when we saw it, we were convinced was a mine. So we de-mined it. It took quite a long time and, as it had to be done tactically, really messed up our best uniforms!' Despite having spent three weeks in hospital, when the course received their results on 4 November, Tony found that he had come top. On 5 November, they spent the day cleaning up the Sully camp then stayed the night in barracks back in Sidi Bel Abbès. They had free passes for the evening, and they made the most of them celebrating the fact that they were now all sergeants. One of the new sergeants subsequently shot himself in the head playing Russian Roulette, '… which slowed him down considerably.'

The next day, Tony returned to Zeralda. His promotion to sergeant was confirmed on 15 November 1959. He moved out of his room at the end of the platoon block and into the company's senior NCO accommodation. Tony could now use the *Mess des Sous-Officiers*, the warrant officers' and sergeants' mess where, every Friday evening, they had open house and champagne for all. He had achieved the aim he had set himself two-and-a-half years before during basic training at Mascara: to become a sergeant. As a sergeant, Tony's status had changed considerably. He was now formally saluted by all those of more junior rank, although he insisted on this only once at the start of the day or at formal meetings. He also had a batman to look after him: *Légionnaire* Marc Ténard.

11

The Beginning of the End

While Tony had been away on his sergeant's course, 1st REP had continued to participate in *Opération Jumelles*. They had cooperated with two Legion infantry regiments, a Legion cavalry regiment and a Legion mechanised demi-brigade also committed to the operation. Meanwhile, events had been moving on the political stage.

Ever since the accession to power of General de Gaulle in May 1958, discontent among the *pieds noirs* had continued to fester. There was growing concern that he was not committed to *Algérie Française* at all costs. The fear was that the Europeans would be driven out of Algeria with a choice between '*le cercueil ou la valise*' (the coffin or the suitcase). De Gaulle's ambiguous and opaque statements did nothing to relieve their concerns, many of which were shared within elements of the Army: what were they fighting for – why should they continue to lose men if it was all to be for nothing? The Army, rightly, felt that they were winning the war on the ground. Were they to see all that they had achieved thrown away by the politicians and government, personified by de Gaulle?

In January 1959, his new constitution having been adopted, de Gaulle was inaugurated as President of the Republic. In his inaugural address, he had spoken of Algeria '… developing her own personality and closely associated with France.' Later that month, he said that '… destiny lies essentially within the Algerians themselves.' In March, this hint was reinforced when he said that '… a new Algeria … will find her face and her soul.' His thinking was diverging from that of his prime minister, Michel Debré. While the latter was saying in August that 'France would do anything, anything at all, to keep Algeria French', de Gaulle's view at the same time was that 'Peace is a necessity. This absurd war …'[1] In August, he took an unusually long holiday, taking with him a paper drafted by Bernard Tricot, his

---

1 Quotations in this paragraph are drawn from Horne, *A Savage War of Peace*, p.342.

advisor on Algerian affairs, on the prospects for a peace settlement. Key elements of the paper were that the FLN must be offered an approach that would not be seen as surrender but rather as a step on the road to definitive talks and consultation of the population on the future of their country. It seems that, during his holiday, he thought through his approach and decided that a referendum would be necessary.

Immediately on his return from holiday, General de Gaulle travelled to Algeria to make a tour of the Army to put his thoughts across to the leaders of the troops fighting so determinedly to bring about victory. He seemed to have realised that his communication with the Army had become less than ideal. Those used to clarity certainly found his enigmatic pronouncements baffling, although it was claimed by Tricot that the Army leadership on occasion exploited ambiguity to pursue their own policies. During his tour, he lost patience with General Faure, chief-of-staff for the Army in Algeria, who repeatedly hammered the point that military operations would be greatly helped if de Gaulle would only make it clear that Algeria would remain French, breaking off the conversation with 'Listen, Faure, I've had enough!'[2]

During his tour, he also visited the Commander-in-Chief's HQ to address around 100 generals and senior staff officers. The address was intended to be confidential and used to orally brief officers throughout the Army in Algeria. The gathered officers were expecting effusive praise for their success. However, while de Gaulle acknowledged that what was being achieved was satisfactory, he said, 'What I have heard and seen here in the course of this inspection gives me full satisfaction. I have to say that to you. But the problem is not solved.'[3] He set out his appreciation of the problem that France faced: the position of the Algerians was intolerable because France had not done enough for them; France was becoming increasingly weak, and the global situation was such that France could no longer ignore world opinion. He emphasised that, to solve France's problems, they needed to carry the Algerian people with them since '… the era of the European administration of the indigenous peoples has run its course.' He finished with a clear statement of what he expected from the Army: 'As for yourselves, mark my words! You are not an army for its own sake. You are the Army of France … It is I who … must be obeyed by the Army in order that France should survive. I am confident of your obedience, and I thank you, gentlemen.'[4]

---

2   Horne, *A Savage War of Peace*, p.343. (Author's translation).
3   Horne, *A Savage War of Peace*, p.343.
4   Horne, *A Savage War of Peace*, pp.343–44.

However, while General de Gaulle was raising his sights to look at the broader problems of modernising France and her place in the world, the Army in Algiers, perhaps not surprisingly, was focused on its immediate problems. De Gaulle later recorded that he had given his audience a hint that he was going to give Algeria the right to self-determination. However, they, including even General Challe, seemed to have failed to understand the message.

On 16 September 1959, de Gaulle addressed the French nation. For the first time, he used the fateful words self-determination. The Algerian people would be allowed to vote on three options: full independence, which he considered would be incredible and disastrous; integration with France with equality of rights; or a close relationship supported by France with a federal structure for Algeria, which would provide guarantees for the different communities. It was clear that he preferred the latter option. He set out a timescale for the referendum to be at the latest four years after the restoration of peace, which he defined as having been achieved when deaths did not exceed 200 per year. The period between peace and the vote would be devoted to resuming normal life, freeing prisoners, and allowing exiles to return. He repeated his appeal to the FLN for a 'peace of the brave'. His choice of words that the question of self-determination would be put to the Algerians as individuals seemed to be ruling out negotiations with the FLN as a body, let alone the handing over of power to them. That left hanging the question: with whom would, or indeed could, he negotiate?

At home in France, the speech attracted wide support, with the National Assembly giving overwhelming backing in October. Only the parties on the extreme left and right remained opposed. However, a huge difference now began to grow between opinion in France on the one hand and the *pieds noirs* and the Army in Algeria on the other. General Challe set out his view clearly in a letter to Prime Minister Debré: 'One does not propose to soldiers to go out and get killed for an imprecise final objective … One can … only ask soldiers of the Army of Algeria today that they die in order for Algeria to remain French.'[5]

At the end of October, Delegate-General Delouvrier returned from Paris with reassurance for Challe from the prime minister that '… we can say both that the government wishes Algeria to remain French and that is what the Army is fighting for.' Although this was inconsistent with de Gaulle's speech, Challe was appeased for the time being. Many of his subordinates were less than convinced. Captain Sergent, commanding 1st Company, 1st REP, told Colonel Dufour, 'For me,

---

5   Horne, *A Savage War of Peace*, p.347.

the FLN flag is floating over Algiers from now on. Algeria will be independent.'[6] Sergent was, of course, to prove correct. In due course, he became a leading figure in the Generals' Putsch of April 1961 and subsequently in the OAS (*Organisation de l'Armée Secrète*).

It is impossible to gauge how the *légionnaires* felt personally about the political situation. However, Tony hints strongly at his own views. He gave a dispassionate account of General de Gaulle's speech; although, in referring to the release of prisoners, his disapproval is clear:

> Three months later he released 7,000 ALN prisoners. This figure represented 58 percent of those we and the other units had captured in combat. Most of them went straight back to the ALN so that we could capture them again ... de Gaulle, having exhorted the armed forces to even greater efforts to win the war, was now saying that he would give Algeria her independence. In their efforts to comply with de Gaulle's wishes for a solid victory very, very many lives had willingly been lost. For the dreadful de Gaulle now to say that it was all for nothing was too much for many.

Among the *pieds noirs*, the reaction was initially mixed, with some seeing some positive aspects but others regarding it as shameful and an insult to those who had lost their lives. Opinion was to harden along these lines. Some moderate Muslims also reacted favourably at first, and even among the FLN and the GPRA (the Provisional Government of the Algerian Republic set up by the FLN a year previously in exile in Tunisia) some saw the proposals as a step in the right direction and announced that they were prepared, under conditions, to open preliminary talks. Of course, Charles de Gaulle did not want to negotiate with them but instead with undefined representatives of the moderate Muslims – if they could be found. However, it was apparent to the FLN that, although faced with military defeat, they had won an important victory. The GPRA Minister of Defence, Belkacem Krim, declared to the ALN in the interior of Algeria, 'Your struggle has obliged the enemy to talk of self-determination, thus renouncing the oft-repeated myth of Algérie Française. His retreat is the fruit of your efforts.' The FLN appreciated that they now had only to continue the battle to ensure that de Gaulle had no option but to negotiate with them and nobody else.

6 Horne, *A Savage War of Peace*, p.347.

THE BEGINNING OF THE END 147

The situation simmering in Algiers would shortly reach boiling point and bring the regiment into the political arena for the first time. Meanwhile, Tony was back on operations a few days after returning to Zeralda from his training. At 0500 hours on 10 November 1959, they set out from the camp. The weather was particularly cold, and they were all issued with hooded anoraks, quilted jackets, long waterproof mittens, and earmuffs:

> This was just as well, as we were hit by a serious snowstorm in the mountains with temperatures down to minus 10°C – not terribly cold, but cold enough for Africa! While we were sitting in the stationary trucks one very cold night in the mountains, waiting to disembark and start marching, a jerrycan in our track caught fire. In our haste to get out I fell from the top of the tailboard, damaging both wrists and breaking my elbow. Such a minor injury did not excuse me from the operation, although I could hardly hold my sub-machine gun, and trying to pull myself up the precipitous mountain by grabbing trees and branches was absolutely agony. Well, it hurt quite a lot anyway. By early January we were back again in Zeralda and I was able to have injections into my elbow, which had by now set at an odd angle. The injections were given with a long flexible needle from the inside of the arm through into the elbow joint from the inside. The first part of the injection was a local anaesthetic followed by, I suppose, cortisone. So it was not too painful and it worked well. In February I was jumping again.

On the plus side, one of the delights of operating in the north of Algeria was that the local wine growers, ever grateful for the presence of the *légionnaires*, kept the company 200-gallon water trailers full of good local red or rosé wine. 'We had to steal a second water trailer for the water.'

By early January 1960, the regiment was back at Zeralda. The balance for 1959 was that 1st REP had accounted for 972 *fellagha* killed in operations while the regiment had lost 42 men killed, including several officers. In the new year, there were changes in the regiment. In April 1960, Captain Ysquierdo moved to regimental HQ and was replaced by Captain Simonot as commander of 2nd Company. Lieutenant Henry Lobel took over command of 2nd Platoon within the company, with Tony as his platoon sergeant.[7]

---

7   Lieutenant Lobel was court martialled for his part in the Generals' Putsch. He was posted to a unit outside the Legion and served with 27th *Bataillon de Chasseurs Alpins* (mountain troops) in Algeria. He deserted when the ceasefire took effect and became an active member of the OAS.

Tony was sent on the sergeants' course in July 1959, and, despite missing three weeks of it in hospital, he passed out top of his intake (again) in November. Back with the 1st REP as platoon sergeant of 2nd Platoon within 2nd Company, he operated at first in the rugged hills of Kabylia, where this snapshot was taken early in 1960. In April, he received his third award of the Cross of Military Valour, and that November he was transferred to Regimental Headquarters, though still taking part in combat operations. (Linda Hunter-Choat).

On 24 January, the regiment was deployed in Algiers at short notice. Tony sums up events in a pithy and somewhat understated fashion:

> The local pied noir population was conducting an anti-government revolt in true French style. They had ripped up the cobbled streets and formed barricades (shades of the French Revolution), and were led by an idiot called Lagaillarde. Shots had been exchanged with the military and the situation was getting out of hand. 1st REP was sent to sort it out. Which we did, but it took a week, then we were back on more routine operations.

Tony's attitude is understandable: helping sort out internal French squabbles was not why men joined the Legion; they much preferred soldiering and fighting the rebels. The regiment's deployment to Algiers was during what became known as 'the week of the barricades'. It marked a further major step in the growing rift between opinion in Metropolitan France and that of the European population and much of the Army in Algeria.

Opposition to General de Gaulle and his policies had been growing steadily over many months. In November 1958, Jo Ortiz, who we met before in connection with the events of May of that year, had formed the FNF (Front National *Française*) to bring together all the militant groups committed to *Algérie Française*. During 1959, Ortiz recruited men to form a para-military militia. They were well armed and, by the end of the year, were appearing in public in uniform. Ortiz was no great orator, but he was an effective rabble rouser:

> We shall go right to the end of the line, even with arms in our hands, to defend Algérie Française ... The determination of the French of Algeria will conquer the self-determination of de Gaulle. Algiers may become Budapest [a reference to the 1956 Hungarian uprising], but we shall remain ... For us henceforth it's either the suitcase or the coffin.[8]

Also towards the end of 1959, the FLN started a growing campaign of terrorism once again, reinforcing outrage amongst the Europeans that the French government could even contemplate negotiating with the rebels. On 26 October, the only living *maréchal de France*, Alphonse Juin, himself a *pied noir*, wrote a forthright article criticising General de Gaulle's policy. It was symptomatic of the growing disenchantment within the Army, particularly prevalent in the elite units, including the paras, who were bearing the brunt of the fighting. At the same time, General Challe had made no secret of his lack of enthusiasm for de Gaulle's proposed self-determination, and a number of colonels in key positions within the Army were in close contact with Ortiz and his FNF. Meanwhile, Delegate-General Delouvrier was becoming increasingly isolated. He was under pressure from the *pieds noirs* while receiving little, if any, guidance or support from de Gaulle.

The 'week of the barricades' was triggered by de Gaulle's understandable removal of General Massu from his post. On 18 January 1960, the German newspaper *Süddeutsche Zeitung* published an interview during which Massu had said that the Army's greatest concern was that:

> ... the government should help us to see the future clearly, in order that we can succeed in maintaining Algérie Française ... We no longer understand the policy of President de Gaulle. The Army could not have anticipated that

---

8   Horne, *A Savage War of Peace*, p.351.

he would adopt such a policy ... Our greatest disillusion has been to see General de Gaulle become a man of the left.

When the journalist pointed out that Massu, along with others, had been instrumental in bringing General de Gaulle to power, Massu replied, 'De Gaulle was the only man available. Perhaps the Army made a mistake ... Myself, and the majority of officers in a position of command, will not execute unconditionally the orders of the Head of State.'[9]

What induced Massu to make such public remarks is unclear. He was not, unlike Salan, a political animal. Perhaps he was lulled into a false sense of security, seeing the newspaper correspondent as a like-minded man (he had been a para in the German Army) with whom he had quickly established an easy relationship. In any case, the interview swept all other news from the French papers. How could a general, particularly one who was such a dogged Gaullist, speak out against the President in such a way? Unsurprisingly, Charles de Gaulle flew into a towering rage and recalled Massu to Paris to explain himself. He was posted to a backwater to command the garrison of Metz. Two days later, Challe and Delouvrier flew to Paris and tried to persuade de Gaulle to leave Massu in place, warning that 'Blood will flow in Algiers.' De Gaulle stuck stubbornly to his decision: 'You exaggerate', he said.[10]

The response was quick to come. The FNF announced a general strike for 24 January 1960, to be accompanied by mass demonstrations centred, as usual, around the war memorial. The impression given was that this was a spontaneous protest against the sacking of Massu. In reality, his removal from his post was simply an excuse for an insurrection a long time in the making. Indeed, Jo Ortiz had little confidence that Massu could be the man that would take them in the direction they wanted. The leaders of the ultras were not united in their objectives. Ortiz wanted a repeat of May 1958, with the *pieds noirs* achieving a total victory for the cause of *Algérie Française*: in other words, the withdrawal of the proposals for self-determination. Others wanted nothing less than a revolution that would spread from Algeria to France. Initially, they had hoped that the Army would be an active participant, but it became apparent that they could not expect the Army to mutiny: the time was not right. However, they were assured that the Army would not fire on the demonstrators and that the paras would be passive. They seemed, however, to take no account of the attitude in Metropolitan France and

9   Horne, *A Savage War of Peace*, p.357.
10   Horne, *A Savage War of Peace*, p.358.

assumed, erroneously, that there was general support for the *pied noir* cause. They also failed to take into account that the man they had brought to power in 1958 was made of sterner stuff than his predecessors.

On Saturday 23 January, the khaki-clad FNF militia and the territorial volunteers were gathering, heavily armed. Meanwhile, Lagaillarde (who had fallen out with Ortiz because he had taken a seat in the National Assembly and had thus been excluded from the planning) acted on his own initiative and seized a building in the university with a handful of armed supporters. He created a barricaded camp and declared that they would not leave until General de Gaulle had conceded to their demands. For all his faults, Lagaillarde, with his military experience, was more organised than Ortiz, and, to the latter's annoyance, men previously supporting Ortiz were drawn to Lagaillarde. Throughout the insurrection, these two men competed for leadership of the *pieds noirs*.

By the time that General Challe had appreciated the gravity of events, Ortiz's men were armed and mustered, and Lagaillarde's were behind their barricades. He did not want to risk bloodshed by attempting to disarm them. To try to contain the situation, he set up roadblocks across routes coming into the city to prevent further armed men joining the demonstrators; ordered the gendarmes, some 2,000 strong, to be deployed to prevent a recurrence of the 1958 seizure of the government buildings; and invited Ortiz to call on him. He also called in army reinforcements, including Tony's regiment, to be ready to deal with what Challe described as 'a little local excitement.'[11] Challe told Ortiz that he had already persuaded de Gaulle to resume death sentences for those convicted of terrorist offences and to continue with pacification. He also said that he had received an assurance that there would be no political talks with the FLN. Ortiz claimed that he and Challe had made a deal that, if public buildings were left untouched, the demonstrators would not be harassed by the police.

An estimated 30,000 demonstrators had gathered by mid-afternoon, and some started to rip up paving stones to create barricades. An Army colonel, Gardes, who had been one of those in contact with the ultras, was seen with Ortiz, which gave encouragement to those who thought that the Army was going to support the demonstrators actively. Meanwhile, the CRS and gendarmes formed up about 200 yards from the mob. Two regiments of paras, 1st REP and 1st RCP, were close at hand. Faced with the deteriorating situation and following an angry conversation with the Delegate-General, Challe had no choice but to act. Gardes, who should in any case by now have left Algiers for another post, was ordered to leave the

---

11 Horne, *A Savage War of Peace*, p.360.

city immediately. Challe still wanted to avoid the police and Army firing on the demonstrators. Orders were given for weapons to be carried unloaded, and a plan was devised for the two para regiments, the CRS and gendarmes, in a coordinated sweep, to herd the demonstrators back to the quarters of the city from which they had come.

At 1800 hours, the gendarmes and the CRS started to move forward in the gathering dark. Suddenly, two pistol shots rang out: it was never established who fired them, but the result was that automatic fire opened up from windows and rooftops on both sides of the boulevard down which the gendarmes were advancing. Homemade bombs were dropped on the gendarmes, and tyres filled with plastic explosive rolled into the boulevard. *Pied noir* youths viciously despatched wounded gendarmes. Caught between shots from both sides and needing to load their weapons before they could return fire, the gendarmes were caught at a severe disadvantage. Having taken 45 minutes to advance 600 yards, Tony's regiment arrived at 1845 hours, and the firing died down. A violent exchange took place between Lieutenant Colonel Debrosse commanding the gendarmes and Colonel Dufour of 1st REP. Where had the paras been? Dufour said that, in his view, the gendarmes had fired first, breaking the agreement with Ortiz. In the subsequent inquiry, the two para colonels argued that they had been held up by Lagaillarde's barricades at the university. In fact, the routes for both para regiments to execute the plan would have taken them clear of the barricades. The real reason for the delay was probably an understandable desire on the part of the two colonels to avoid being drawn into a situation where they had to fire on the insurgents. In any case, whether the earlier arrival of the paras would have prevented the violence is arguable.

Whatever the circumstances, the result was six demonstrators killed and 24 wounded, and 14 killed and 123 wounded among the gendarmes and CRS. A dangerous line had been crossed in the Algerian War: for the first time since the Second World War, Frenchmen had fired on Frenchmen. The seriousness of the situation was lost on neither Delouvrier nor Challe. General Crépin, who had replaced Massu, and other senior commanders made it clear that, other than by using tanks, the well-organised barricades of Lagaillarde could not be breached. The para colonels also made it clear that they would do no more than maintain a perimeter around the barricades. It was unthinkable that Challe would use the necessary force, let alone armour, to disperse the European civilian insurgents, and a stalemate set in. Fraternisation between the paras and those behind the barricades developed quickly. Captain Pierre Sergent, commanding 1st Company, 1st REP, shook hands with Lagaillarde and assured him that his men would never fire on the insurgents. *Pied noir* women were allowed to pass freely with supplies

THE BEGINNING OF THE END 153

for those manning the barricades, and coffee and croissants were shared with the paras. There was a holiday spirit about the whole affair for the next three days. The feeling among the *pied noir* leaders and those in the Army sympathetic to their cause was that they must have won the day and that de Gaulle would have no choice but to concede.

During the night of Sunday 24 January, General Challe declared a state of emergency and made a radio broadcast. On Monday, General de Gaulle also broadcast, exhorting all to return to order. He said that he had been brought to power to find a French solution for Algeria, an ambiguous phrase that as usual did nothing to reassure the *pieds noirs*. Neither broadcast had any noticeable effect. Those in the Army who sympathised with the insurgents tried to persuade Challe to come out openly in support. On Wednesday 27 January, he made a broadcast aimed at the Army, declaring that '… the French Army is fighting in order that Algeria shall remain definitively French.' This was not repudiated by de Gaulle, and Challe's remarks went some way to reassure many in the Army. He would later feel that he had been deceived by Charles de Gaulle and, in effect, coerced into telling a lie. The next day, Challe and Delouvrier slipped quietly out of Algiers and set up their HQ at a French Air Force base outside the city. Before leaving, Delouvrier had recorded a speech calling for a return to order. He offered to shake hands with Ortiz and Lagaillarde and go with them to the war memorial '… to pray and weep for the dead of Sunday, dead in the faith that Algeria should remain French and that Algeria should obey General de Gaulle.'[12]

De Gaulle was furious with Delouvrier's speech, in particular with the offer to shake the insurgent leaders by the hand. However, the speech and the withdrawal from Algiers by Delouvrier and Challe marked the turning point in the crisis. The insurgents were wrong-footed by the withdrawal: did this mean that the Army had pulled back to lull the insurgents into a false sense of security before attacking the barricades – much as the Soviet Army had done in Budapest in 1956? On Friday 29 January, the tide turned against the insurgents. First of all, the fine weather changed to become cold, wet, and windy – dampening the spirits of those behind the barricades. Then, that evening, de Gaulle made a televised address. He wore uniform to emphasise, as he made clear, that he spoke as both General de Gaulle and head of state. He was uncompromising. The Algerians would have '… free choice of their destiny … self-determination is the only policy that is worthy of France. It is the only possible outcome.' In addressing the army, he made it clear that he expected obedience in all circumstances: 'Listen to me carefully … no

---

12 Horne, *A Savage War of Peace*, p.368.

soldier, under penalty of being guilty of a serious offence, may associate himself at any time, even passively, with the insurrection. In the last analysis, law and order must be re-established … your duty is to bring this about. I have given, and am giving, this order.'[13]

Army units quickly rallied to the call, with Delouvrier receiving signals pledging loyalty. Needless to say, General de Gaulle had done nothing to reassure the hard-liners in the Army, in particular the para officers, but the insurgence, although it dragged on for 48 hours, was over for all intents and purposes. Not only had the weather turned against the insurgents, but the men behind the barricades were now also cut off from the support they had from family and sympathisers. The sympathetic paras, including Tony's regiment, were replaced by other units who neither fraternised with the insurgents nor allowed supplies to pass. Men started slipping away from the barricades. De Gaulle made it clear to Delouvrier that he should not shy away from the use of force. However, the Delegate-General managed to bring off a peaceful solution.

Ortiz disappeared from Algiers on Monday 1 February; Lagaillarde and his men, under terms negotiated by Colonel Dufour of 1st REP, marched out of their redoubt (which they had called 'The Alcazar') the same day. They did so with flags flying and bearing arms, accorded full honours by 1st REP. However, they were not allowed to march through Algiers: they boarded trucks and were taken to Zeralda. Under the terms of the agreement, Lagaillarde surrendered to the authorities and was flown to prison in Paris to await trial. The rank-and-file insurgents were pardoned. Those who wished to do so were allowed to form The Alcazar Commando to fight alongside the Legion. Some 120 chose this option and were taken under the wing of 1st Company, 1st REP. The harsh realities of fighting against the ALN in the bled were far from the romantic image gained behind the barricades. By the beginning of March, the dream was over: the men from Algiers dispersed and returned to their homes and their jobs.

With normality more or less restored in Algiers, the regiment returned to barracks at Zeralda. The events of barricades week had left a deep mark on many of the officers of the para regiments. Their dissatisfaction and disillusionment with de Gaulle's policy would lead many down the road to mutiny in little more than a year, and some would go on to struggle for *Algérie Française* as members of the OAS. For the moment, the officers would do their duty, even if some felt that to continue to fight and lose lives for what looked increasingly like a lost cause was futile. As Tony pointed out, many of the French see the Legion as fighting for

---

13   Horne, *A Savage War of Peace*, p.369.

France, but the *légionnaires* see their loyalty as being to the Legion itself. How the men from many nations felt about the future of French Algeria can only be a matter of speculation. However, they knew that they were winning the war militarily against the ALN. To know that more of their comrades would fall in combat in order to create a situation where the FLN would, in all likelihood, achieve their political objectives must have had a debilitating effect on their morale. Nevertheless, they were first and foremost soldiers of vocation with the highest of professional standards, and, as we shall see, they continued to fight to the best of their ability. As *légionnaires*, it was unthinkable that they could do otherwise. In the final analysis, the ambiguity of the status of the Legion within the French body politic would result in those officers of the Legion brought to trial after the putsch against General de Gaulle in 1961 receiving heavier sentences than officers from the regular Army. As Frenchmen, their crime was to have used foreigners to intervene in French affairs. However, for now, 1st REP returned to the fray and continued to fight.

Tony recalls that, on 27 February 1960, they were deployed in the region of Béjaïa, a coastal town in Kabylia about 100 miles east of Algiers. The people of the Kabylia are Berbers and speak their own dialect. Tony found their villages to be immaculate 'by Algerian standards', with solid stone houses, however tiny the village, and paved streets in the bigger villages even if they often led nowhere. The Kabyle people were extremely tough, and the region very mountainous and rugged with deep ravines and very dense undergrowth. Conditions were so challenging that often the *légionnaires* could only make two or three miles a day. On one occasion, making their way through particularly difficult country, Tony was struggling through matted brambles that, unknown to him, spanned a small, deep-sided wadi:

> Suddenly, I fell right through and there I was at the bottom of the wadi, with no means of climbing back up through the thick brambles, and with the war going on merrily above me. I was particularly concerned that grenades thrown by either side would fall through the brambles and find me. I couldn't make myself heard and had to go down the wadi until I could find somewhere to climb out; here again I had a problem, as I didn't know which side would be above me as I emerged. Luckily it was our side. No-one had noticed I was missing anyway.

Kabylia, 1960: paras unloading captured weapons, munitions, and equipment; again, the rifles on the truck seem to be SMLEs. (Linda Hunter-Choat).

The regiment operated all over the Kabylia highlands pursuing and tracking down *fellagha*. The problems of the terrain were compounded by the rebels sheltering in huge limestone cave complexes. Rather than trying to fight in pitch-black caves stretching back miles, the *légionnaires* often resorted to blowing them up with large quantities of explosives flown in by helicopter. On one occasion that they did this, they subsequently captured a *fellagha* who had been inside the cave. The *légionnaires* were astonished that he was still alive. He explained that '... while we were busy flying in explosives and stacking them at the entrance, they simply trotted through the cave complex exiting some two miles away just in time to watch the bang.'

If a cave complex had only a small entrance, the *légionnaires* often used Soler Oviedo's Spanish wild-boar hunting technique. A teargas grenade, with a long cord attached to the loosened pin, would be pushed as far as possible into the cave using a long pole. The cord would be pulled to set off the grenade and the entrance blocked. Any escaping gas was also blocked off. Before long the *fellagha*:

> ... would be struggling to get out and would emerge: 'Bonzour, bonzour, vive la France!', in the manner of Germans in the Second World War who would call out, 'Kamerad, Kamerad!' as they surrendered. We interrogated them immediately, 'How many are you, how many weapons?' 'Seven men, six moukallas and a machine gun.'[14] One day we captured a young Algerian lad with the enemy. He was only a boy and we called him 'Ouled' – boy. He stayed with us through to the end of the war. Many of those we captured and treated well stayed with us, embodied in 1st REP, acting as scouts, at which they excelled, and interpreters. I dread to think what happened to them at independence.

Ouled, a young boy captured by 1st REP, who was adopted by the regiment and stayed with them until the end of the war. (Linda Hunter-Choat).

14 The moukalla was a black-powder musket with a long barrel and large calibre. It was common in the Kabylia region of Algeria but also found throughout North Africa.

As Tony went on to point out, when Algeria became independent, France abandoned to their fate many thousands of Algerian Arabs and Berbers who had remained loyal to the French throughout the war. The retribution after independence was on a massive scale and marked by many atrocities. Figures vary between 30,000 and 150,000 Algerians who died in the purges after independence, including many women and children.

Much of the time was spent searching villages for weapons. The villages smelt of olives, wood smoke, and sometimes fear. The men were usually not there, except for a few who were very old, and the women and children were not particularly antagonistic. The Kabyle people were, '... when they were not shooting at us, delightful. Life in their rugged hills was hard; many of the women suffered from severe goitre caused by a general lack of iodine, their necks swollen and heavily tattooed.' However, despite the lack of overt antagonism, the appearance on the surface that all was tranquil and innocent was often deceptive. They had to go through the villages with a fine-tooth comb. Usually the *légionnaires* found only chickens, but, from time to time, instinct or a tell-tale sign would lead to the discovery of documents or weapons.

Despite the pace of operations, Tony had time off occasionally and remembered fondly a day in Annaba with a friend: 'It was a wonderfully relaxing day, window-shopping, strolling through the streets without a care in the world, a pleasant lunch, some pastis and a glass or so of wine. I bought my parents a pair of pretty Limoges china coffee cups, which, amazingly, arrived home in one piece.'

Tony's platoon commander at this time, Lieutenant Henry Lobel:

> ... was tall, attractive, very, very fit and a great athlete. He tore up and down mountains at a tremendous rate, carrying very little, while we struggled along behind carrying huge quantities of kit, ammunition, grenades, spare belts for the light machine guns, rifle grenades for the rifle-grenadier, rations, sleeping bag, water, magazines. Although all that was a manageable load it was not conducive to speed and agility. Despite our fatigue, Henry Lobel managed to remain cheerful throughout.

Most of the men in Tony's platoon had now been known to him for some time. He considered them all to be very good men. One of them was Peter Behr, a 'big, strong but gentle person, extremely kind and always happy. He was a good soldier too.' In August 1960, Behr was killed in a fairly minor but fierce contact: '... for once I, who had become fairly blasé about such things, was sad.'

There was a short break from operations in March 1960 when the regiment returned to Zeralda and carried out some parachuting from Bilda airfield.

However, the respite was not long, and, for an engagement on 25 March 1960, Tony received his third decoration. The citation for the Cross of Military Valour with Bronze Star describes Tony and the action as follows:

> A young [section] commander, ardent in combat and possessing fine qualities as a trainer of men. On 25 March 1960 at Douar Beni Amrou at the head of his team, he participated in a lively engagement at close quarters with a heavily armed group who left on the battlefield ... seven dead and seven weapons including a light machine gun.

Tony relates that this was the first contact during which 'I was seriously nervous. Afraid. Fortunately it passed.'

In May and June, the regiment was involved in several operations away from Zeralda, first in the region of Bou Saâda, about 125 miles south of Algeria, and then in the Hodna mountains 80 miles south-east of Algiers. In late June, they were deployed briefly to Collo on the coast about 100 miles from the Tunisian border. In late July, 1st REP moved again to the Ouarsenis region, where they remained until early September participating in *Opération Cigale*, resulting in 115 rebels killed in action by the regiment.

A break in operations gave Tony time once again to attend the Queen's Birthday reception at the British Consulate on 15 June 1960: 'I was much smarter this time as a sergeant and with a few medals to boot.' While out on operations, Tony developed:

> ... the most agonizing toothache, but there was nothing I could do about it other than take lots and lots of aspirin to keep the pain down. By the time we came back in from operations to our temporary base my face was swollen and my jaw had locked solid, to the point that the dentist couldn't open it to operate on the tooth. For several days I was fed on soup and antibiotics until the jaw unlocked and the tooth could be extracted.

The reduced pace of operations in the summer also gave the regiment time for more training and parachuting. Tony recalls a regimental jump with the sky full of parachutes as '... an impressive sight'. With the many jumps, Tony admits that he had become somewhat blasé and on one occasion had failed to carry out the normal checks, including that of ensuring that the parachute canopy was fully open. Looking around him, it appeared as though his fellow parachutists were all going up:

... as I raised my head to watch the nearest one it occurred to me that my view was not blocked by a canopy above me, which had candled. I was going down very quickly indeed. I had two choices – either to deploy my reserve or to try to shake my candled chute open. I tried the latter by pulling the rigging lines sharply outwards and it worked. It was lucky that it worked, as by now I was too low to have time to deploy my reserve and I would have been dead.

Tony recounts another experience during this period of jump training:

One day, standing at the edge of the DZ idly watching our fellow paras jumping from subsequent lifts, we saw one para release himself from his harness at about 1,000 feet and just let go. There was a dull thud and he bounced about three feet. Why he chose such a complicated way to die was beyond us. At all times we had weapons and live ammunition with us, and he could have shot himself at any time. Sad. And odd.

During this period, there was also time to relax and go into Algiers. At the end of one very long evening out, Tony was at the foot of the Casbah waiting for the midnight truck back to Zeralda. Three staff sergeants, including his friend Johann Wallisch, appeared and announced that they had come to town in Wallisch's car but that they were all too drunk to drive the 30 miles back to Zeralda at night along the winding coast road: 'Johnny, you are hereby designated duty driver. Off you go, onwards to Zeralda.' Tony had never driven a car before but had some experience on Ferguson tractors:

It turned out that the principles were the same: gear, clutch, accelerator, brake. Wallisch's car was a Panhard with a column gear lever which fooled me for a bit, but as all the others had promptly gone to sleep there was no one I could consult and had to work it out for myself. As I was as drunk as they were, but less sleepy, it was amazing that we got there. But we did.

On 28 July, the regiment was deployed away from Zeralda for *Opération Cigale*. They moved all day by truck the 100 miles south-west to Orléansville (now Chlef) for operations in the Djebel Ouarsenis south of Chlef and east towards Miliana and Médéa. The French Air Force was now using more napalm, '… and the smell of burning bodies mixed with the smell of cordite, artillery and burning bushes.' As a contrast to the horrors of war, two of Tony's great pleasures on operations were the first cigarette of the day and chewing as they marched the raw garlic that he always carried in his combat jacket pocket.

Because of the high rate of consumption of French grenades during their *rouleau compresseur* tactics, the regiment had been issued American 'pineapple' grenades. During this operation, two serious incidents arose with these weapons. The *légionnaires* carried six grenades ready for immediate use in a pouch with three 2-grenade pockets. The pouch hung from the belt and was strapped to the leg so that it did not crash about. They usually had several more grenades in their packs. Driving back to their temporary camp one day from an operation, there was suddenly a huge explosion, and:

> ... in the back of the truck was half a légionnaire, while the légionnaire sitting on his right had lost his left leg, and the man on his left had lost his right leg. We used grenades all the time and there was no question of operator error; one of the grenades had had a dodgy fuse, had self-activated and set off the other five. Two days later, on reaching the trucks at the end of another operation, one of the légionnaires threw his pack into the back of the GMC [truck], whereupon the grenades in it exploded killing him outright. For us that was quite enough, and we refused to use the American grenades thereafter.

As if grenade problems were not enough, during these operations, a staff sergeant was shot by a *fellagha* firing from a well-concealed cache at the side of a track. Shooting up from ground level, he shot the staff sergeant in the lower stomach, with the bullet '... taking off his testicles and half his penis and exiting through his rectum.' Tony does not tell us whether or not the unfortunate Max Sokolowski survived his wound.

All the operations that were based on good intelligence started with the *légionnaires* moving fast towards the area of anticipated contact with the rebels. The aim was to get there quickly before the *fellagha* realised that they were coming, to get blocking groups in place to stop the rebels escaping the net, and to ensure that the *légionnaires* had the advantage of the ground when the combat started. The *légionnaires* were very fit but so were the *fellagha*, who often carried just backpacks crammed with ammunition. The operations in the Ouarsenis came to an end on 4 September 1960, having finished with two weeks' continuous deployment in the mountains. Tony took the opportunity over this fortnight to grow a moustache, which, as he ruefully admitted, was not necessarily a great improvement.

In October, the regiment was deployed once again for *Opération Ariège* in the Aurès region about 60 miles south of Constantine. Tony now had a new role, having been transferred to the intelligence section at regimental headquarters to serve alongside Captain Ysquierdo and Lieutenant Favreau.[15] On 16 October, he had his first operation in his new capacity as NCO in charge of maps. His first task was to give the necessary maps to a young second lieutenant medical officer, Jean-Michel Default, who had only just joined the regiment. Tony went to see him, saluted smartly at the regulation distance, presented himself and announced, 'Here are the maps for the forthcoming operation, sir'. So brand new was the doctor that he had hardly ever been saluted before and was somewhat taken aback. He was also taken aback by the mass of maps since he had no understanding whatsoever of map reading. (Tony was to remain in contact with Default, and they jumped together 30 years later.)

By 3 November, the regiment was back in barracks at Zeralda, and Tony had become Head of the Observation Team. The task of his team – using binoculars, large tripod-mounted wide-angle binoculars, and the radio – was to keep the commanding officer always in touch with a running commentary on the location of the various companies. They also kept the operational map up to date. It was a big change from the life of a sergeant in a combat company, but '… a welcome break after three-years' non-stop fighting. I was sad, though, not to be with my old friends, sharing their hardships and discomforts, but also their victories.'

With his new responsibilities at regimental HQ, and without a platoon to look after, Tony had more leisure time. If he wanted leave to go to Algiers, then it was to Lieutenant Favreau, his immediate commander, that he had to go for approval:

> He knew that I went from time to time to the British Consulate; he, however, fancied one of the consul's daughters, and suspected my motive – which did not involve the consul's daughter, though he thought it did – so that whenever he planned to be in town and was thinking of popping into the consulate he would refuse my application for a leave pass. Bugger.

While back in Zeralda at this period, Tony learnt to drive, using the regiment's US Second World War-vintage Jeeps with three forward gears, reverse, high and low ratio, and a differential lock. 'It could go practically anywhere and was a wonderfully simple machine'. The course was run by the mechanical transport warrant officer, and there were normally two students to a jeep: one driving and one waiting to drive. Tony was with an Italian *légionnaire* one day, and, when it was the Italian's turn to drive, it was apparent that he was not a very good driver

---

15 Jacques Favreau was severely wounded later in the year but went on to have a successful career in the French Army, retiring as a major-general.

and a very slow learner. Driving along a track outside the camp one morning, he managed to get the wheels over the edge of the road, and they all rolled down a hill: 'Fortunately, we finished, by pure chance, the right way up and although the superstructure of the canopy was pretty bent it was easy to drive back up the hill to the track. I passed my test, though the Italian had to do the course again.'

The time in barracks also gave time to relax, but not without risks: promotion and new responsibilities do not necessarily seem to have taught Tony to be either sensible or prudent. One evening off duty, Tony and a friend:

> ... went to Zeralda village for a drink in one of the bars where, after several pints, we both fell in love with the barmaid. It was late by then but we walked back to camp and picked all the flowers outside the company offices, made two attractive bouquets, walked back to Zeralda and presented them to the barmaid. Who couldn't have cared less. Somewhat sobered by her rejection we came to the conclusion that stealing the company commander's flowers was, perhaps, not such a good idea after all, particularly as it had got us nowhere. We had a brainwave. After much hammering and shouting we managed to wake the Arab owner of the nearby grocery shop demanding service. We bought, at considerable expense, all the boxes of camembert he had. In each little box as well as the camembert was a plastic flower as a promotional gimmick. We threw away the huge quantities of camembert and carefully planted the plastic flowers in the company garden. We thought that they looked wonderful and went to bed. The company commander did not think that they looked wonderful but never found out who had done it.

On 8 November 1960, the short break from operations came to an end, and the regiment was deployed once again to the Ouarsenis mountains. The route initially took them through gently rolling green hills with wooded slopes of olives, firs, and oaks. Then, it was on through rocky gorges and into the open, yellow, arid plain studded with rugged, rocky mountainous outcrops. The trucks travelled on roads and tracks that the rebels had cut and booby-trapped. Bridges had also been blown, and long detours were required across country in pitch dark without lights, preceded by *légionnaires* reconnoitring on foot.

On 10 November, the regiment became involved in combat with a rebel unit some 100 men strong, which was to prove one of the bloodiest days in the unit's war in Algeria. The second wave of a company deploying by helicopter was caught by fire from rebels well concealed and protected by dugouts constructed with wooden poles. Armed helicopters and reinforcements were deployed, but, as night fell, most of the rebels were able to slip away. The regiment had suffered 11 killed and six wounded for the loss of nine rebels killed. They now moved deeper into the mountains, along narrow hairpin tracks, through narrow gorges onto a high sheltered plateau of green grass with clear streams, complete with wild horses, sheep, and goats. Regimental HQ moved from hilltop to hilltop to ensure the best possible communications and views of the terrain. The weather '... deteriorated into howling, steady gales, not gusting, just on and on with winds reaching 100 mph. To boot there were snowstorms, the ammunition tent caught fire and blew up, and then all the tents blew away: it was not a fun operation.'

On 15 November, they were back at Zeralda, and a funeral ceremony was held for the 11 men killed five days before. The funeral orations of the officer commanding, Colonel Dufour, and the regimental padre, Père Delarue, no doubt reflected the thoughts of many who were fighting in the Legion and the regular French Army, but they were not well received in higher places. Tony recorded Dufour's words: 'It is not possible that your sacrifice will be wasted. It is not possible that our countrymen in Metropolitan France will not hear us.' Delarue's blessing for the dead had been approved by Dufour:

> You have come from all these countries of Europe where people still love liberty, to give freedom to this country ... Death has struck you full in the chest, full in the face, like men, at the moment when you were rejoicing at having at last uncovered an enemy elusive until now ... You have fallen at the moment when, if we are to believe what we hear, we no longer know what we are dying for ...[16]

The words of the regimental commander and his padre, coming after the events during barricades week in Algiers in January, and Dufour's well-known and unconcealed sympathy for *Algérie Française*, were too much for the authorities. Dufour was relieved of his command and ordered to report to a post in Germany. Initially, he disappeared and refused to leave Algeria. At the same time, two junior officers stole the regimental standard, symbolically important for the passing of command to the new CO, Lieutenant Colonel Guiraud. Command passed to Guiraud without the standard on 7 December, but the next day Dufour, who had

---

16   Montagnon, *Les parachutistes de la Légion*, p.267. (Author's translation).

THE BEGINNING OF THE END

given himself up and now had it in his possession, handed the standard back. He was then taken under guard for a flight back to France and his new post.

Dufour had been in the thick of plotting against General de Gaulle for some months and had been under surveillance.[17] Although his funeral address was the last straw, it is likely that the authorities wanted him well out of the way before a visit to Algeria by de Gaulle planned to begin on 9 December. In July, Dufour had tried to enlist the support in France of retired General Marie-André Zeller, former chief-of-staff of the armed forces, for a two-pronged coup in France and Algeria. His plan was that, on the 14 July Bastille Day parade in Algiers, the 1st REP would seize Delegate-General Delouvrier and General Crépin, the Army chief in Algiers, while in France de Gaulle and his ministers would be rounded up. On 13 July, the word came from Zeller: 'Do nothing. It's not ready here.' Dufour contented himself with marching past the saluting base without his medals in protest at General de Gaulle's policy.

Captain Pierre Sergent of 1st REP had also been plotting, in his case with General Edmond Jouhaud, a *pied noir* who had recently retired as Air Force chief-of-staff.[18] The plan was that, in coordination with the *pied noir* FNF, a general strike would be organised in Algiers to coincide with de Gaulle's visit. The strike would be accompanied by scattered demonstrations, which would be difficult to control by the CRS and gendarmes. Thus, it was hoped that, to control the situation, the Army would be called in. They would then capture General de Gaulle. Although some unit commanders seemed initially well disposed to the plan, it came to nothing when insufficient support materialised. Four separate attempts were made to assassinate Charles de Gaulle during his visit. The most dangerous plan was for a CRS motorcycle escort to shoot the president; he was ready to do so but, at the last minute, was ordered not to proceed. A further plot was for de Gaulle to be ambushed when he entered Orléansville, but, after a tip-off by the Israeli intelligence services, his route was changed, and the waiting would-be assassins bypassed. The next two attempts were freelance and farcical: the first involved a disenchanted *pied noir* flying his private aeroplane into de

---

17   After the Generals' Putsch in April 1961, Colonel Dufour joined the OAS. He was dismissed from the Army and stripped of his decorations and civil rights, which were subsequently restored in 1968.
18   After the defeat of France in 1940, Edmond Jouhaud had initially joined the Vichy forces but, in 1943, had taken leave. He subsequently made two attempts, without success, to join the Free French in England. He joined the Resistance and, in late 1944, rejoined the French Air Force.

Gaulle's helicopter. However, when he arrived over Bilda aerodrome, there were so many helicopters that he could not decide which one was carrying the president and aborted his attempt. The final plot was by a veteran *pied noir* junior officer who, during the inspection of his para commando by de Gaulle, would shoot the president. Fortunately for General de Gaulle, the officer got entangled in a Muslim demonstration on his way to the base and arrived too late.

Meanwhile, the planned demonstrations in Algiers had started on Friday 9 December and rapidly turned violent, with 6,000 CRS and gendarmes with armoured cars and tanks attempting to restore order. The violence continued unabated on the following day, and, on the Sunday, the Muslims took to the streets.

Eventually, as the plotters had hoped, the Army was called to intervene. Tony's regiment was away on operations: 'On 11 December we heard of great excitement in Algiers but had no idea what it was, and the radio news was censored.' In view of events in January, it is unlikely that either 1st REP or 1st RCP would have been used, but there was, and remains, a belief that both regiments were deliberately kept busy after barricades week to keep them out of the way. It may, of course, just be that, in view of their proven effectiveness, they were the best men to be employed operationally. In any event, it was Colonel Masselot's 18th RCP that was called in to reinforce the CRS and gendarmes. Masselot was a *pied noir* and disgusted by de Gaulle's policy. He was also sympathetic to the Army conspirators, but he was disillusioned by the *pied noir* ultras. One of the FNF leaders told Masselot that he could not hold his men back and that they would rampage through the Muslim quarters of the city; Masselot was outraged: 'I too am a *pied noir*, but get into your head that there cannot be an Algérie Française without the Arabs.'[19] In the event, de Gaulle avoided Algiers, but the coup failed largely because of a lack of resolve on the part of General Jouhaud and recognition of a lack of support in Metropolitan France. Nevertheless, another step had been taken towards the turmoil that was to follow a few months later.

---

19   Horne, *A Savage War of Peace*, p.432.

12

The Last Months of 1st REP: January–April 1961

On 8 January 1961, France and Algeria voted in a referendum: 'Do you approve the bill submitted to the French people by the President of the Republic concerning the self-determination of the Algerian population and the organisation of the public powers in Algeria prior to self-determination?'[1] The formulation had been cleverly constructed to give Charles de Gaulle a free hand for negotiations. The reaction to the wording was, not surprisingly, divided in both France and Algeria.

Those in France who were opposed to a yes vote had diverging, and sometimes contradictory, reasons for their positions. Supporters of *Algérie Française* in Metropolitan France, including former Governor-General Jacques Soustelle, argued that the referendum was unconstitutional since no one could dispose of French territory. Prominent retired generals argued for a no vote on the grounds that an independent Algeria would extend Soviet influence in the Mediterranean. Perversely, the French Communist Party took a somewhat confused line by urging its supporters to vote no, arguing that they would not be supporting the ultra *pieds noirs* but voting against the war.

In Algeria, the *pieds noirs* were, of course, overwhelmingly going to vote no. Amongst the Muslim population, there were those who supported the referendum as a way of achieving independence, but the official GPRA/FLN line was to encourage a boycott. An underlying fear within the FLN had long been, and would remain, that de Gaulle would try to find a more liberal negotiating partner than them, and they were concerned that a yes would give him the mandate he wanted. Their fears were justified to the extent that de Gaulle did, indeed, want to negotiate with a third force if one could be found. However, his hopes would

---

1 Horne, *A Savage War of Peace*, p.434.

rapidly evaporate, and he would have no choice but to come to terms with the FLN. In the event, the turnout in Metropolitan France was 76 percent and in Algeria 59 percent of those registered to vote. In France, 75 percent voted yes. In Algeria, the figure in favour was 70 percent, but among the European population, around 70 percent opposed General de Gaulle. Nevertheless, as far as de Gaulle was concerned, the electorate as a whole had agreed his position.

Amongst the Legion parachute regiments, the officers remained vehemently opposed to any solution other than *Algérie Française*. On either 7 or 8 January (accounts vary on the precise date although the majority lean towards the day of the referendum), an extraordinary event occurred. Three combat companies and the HQ Company of 1st REP, which was at that time deployed near Lamy close to the Tunisian frontier, went on strike. The losses in November 1960, the speeches of the commanding officer and the padre at the funeral of the men killed in action, the posting of Colonel Dufour in reprisal, and the policy of de Gaulle had all come to a head. Led by their officers, the four companies refused to take part in operations and remained in camp to undertake routine tasks. The officers concerned argued that they were not refusing to fight but that they wanted to have a clear reason to do so and wanted their feelings to be known at the highest levels. In that, they achieved their aim, and action followed quickly. Captains Sergent, Simonot, Ponsolle, and La Forest Divonne and three lieutenants were posted back to France out of the Legion to regular units and away from airborne duties. That Colonel Guiraud, the new officer commanding, had been disobeyed was clearly a concern. Major Hélie de Saint-Marc was posted in as second-in-command to strengthen the command structure, being recalled to duty having retired one year earlier. A former resistance fighter, survivor of Buchenwald concentration camp, a Legion officer since 1948, a member of 1st BEP in Indochina, and an officer on General Massu's staff during the Battle of Algiers, he must have seemed a safe pair of hands. In the event, he was to lead 1st REP in support of the Generals' Putsch and would be condemned to 10-years' imprisonment for his pains.[2]

The strike behind them, the *légionnaires* of 1st REP went back to operations throughout the rest of January, February, and March and into April. January and February were marked by gales and cold weather, but, by March, it had become warmer. Several hundred rebels were killed, wounded, or captured during these operations as, despite misgivings over the political situation, the regiment

---

2   Saint-Marc was amnestied in 1966 after five years in prison. His decorations and civil rights were restored in 1978. He was awarded the Grand Cross of the Legion of Honour in 2011.

THE LAST MONTHS OF 1ST REP: JANUARY–APRIL 1961

continued to fight professionally. Tony records that the last real battle that the regiment fought was on 28 March 1961 in the Aures region. After a rapid 10-mile march during the night followed by a river crossing at first light, the *légionnaires* took up position to trap the *fellagha* in a wide, deep valley. Tony recalls looking down on low-flying B-24 Liberator bombers and hearing the satisfying heavy crump of their bombs as they attacked the rebels in the valley. On 8 April, the regiment came down from the mountains by truck and returned to their temporary camp. Five days later, they moved out of camp for the journey back to Zeralda.

Discontent within the Army in Algeria had continued to grow throughout the early months of 1961. The announcement at the end of March that peace talks would start between the French government and the FLN on 7 April only added to the growing movement towards open revolt. On 11 April, General de Gaulle gave a press conference: he declared that maintaining colonies was costly, bloody, and a situation without an end. The French colonies stood in the way of the essential renewal of France. Algeria would be sovereign, and France would place no obstacle in its way. Plans for a coup had been under way for some time, but this was the final straw.

While there was widespread discontent at junior levels, much of the plotting was carried out by disaffected colonels. However, if they were to succeed, they recognised that they would need the support of more prominent figures. Attempts to recruit General Massu had failed: despite his earlier outspoken remarks, he would not countenance turning against General de Gaulle. A story recounts that, on one occasion, de Gaulle had said to Massu, 'Still an ass Massu?' He had then replied, 'Yes, general, still a Gaullist.'[3] Earlier, shortly after his posting away from Algeria, he had been approached by the ultra *pieds noirs* to enlist his support for their position. He had made his thoughts clear on the leadership of France: '*He* [de Gaulle] is a leader. I have also seen Bidault. He is small and sick, and his overcoat has a fur edging. You cannot replace de Gaulle with Bidault. Well then, *who have you got?*'[4]

General Salan, in exile in Madrid, was an obvious candidate to lead the putsch for the Army, but he was not popular with the *pieds noirs*. General Challe, who had earned much respect among both soldiers and the civilian population, was very

---

3   Horne, *A Savage War of Peace*, p.438.
4   Horne, *A Savage War of Peace*, p.438. Georges Bidault, twice prime minister in the immediate post-war years, was a member of the Chamber of Deputies and unequivocally committed to *Algérie Française*. He went on to become heavily involved in the OAS.

likely to be popular and was finally selected as the leader. Despite his sympathies for the cause, he was initially hesitant to throw in his lot with the conspirators, and he was warned by some of his subordinates of the folly of joining the plot: there would be little support in Metropolitan France, and support for a putsch from the Army outside Algeria could not be counted on. In the end, he was pushed over the edge by General de Gaulle's press conference of 11 April and agreed to lead the putsch. He would be responsible for military matters, General Jouhaud would take responsibility for information and propaganda, and General Zeller would cover economic affairs and administration. Salan, when he could travel from Spain, would take on civil affairs.

Meanwhile, the OAS had been born and had already started a campaign of terrorism both in Algeria and France. On 25 January 1961, a young liberal European lawyer was stabbed to death in Algiers, and at the beginning of March, an unsuccessful attempt was made on the life of a prominent *pied noir* supporter of de Gaulle. In France, on 31 March, the mayor of the town of Evian, where the peace talks were scheduled to take place, was assassinated. On 2 April, a bomb exploded near the Paris apartment of François Mitterand (why is anybody's guess since Mitterand was an opponent of General de Gaulle), and two days later, 14 people were injured by a bomb outside the stock exchange. Also in April, in a plot that perhaps was the origin of the later Frederick Forsyth novel *The Day of the Jackal*, an ex-*légionnaire* was contracted to shoot de Gaulle with a rifle with a telescopic sight. For his pains, he was to receive the princely sum of 40,000,000 old francs (about £55,000). The would-be assassin, having collected a 50 percent advance, tipped off the police and disappeared into thin air.

On 20 April, Generals Challe and Zeller left France for Algeria, flying in an aircraft purloined from the Air Force. The commander of the French Air Force was complicit in the provision of the aircraft but sent Challe off with the words, 'I am convinced that you are committing a stupidity …'[5] Jouhaud was living in Algeria waiting for their arrival. Salan flew from Madrid to join the others on 23 April. There were hitches from the start. First of all, Challe's aircraft landed at Algiers when his reception party was awaiting him at Blida and had to take off again. Next, Challe found that an order had been issued in his name, apparently on the initiative of 1st REP, delaying the start of the putsch for no obvious reason. To cap it all, Colonel Godard, the intelligence mastermind, had left his briefcase with all the plans for the coup in a public place. However, this breach of security was of

---

5   Horne, *A Savage War of Peace*, p.448.

little consequence: leaks were widespread, including to those unsympathetic to the cause of the conspirators.

The leaders established a headquarters and spent 21 April checking plans and telephoning those unit commanders who had expressed support to confirm their loyalty. Key to the plan was the support of 1st REP. Colonel Guiraud was absent on leave in Paris for a few days, and Major Saint-Marc was acting as commanding officer. Captain Besineau, commanding the HQ Company, was the first to hear of the arrival of Challe and Zeller:

> Major, I have something very serious, very important to tell you.
>
> If you can avoid telling me, Besineau, I should prefer it. I have quite enough worries with the regiment and I would like not to have more.
>
> That's impossible, major, I have a message for you from General Challe.
>
> The general is in Algiers?
>
> Since last night![6]

Saint-Marc had been summoned to go to see Challe at his HQ. Waiting for him were Captain Sergent, who had made his way back to Algiers from France covertly, and another former member of 1st REP, Lieutenant Roger Degueldre, who – rather than be transferred out of the regiment – had deserted after the events of December during de Gaulle's visit.[7] The two waited outside while Challe met with Saint-Marc. They were clear: they had burnt their boats, they were committed. If Saint-Marc did not go along with the putsch, they would arrest him to give themselves a free hand with the regiment.

Challe could not be certain of Saint-Marc, who was known for his loyalty. Would he rebel against authority? Challe put his cards on the table:

---

6   Montagnon, *Les parachutistes de la Légion*, pp.290–91. (Author's translation).
7   Degueldre had fought in the Resistance. After the war, he joined the army, transferring shortly thereafter to the Legion. He had a distinguished career in Indochina and Algeria and had been decorated with the *Médaille Militaire* and as a *Chevalier de la Légion d'Honneur*. He became a ruthless leader of the OAS, forming the Delta Commandos. A remark of his became the watchword of the OAS: 'It is of little importance if we win or we lose, the essential is to fight'. In March 1962, a Delta Commando put six *pieds noirs* and Muslim administrators of a social centre in Algeria against a wall and machine-gunned them. The next month, Degueldre was arrested; he was tried and executed by firing squad in France in July 1962.

We are only here to keep the promises of 13 May [an allusion to the return to power of de Gaulle in 1958]. I am a democrat, Saint-Marc, this will not be a fascist *coup d'état*, nor a racist backlash. Are you with us?

On one condition: that there will be no unnecessary violence on our part, nor any settling of accounts, and in that case, mon général, I am at your service.[8]

Five other officers of 1st REP who had been posted out had also returned covertly for the putsch. Sergent and Degueldre, having considered the possibility that Saint-Marc might refuse to go along with them, had earmarked these men to replace other officers in the regiment who might baulk at both disobeying Saint-Marc and mutinying against the government. In the event, this was unnecessary. Saint-Marc returned to Zeralda and briefed his company commanders:

So, here is what I have decided. What we are going to do is very serious. We risk our skins. In any case I will take it all on my shoulders. If ever this goes wrong, it is me who will take responsibility for this adventure. You are seven company commanders. You are adults. If any of you have misgivings, I understand. I will confine you to your room and I will take the regiment with me without you. We are going to take control of Algiers tonight.[9]

Two company commanders were hesitant. However, Saint-Marc commanded great respect among the officers of 1st REP, and they threw in their lot with the putsch.

The objectives were set for the company commanders. Two companies would take control of the regular Army barracks, the HQ Company would seize the Army Corps HQ, a further company would take the radio station, another the police school, and the sixth would arrest Delegate-General Jean Morin. The final company would be held in reserve. One of the senior Army generals who would remain loyal to General de Gaulle throughout, General Simon, got wind of what was going on. He was some 60 miles away from Algiers at Tizi-Ouzou, too far from the centre of events to intervene. He telephoned Morin to warn him. Morin in turn called General Gambiez, Commander-in-Chief in Algeria since January. Gambiez called back around midnight on 21 April and, somewhat annoyed at having his evening disrupted, said he had spoken to Saint-Marc at Zeralda: 'He's just returned from dining with General Saint-Hillier. When I mentioned the

---

8   Montagnon, *Les parachutistes de la Légion*, p.291. (Author's translation).
9   Montagnon, *Les parachutistes de la Légion*, p.292. (Author's translation).

movement of troops of the general reserve, why, that made him laugh. Everything at his end is perfectly quiet.'[10]

A telephone call from Paris gave Morin entirely different intelligence. Two more conversations with an irritated Commander-in-Chief followed. Gambiez decided that he would find out for himself and set out in his staff car. On the outskirts of Algiers, he ran into the Motorised Company of 1st REP, whereupon the commander, Lieutenant Durant-Ruel, arrested him: 'In my time, young man, lieutenants did not arrest generals.' 'In your time generals didn't sell off empires!'[11]

The plan for 1st REP went well for the most part. There was only one casualty: a regular Army NCO shot in self-defence by a warrant officer of 1st REP. More amusingly, General Venizet, the Algiers Corps commander, was stopped by a *légionnaire* from drawing his side-arm, but in the struggle, a portrait of de Gaulle fell from the wall. It was said that Venizet was trapped by the frame, giving rise to the story that he had been framed by 1st REP. However, more widely, not all had been either well thought out or executed by the plotters: with extraordinary incompetence, the telephone lines from the government offices had not been cut. Morin was able to alert Paris and outlying command posts. The generals commanding in Oran and Constantine declared their loyalty to de Gaulle. The Navy commander also declared for the President, and the Air Force commander expressed his ignorance and surprise. Nevertheless, on the morning of Saturday 22 April, all seemed well set, with the objectives met and the principal opponents in custody. Roger Degueldre entered the office of Colonel Godard: 'Colonel, I have in my hands some bastards, Morin, Gambiez and company, I am going to shoot them.' 'Degueldre, you are mad!' 'Fine, then it's all fucked! I'm taking to the hills!'[12]

While all the excitement was kicking off, Tony was in town with friends – a South African and his *pied noir* wife, Eric and Yvette Coetzes. Tony often spent time with them; he wore civilian clothes that he had bought in Algiers, strictly against the rules, and drove around in their blue and cream 1957 Buick convertible. His

---

10   Horne, *A Savage War of Peace*, p.448.
11   Montagnon, *Les parachutistes de la Légion*, p.293.
12   Montagnon, *Les parachutistes de la Légion*, p.293.

friend, Ray Palin, often joined him but could not be depended on to behave for more than a couple of hours: 'One day in a fit of scouse pique he ripped the sliding door off Eric's work van and chucked it down the road. He wasn't invited again.'[13]

Tony caught up with the regiment on the Saturday:

> ... just in time to escort, in my Dodge 4x4 truck, a four-star general to his temporary prison, which was quite fun for a young sergeant.[14] In the space of twenty-four hours we took over the whole of the administration of Algiers, including all government offices, the radio station and the airport, and disarmed and locked up the hated (by us) CRS, a counter-terrorist force infamous for their heavy-handed actions, including against us if we were being difficult. It took one under-strength platoon of the Legion to disarm this fearsome body of men. We left them locked in their own barracks. We had a wild few days in Algiers, feted by the European population, drinking their champagne.

Clouds quickly began to gather over the mutineers. General Zeller, who was responsible for logistics, assessed that, in the face of a blockade imposed by France, Algeria could hold out for a fortnight – the original assessment had been three months. More importantly, they did not have widespread support within the armed forces. The French Navy was at best neutral, with its commander holed up in the well-fortified Mers El Kébir naval base. The French Air Force was also keeping its distance and, from 24 April, started sending all its transport aircraft back to France. Some Army commanders were resolutely opposed to the putsch, and others were simply irresolute. Even the Legion units were not unanimously in support. On the Sunday, Salan arrived to a lukewarm reception by his co-conspirators, with Challe concerned that he would try to take over. Problems were also emerging with the ultra *pieds noirs*, who were critical of Challe's reluctance to take any action that might lead to civil war. Some wanted to round up opponents – just the sort of settling of scores that Saint-Marc would have nothing to do with.

---

13 Caporal-Chef Palin served at least 20 years with the Legion and was awarded the *Médaille Militaire*.
14 This was probably General Venizet.

THE LAST MONTHS OF 1ST REP: JANUARY–APRIL 1961

In Paris, President de Gaulle exhibited his characteristic coolness: 'What is serious about this business, gentlemen, is its amateurishness ...'[15] He reckoned that it would last three days, and he was not far off the mark. The Minister of the Interior acted quickly to arrest General Faure, who was supposed to lead some 2,200 lightly armed paras and some armoured units to take Paris. Lacking leadership, the paras dispersed quietly when ordered to do so by the gendarmerie. Meanwhile, General Crépin, until recently commander-in-chief in Algeria and now commanding French forces in Germany, signalled his support for General de Gaulle, and other commanders throughout France did likewise. De Gaulle had been dismissive of the threat of invasion from Algeria: 'If they want to land in France, they will land. That's up to them. There won't be much to stop them. What will happen? Oh, it's not difficult to guess: these are men of narrow vision; they will soon be faced with problems that will be beyond them ...'[16]

He was right that there would not be much to stop them: a few decrepit Second World War Sherman tanks, but little else. However, with the withdrawal of the transport planes of the French Air Force, there was no likelihood of landings in France, and, in any case, that had not been the intention of the leaders of the putsch.

On the evening of Sunday 23 April, Charles de Gaulle addressed one of his greatest speeches to the nation on television. He ordered that 'In the name of France ... all means, I repeat *all means*, be employed to block the road everywhere to those men ... I forbid every Frenchman, and above all every soldier, to execute their orders ...'[17] The appeal was most closely felt by the reservists and conscripts. The President had appealed to them directly, giving them the authority to disobey commanders who took the side of the putsch.

By Tuesday, Challe had decided that all was lost. There were some hard-liners who contemplated a putsch within the putsch, replacing Challe by Salan, but this came to nothing. Challe headed off to Zeralda with 1st REP late on Tuesday 25 April. He held on until the early hours of Wednesday and then decided to give himself up. He urged Saint-Marc to get out, telling him, '... let me pay the bill alone.'[18] The Acting Commander of 1st REP refused: he had led the regiment into the revolt and would remain with them until arrested. General Challe flew out

---

15 Horne, *A Savage War of Peace*, p.454. (Author's translation).
16 Horne, *A Savage War of Peace*, p.454.
17 Horne, *A Savage War of Peace*, p.455.
18 Horne, *A Savage War of Peace*, pp.458–59.

at 1000 hours to face the music in France.[19] General Zeller had already put on civilian clothes and melted into the local population.[20] Generals Jouhaud[21] and Salan[22] followed suit, vowing to continue the fight by other means. Many other leaders of the putsch also fled, including Captain Sergent.[23]

Tony's analysis of the failure of the putsch was succinct and to the point: 'The story of the putsch and its failure is complex. Essentially the four generals, in good French fashion, had failed to make a proper plan, had failed to ensure sufficient support, had totally ignored the logistics, and it reached a point where they simply gave up. With, I suppose, a Gallic shrug of the shoulders.'

Back at Zeralda on 26 April, 1st REP found itself surrounded by police and Army units with helicopters overhead:

> One police unit approached the front gate, but we set up an anti-tank gun and they withdrew. Off the coast, barely one mile away, lay a battleship with its sixteen-inch guns trained on our camp. We had little choice. We blew up as much of the camp as we could, packed our kit, kept our weapons and got on the trucks to leave Zeralda for the last time. We were [soon] in a barbed wire compound on an old USAF base at Thiersville [now Ghriss], 25 miles from Sidi Bel Abbès, awaiting our fate. Although we were surrounded by

---

19   General Challe was sentenced to 15-years' imprisonment. He was freed in 1966 and amnestied in 1968.
20   General Zeller gave himself up in May 1961. He was sentenced to 15-years' imprisonment but was freed in 1966 and amnestied in 1968.
21   General Jouhaud remained in Algeria as a leader of the OAS. He was arrested in March 1962. He was sentenced to death, but his sentence was commuted to life imprisonment. He was freed in 1967 and amnestied in 1968.
22   General Salan, who had also remained in Algeria and headed the OAS leadership, was captured almost by accident in Algiers in April 1962. He was condemned to life imprisonment in 1962 – to the annoyance of de Gaulle, who had wanted the death penalty – but was pardoned and freed in 1968.
23   Pierre Sergent returned to France to continue the struggle as an active member of the OAS. He was sentenced to death in absentia in 1962. He managed to avoid arrest, taking refuge in Belgium and Switzerland until he was amnestied in 1968.

military loyal to de Gaulle, we still had our weapons and they left us alone, very wisely.

Legend has it that, as 1st REP left Zeralda, they sang Édith Piaf's song '*Je ne regrette rien*' while *pieds noirs* lined the road weeping.[24] The putsch had lasted four days and five nights. The regiment celebrated its last Camerone on 30 April 1961 and was disbanded the next day, along with two regiments of the regular Army that had also played a prominent role in the putsch. Many *légionnaires* deserted to join the OAS.

One of those to desert was Tony's batman Claude Tenne, serving in the Legion under the pseudonym Marc Ténard. The following month, he was involved in the murder of Commissaire Gavoury of the French police in Algiers. He, along with others involved, was captured later in the year. The two perpetrators of the crime, including a Yugoslav *légionnaire* known to Tony, Sergeant Dovecar, were sentenced to death. Tenne was imprisoned for life on the Île de Ré for his role as an accomplice. In 1967, due to an extraordinary lapse of security, he escaped in a fashion reminiscent of a boys' adventure story. Prisoners due for release were allowed to take a trunk with them containing their personal possessions, and, noting that these were not routinely searched, Tenne hid in the trunk of a prisoner due for release. This was another of Tony's ex-comrades, the Hungarian László Varga, who convinced the prison authorities that the trunk contained books. Despite a massive search, Tenne evaded capture and fled to Spain. He returned to France in 1968 under amnesty.

Those who did not desert were posted to other units within the Legion. Tony was initially posted to 1st RE (Foreign Regiment).[25] He subsequently joined its newly formed 7th Intervention Company.

---

24   Tony makes no mention of the singing, and there is some doubt over the authenticity of the legend. However, Captain Bonelli was with 1st REP that day, and his biography mentions the singing – Helcégé, *Capitaine Bonelli, L'arbre à papillons*, p.221; Pierre Montagnon, who was with 2nd REP gives a second-hand account that supports the story – Montagnon, *Les parachutistes de la Légion*, p.300. Captain Sergent, who as we have seen played a prominent role on the putsch, also records the singing of Piaf's song – Sergent, *Je ne regrette rien*, p.654.
25   1st RE was the Legion's depot regiment, formed from 1st REI, 1st Foreign Infantry Regiment in 1955.

13

Final Months

After the disbandment of 1st REP, Tony still had almost a year to serve until his initial contract came to an end. His last months were marked by a reduction in intensity of the war with the ALN, but the situation in Algeria between, and within, the European and Muslim communities became increasingly unstable and complex. The OAS stepped up its terrorist activity against both Muslims and *pied noir* liberals, thus provoking increasing FLN-instigated reprisals, and the French security forces were struggling to eliminate the organisation. To add to the complexity within Algeria, a motley, and pretty amateur, group of hard-line Gaullist supporters started, and lost, a mini civil war with the OAS. On the broader political front, peace negotiations moved inexorably but stutteringly towards a conclusion. In Metropolitan France, the OAS waged an ultimately counterproductive war of bombings and attacks on pro-Algerian liberals and left-thinking intellectuals, which soon turned into simple gangsterism that cost many innocent lives.

Tony was no doubt delighted to be out of this chaos and with his new unit, 7th Intervention Company, at Mercier Lacombe (now Sfisef) about 25 miles east of Sidi Bel Abbès. The new company established itself in a commandeered vacant farm that they quickly brought up to the standards they required. The unit brought together a number of Tony's comrades from 1st REP, others in the regiment that he had known less well, some newly trained recruits from Sidi Bel Abbès, and some seasoned *légionnaires* from other units. To command:

> ... this rather politically dangerous body of men, thrown together without the usual development of relationships, and with disparate levels of training

and combat experience, Colonel Vaillant, commanding the Legion at Sidi Bel Abbès, selected Captain Henri Billot. Not a para, not a revolutionary, but an outstanding commander and administrator ... He decided that the best way to keep us, and him, out of trouble was to keep us busy; we were on operations nearly all the time.[1]

The farm at Mercier Lacombe was 'just about perfect'. They were miles away from the authority of Sidi Bel Abbès but near enough to be able to take a truck to town when they were not on operations. The buildings, newly painted white, were in excellent condition and provided ample accommodation for the 130 officers and men. Each of the senior NCOs had his own room and a batman to look after him. His duties were not onerous as the NCOs took care of their own kit, but '... he did bring us coffee in the morning, which was essential, and ensured that we were kept supplied with beer when off duty.' There were small officers' and sergeants' messes and good living accommodation for the junior NCOs and *légionnaires*. The sergeants' mess had a pleasant bar-cum-lounge with comfortable sofas and armchairs and a black-and-white television set. Every so often, an Arab programme would appear on the television. Staff Sergeant Rathlau, who had been in 1st REP with Tony, '... absolutely hated Algerian Arabs, and when such programmes were screened he became incensed and from the bar behind those of us watching the TV would shoot it to bits with his 9mm pistol, firing between our heads. He always paid for a new one.'

Control of ammunition, which was plentiful for operations and training, was evidently lax. There was enough to go round for rat hunting. The ceilings of the accommodation rooms were made of suspended whitewashed canvas attached to frames. Lying in bed:

> ... one could follow the passage of the rats as they travelled across the ceiling, their weight making it sag. From the comfort of one's bed one could shoot the rats, aiming at the indentations. The problem was that there would be soon one or more rats above the false ceiling which, in the heat, deteriorated rapidly. This was the moment to summon the batman.

When not on operations, the company spent its time training: '... not too hard but enough to keep us busy. Life was not exciting but very good nonetheless.'

---

1   Henri Billot had fought with the Free French towards the end of the Second World War and then served in Algeria. He was decorated numerous times and finished his career as a general. He remained a friend of Tony's.

A seasoned workman with the tool of his trade – the splendid and reliable MAT49. Tony photographed near Sidi Bel Abbès, late 1961, while serving as a sergeant with the new 7th Intervention Company of the depot formation, 1st RE, after the disbandment of 1st REP following the failed Generals' Putsch of April 1961. He now wears on his green beret, the cut-out gold grenade badge of 1st RE, instead of the silver encircled wing and dagger of the airborne troops. He was still only 24 years old, but his face shows the legacy of five-years' hard soldiering, wounds, injuries, and sickness. (Linda Hunter-Choat).

They dined well and preceded more formal meals with a robust rendering of the Legion song *Le Boudin* accompanied by a toast with full glasses downed in one go. When on duty, however, Tony did not rate the quality of the junior officers in the company very highly: '[They were] all good sensible loyal Gaullists. One was downright rubbish, a young second lieutenant from the Officers' School in Cherchell; he should never have been in the Legion – his only recognisable skill was to do superb handbrake turns at high speed in a narrow lane. For all military activities he was useless.'

However, Tony's platoon commander, for whom he was platoon sergeant, Lieutenant Remy, '... wasn't bad, just young and inexperienced in combat. He had a delightful nature, though not as relaxed in the company of his troops as were the officers of 1st REP who had had the advantage of being on continuous operations with theirs for years in both Indochina and Algeria.'

Tony also considered himself very fortunate to have a good caporal-chef as his second-in- command. Kasjic had '... a lovely dry sense of humour and between us we kept each other cheerful and the platoon happy.'

With the rank of sergeant came administrative responsibilities. One of the more unusual jobs that came Tony's way, conferred on him by Captain Billot, was the:

> ... onerous task ... of organising and staffing the small company brothel, the BMC, (Bordel Militaire Contrôlé). Through old contacts with 1st REP I managed to get the madame from the Zeralda regimental BMC – who in the absence of the regiment and the camp was now out of a job – to come and work for us. I sent her off to Sidi Bel Abbès on a recruiting tour. I built up a smart little establishment with rooms for the girls, and a bar. The downside was that I was responsible for the accounts. Fortunately the madame had kept the accounts at Zeralda and knew the form. After a few months I requested an interview with Captain Billot and asked him to take me off the task as it was not quite my idea of soldiering.

When Tony wasn't busy with the brothel, on operations, or training, he was free to go into the town of Mercier Lacombe, where he spent happy evenings with the local *pieds noirs*:

> ... drinking beer and very good wine, and having mechouis and civilised, sensible conversations. Within a year they would all be either dead or left for France, abandoning all their farms, all their lives. It was all very like Rhodesia, inevitable in the great scheme of things but very unpleasant nonetheless. Although spending all this time with the younger set of Mercier Lacombe was great fun, it was an awful let-down after 1st REP ... after four years of Legion [life] I found it difficult to communicate with civilians. I still do.

Tony's unit was essentially an independent intervention company. Their operations were conducted with no external support other than intelligence and transport from 1st RE at Sidi Bel Abbès. The roles of 1st RE were largely the administration of the Legion and training of *légionnaires*, rather than conducting operations, and:

> Inevitably the quality of intelligence was low, but the transport was good, and one can't have everything. In any case the whole war was running down; Algerian independence was now inevitable and just a question of time, and our role was that of peace-keeping rather than that of an aggressive fighting force. All this could not be blamed on the Legion, but it was quite a different kind of soldiering from what I had become used to. Operating around Sidi Bel Abbès had its compensations [however] with endless delicious watermelons, grapes and sweet, sweet pomegranates to be plucked on our way.

On 3 September 1961, Tony went to Oran for a full week of examinations for promotion. As usual, Tony did exceptionally well, coming top of the candidates throughout the armed forces in Algeria. When the results came through in the middle of October, he was called for an interview with Colonel Vaillant, the commanding officer of 1st RE, at Sidi Bel Abbès. Tony had met the colonel before and was greeted warmly and congratulated on the results of his promotion examinations. He was also told that he had been awarded the *Médaille Militaire* for 'exceptional acts of war' and also selected for officer training at Montpellier in early 1962.[2] All officers in the Legion are French nationals, and accepting a commission would have brought naturalisation as a French citizen. Tony found the offer:

> ... extremely flattering [but] although the thought of becoming an officer appealed to me a great deal, I was starting to have doubts – about continuing a career in a Legion without an Algeria, about being in an independent Algeria where the Algerians would be in command, or being in France in a military backwater. I thanked Colonel Vaillant very much, but kept my reservations to myself. My five-year contract was coming to an end [on] 17 March 1962, but I had twenty-four days leave due to me; Colonel Vaillant signed my leave pass and we had our last talk together. I explained that I intended to go home, see how things were with my family and then make a

---

2   The *Médaille Militaire* is an important gallantry decoration reserved for NCOs (or on occasions for very senior commanders). Equivalence of decorations is always imprecise, but, in British terms, it might approximate to the Distinguished Service Medal.

decision whether or not to renew my contract. I knew that I could be away for six months without that counting as an interruption of service, for a year and retain my rank but with an interruption of service, and longer if the Legion agreed, but with a reduction of one rank. Which would soon be recovered. So I had plenty of time to think about it. I planned to go back, and left three large metal trunks full of my uniforms and souvenirs at Mercier Lacombe, including a mass of Algerian silver recovered from a well where it had been dumped by a FLN 'tax collector' on the run from us.

Farewell to Colonel Vaillant, farewell to Captain Billot, farewell Remy, farewell Kasjic, farewell to all my Legion and civilian friends at Mercier Lacombe, farewell to the girls in the BMC, then away. First by truck to Sidi Bel Abbès, where I was de-kitted and had returned to me the clothes I had surrendered in Paris five years earlier. Then by train to Oran, by the Sidi Bel Abbès [SS *Sidi Bel Abbès*] to Marseille, where I stayed one night, and then took the train to Paris. This time I was not locked in and spent most of the journey in the buffet car, where, with another légionnaire, we emptied the beer stock and started on the cognac. I stayed a few days in Paris, in a cheap hotel in Saint-Denis [a Parisian suburb]. Selling a couple of souvenirs allowed me to buy an air ticket to London and stay in Paris a little longer. My first flight in a jet plane, a Caravelle, took me from Le Bourget to Heathrow together with all my kit including a large tin trunk. So I decided to take a taxi to our home in Ascot; unfortunately I [had] only half a crown (twelve-and-a-half pence) left, which would hardly have got me out of the airport. Dad paid when I got home.

While Tony was serving his last months in the Legion with 7th Intervention Company, 1st RE, France and the GPRA were hesitantly but inexorably moving towards a peace agreement. The first talks at Evian started in May 1961, the prospect of which had triggered the Generals' Putsch, but broke up in failure in June, much to the delight of the *pieds noirs* and the OAS. De Gaulle had tried to include moderate Algerians in the talks, but the GPRA refused outright. They understandably saw themselves as the only legitimate party to represent the Algerian people and saw this as an attempt to find a settlement that would suit General de Gaulle but would fall short of their objectives. There were many points of disagreement, but a key sticking point was the French demand that there should be a ceasefire pending a negotiated political settlement. The GPRA had been, and remained until the end, adamant that they would not agree to a ceasefire before they had a political agreement with France. To accept a ceasefire would make it very difficult for them to renew operations subsequently if necessary, would remove the pressure on the French to reach a settlement, and would drag out negotiations. In an attempt to persuade the GPRA to soften their line, de Gaulle implemented a unilateral French ceasefire, with offensive operations against the ALN ceasing, military action limited to defensive measures, and several thousand prisoners released. The response of the ALN was to step up attacks on civilian targets in Algiers and the country at large. In turn, the OAS stepped up their terrorism both in Algeria and France. Talks resumed in July at Lugrin but failed after only six sessions. The French had little choice but to resume the war in August, albeit in a more limited manner than hitherto.

By the autumn of 1961, Charles de Gaulle was thoroughly frustrated by the lack of progress. The French public was tired of the war, the Army had been torn apart by the Generals' Putsch, and de Gaulle's government was beset by problems with the trade unions. Achievement of his vision for a France with a revitalised economy and modernised armed forces, able to play a leading role in world affairs, was hamstrung by the Algerian problem, both as a drain on resources and because of the country's image in the eyes of the world. One by one, French initial demands were conceded. Dual nationality for *pieds noirs* after independence, a permanent military enclave at Mers El Kébir, retention of property rights for Europeans, and the idea of some form of close association between an independent Algeria and France were all given up. Most importantly, in September, Charles de Gaulle conceded as untenable France's original demand that the negotiations should embrace the coastal strip to the north and exclude the Sahara region in the south of Algeria, in part to preserve nuclear test facilities but also because of the newly developed oil and gas fields.

Although the formal talks had broken down in July 1961, contacts continued, and in November, a series of meetings were held to try to find a way forward. Further sessions were held in January 1962, and formal negotiations resumed in February. These seemed on the brink of failure until de Gaulle – consistent with an earlier remark, 'Il faut en finir!'[3] (We must finish with it!) – sliced through the Gordian knot. Demands to retain Mers El Kébir and test facilities in the Sahara had already been trimmed back to leases for defined periods. On 17 February, de Gaulle told his chief negotiator that these points were unimportant in the overall

---

3   Horne, *A Savage War of Peace*, p.505.

scheme of things: the essentials were a ceasefire and self-determination as soon as possible. The outlines of a settlement were quickly agreed. It was now a question of drafting a text and finalising agreement. The final talks resumed at Evian on 7 March 1962, but internal divisions amongst the Algerians then brought things to the brink of failure once again. An increasingly frustrated Charles de Gaulle threatened unilateral measures, including partition and creation of a *pied noir* state centred on Oran and Algiers (an idea aired earlier, which had caused much alarm among the Algerians). On 16 March, there was still an impasse, and then, suddenly two days later, it was all over: an agreement was signed, and a ceasefire agreed for the following day. Two days after the end of Tony's contract with the Legion, the ceasefire took effect.

Epilogue

The terms of the agreement at Evian provided complete independence for Algeria. French forces would be drawn down to 80,000 men within a year and completely withdrawn over three years. France was to be granted a five-year lease on nuclear test facilities in the Sahara and a 15-year lease, renewable, on the naval base at Mers-el-Kébir. In the event, the French left the base in 1967. Concessions were granted to French companies for exploitation of the gas and oil fields for six years, and Algeria would remain in the franc currency zone. In return, the French would give economic aid for three years at the same level as already planned for development of the country. Europeans would have the same rights as native Algerians for a transition period of three years; after that, they would have to choose between French and Algerian nationality. If they did not adopt Algerian nationality but chose to stay, they would have the same status as other foreigners.

Nevertheless, despite the ceasefire between the ALN and the French, in the short term the bloodshed was far from over. The OAS continued with acts of terrorism against the Muslim population and now considered the French Army the enemy. The response of the French forces was vigorous and violent, including use of tanks and aircraft to reduce OAS enclaves in Algeria. There was also a settling of scores by the FLN with those Muslims who were considered to have supported the French. The ALN also attacked bars and other public places frequented by the OAS and their supporters, with the French forces powerless to intervene under the terms of the Evian agreement. Unexpectedly, a truce was agreed between the FLN and the OAS in June 1962, and, save for a few isolated freelance attacks, the war was finally over. In less than a year, the OAS had inflicted three times more civilian casualties in the region of Algiers than the FLN/ALN had in the preceding six years.

On 1 July 1962, a referendum was held, and the Algerians voted overwhelmingly in favour of the Evian agreement. De Gaulle recognised the independence of Algeria. This was followed by the exodus of the vast majority of the *pieds noirs*, around 1,000,000 people, abandoning homes, possessions, and businesses to flee to France. Those Muslims who had supported France, including those who had fought alongside French troops, were abandoned to their unenviable fate at the hands of the FLN; many were slaughtered, but thousands also fled to France. Algeria had a difficult road to follow in the decades to come, but that is beyond the scope of this book.

In the longer term, the end of the war brought, as de Gaulle had anticipated, the opportunity to divert resources from Algeria to economic recovery and modernisation of the French armed forces. The French describe the period of economic growth during the three decades from the end of the Second World War until the oil crisis in 1973 as '*Les trente glorieuses*'. The term applies broadly to European post-war recovery, but it is clear that the end of the war in Algeria was a significant factor in French economic growth in in the 1960s and early 1970s.

Tony could not have anticipated the precise turn of the events after his departure from Algeria, although as we have seen, he clearly did not relish remaining in an independent Algeria. One of the criticisms of the Generals' Putsch was that the Legion, composed predominantly of foreigners, had meddled in French affairs. In view of this, it is unlikely, particularly in view of mixed loyalties, that Legion units would have been deployed against the OAS. However, if he had renewed his contract immediately, it could not be ruled out that Tony would perhaps have found himself pitted against the many ex-comrades who had deserted to join the OAS. He makes no comment in his memoirs, but it is hard to believe that he would have relished such a prospect. In the event, in May 1962, he joined the British Army for a long and successful career.

As usual, he did well from the outset, passing out the top in his course at Mons Officer Cadet School. He joined the 7th Duke of Edinburgh's Own Gurkha Rifles in Malaya and subsequently served in Sarawak and Borneo, where he fought in the Indonesia–Malaysia confrontation, taking part in coastal raids and cross-border infiltrations into Indonesia.

Too old for a regular commission in the infantry, he transferred to the RA (Royal Artillery) in 1964. He remained in Borneo as a forward observer officer until 1966, when he returned to the United Kingdom. From 1969 to 1970, he attended the Staff College, Camberley, and then served in 45th Field Regiment RA. He became a battery commander and was then appointed second-in-command of 3rd Regiment Royal Horse Artillery in Hong Kong. He served on the directing staff of the Junior Staff College, Warminster, from 1975 to 1977.

In 1977, Tony was offered command of 23rd Special Air Service Regiment (Reserve), which was unusual for an officer without a British special forces background. He commanded the regiment until 1981. He was awarded the OBE in 1983. Tony then served until 1986 as a senior staff officer at the NATO headquarters in Naples and at SHAPE (Supreme Headquarters Allied Powers Europe) as a special forces adviser to the SACEUR (Supreme Allied Commander Europe). His last post in the British Army was as a personal liaison officer between the commander-in-chief of the British Army of the Rhine in Germany and his US counterpart. He retired from the Army in 1989 in the rank of colonel.

Immediately after retiring from the British Army, Tony became commander of the SSF (Sultan of Oman's Special Force), initially in the rank of colonel. His responsibilities included increasing the numbers in the SSF from under 1,000 to more than 2,000 and improving their equipment and capability. In 1993, in recognition of his achievements and leadership, he was promoted to brigadier. In 1995, he was awarded the Omani Order of Achievement by Sultan Qaboos. He retired from the Omani Army in 1997. From 1998 to 1999, he was a member of the Kosovo Verification Mission monitoring the cease fire. He subsequently became the head of security for Aga Khan IV.

After the 2003 invasion of Iraq, Tony became head of security for the Coalition Provisional Authority's Program Management Office, which was responsible for funding reconstruction projects in the country. He was later responsible for making security plans for USAID in Afghanistan and was an accomplished lecturer on leadership and security. Brigadier Tony Hunter-Choat died in Hereford on 12 April 2012 at the age of 76.

Bibliography

Branche, Raphaëlle, *La torture et l'armée pendant la guerre d'Algérie, 1954–1962* (Paris: Gallimard, 2016)
Branche, Raphaëlle, *Papa, qu'as-tu fait en Algérie ?* (Paris: La Découverte, 2020)
Geraghty, Tony, *March or Die, France and the Foreign Legion* (London: Grafton Books, 1986)
Helcégé, Bénédicte, *Capitaine Bonelli, L'arbre à papillons* (Sceaux: L'Esprit du Livre Editions, 2009)
Horne, Alistair, *A Savage War of Peace, Algeria 1954–1962* (New York: New York Review of Books, 2006)
Montagnon, Pierre, *La Guerre d'Algérie, Genèse et engrenage d'une tragédie (1954–1962)* (Paris: Pygmalion, 1984)
Montagnon, Pierre, *Les parachutistes de la Légion, 1948–1962* (Paris: Pygmalion, 2005)
Sergent, Pierre, *Je ne regrette rien* (Paris: Fayard, 1972)
Windrow, Martin, *The Last Valley, Dien Bien Phu and the French Defeat in Vietnam* (London: Wiedenfeld and Nicholson, 2004) and (London: Cassell, 2005)

Author's Note

My primary source, of course, has been the memoirs left by Tony. They have given me a new insight into the character of the man I first met at SHAPE in the 1980s – they have also deepened my respect for him. I knew little of Tony's background when I met him, although it was clear that he was remarkable man. I have two distinct memories of him. The first relates to his fitness and agility. On one occasion, he came into the office that I shared with his good friend, the then Lieutenant Colonel John Griffin, who kindly wrote the foreword to this book. He somehow contrived to leap effortlessly backwards from a standing position to end up sitting atop a four-draw steel filing cabinet. My second memory relates to his French. This was, as perhaps one could expect, fluent, to the extent that I remember a puzzled Belgian barman asking, 'Where are you from in France? I can't quite place your accent.' Tony's story is extraordinary, but his understated way of recording his experiences might lead some to underestimate what he achieved and went through. I once met a French ex-*légionnaire* who had also fought in Algeria. He was very macho and shared none of Tony's modesty, but he stopped in his tracks when I mentioned that I knew someone who had served in 1st REP: 'They were not *légionnaires*, they were supermen!'

Something that shines through in Tony's memoirs, and I hope I have been able to reflect in this book, is the extraordinary comradeship engendered by service in the French Foreign Legion. Service in the armed forces of any nation, and whatever the branch, brings friendships and comradeship, which last a lifetime. However, it is clear that there is something exceptional about the Legion, with deep and lasting friendships built across the barriers of rank between *légionnaires*, NCOs, and officers. To build such relationships and maintain the necessary military discipline says a great deal for the quality of the officers, NCOs, and men of this exceptional fighting force.

Much has been written about the war in Algeria. Alistair Horne's book *A Savage War of Peace, Algeria 1954–1962* is an outstanding account in English. Two important sources in French have been Pierre Montagnon's *La Guerre d'Algérie, Genèse et engrenage d'une tragédie (1954–1962)* and *Les parachutistes de la Légion,*

1948–1962. Pierre Montagnon served in Algeria as a para officer with the Legion's 2nd REP and, after the Generals' Putsch of 1961, deserted to join the OAS. After the cease fire in 1962, he led a resistance group of 80 men fighting to preserve French Algeria. Surrounded by greatly superior French forces, he surrendered and, in 1963, was sentenced to six-years' imprisonment. He was amnestied and freed in 1964. He went on to become a much-respected historian and was awarded a prestigious prize by the *Académie Française* for the first of the above books. In addition to his academic rigour, he brings the insight of someone closely involved with events and many of the key personalities. Also, in French, are two books concerning former members of 1st REP. First of these is the biography of Captain Bonelli, who we meet in the early days of Tony at Zeralda, *Capitaine Bonelli, L'arbre à papillons* by Bénédict Helcégé, which provides a personal view of some of the exploits of 1st REP. The second, *Je ne regrette rien*, is by Pierre Sergent, who was so prominent in the Generals' Putsch. He records the exploits of 1st REP from its formation as 1st BEP in 1948 until its dissolution after the Putsch in 1961, but he surprisingly tells us little of his part in events.